ABOUT JIM HAYNES

Before becoming a professional entertainer in 1988, Jim Haynes taught in schools and universities from outback New South Wales to the UK and back again. He has two masters degrees in literature, from the University of New England and the University of Wales.

He has won the Bush Laureate Book of the Year award three times. Jim has also made many recordings of Australian humour, verse and songs, and appears regularly on television and radio.

COBBERS

Stories of Gallipoli 1915

JIM HAYNES

ABC
Books

First published by ABC Books for the
AUSTRALIAN BROADCASTING CORPORATION
GPO Box 9994 Sydney NSW 2001

First published in August 2005

ISBN 0 7333 1593 3.

Cover image courtesy of Australian War Memorial
Cover and internal design by Christabella Designs
Typeset by Kirby Jones in 11/15pt Sabon
Printed by Griffin Press, Adelaide

5 4 3 2 1

This book is dedicated to the memory of
Kitty McMillan 1908 – 2005

ACKNOWLEDGEMENTS

THANKS TO:
> Alan Murphy for the maps
> Sally Cohen and Nicole Levett for the typing
> Ali Salih Dirik for his insights and knowledge
> Jennifer Blau for her advice, enthusiasm and help with photos
> Brigitta Doyle and Stuart Neal for their support
> Janet Hutchinson for copy-editing
> Christabella Design
> Kirby Jones Typesetting
> HarperCollins Australia for the use of Leon Gellert's, *Anzac Cove*
> The Australian War Memorial
> The Mitchell Library, State Library of NSW
> Embassy of Turkey, Canberra
> Jillian Dellit for help online
> Robyn for support and suggestions
> Lorrae and Norval McClean, Norm and Beryl Mackenzie
> Frank Daniel
> Our driver, Mehemet
> NUR Travel, Istanbul

CONTENTS

HOLDING THE LINE

GLIMPSES OF ANZAC

THE BREAKOUT

Enlistment poster, C. Wall, 'Remember Gallipoli' 1916–1918
Photolithograph Overall: 54.2 x 64.8 cm.

INTRODUCTION

This book is primarily a collection of fiction and verse inspired by the Gallipoli campaign. Some of the writing reflects the experiences of the troops themselves. Other stories and verses chronicle the impact of the conflict on those waiting at home and the reactions of writers and journalists to the whole affair once they had met with, and spoken to, the survivors of the campaign.

Also included are some narrative first- and second-hand accounts of the experiences of the Anzacs at Gallipoli. These are included in order to stand with the rest as stories. I found that these accounts often gave a different angle or perspective on the characters involved, or the campaign itself.

I need to state at the outset that this collection is not an attempt to give the history of the Gallipoli campaign or to analyse it. There are plenty of books that do that, and readers will find some listed in the bibliography. Of those still generally available on bookshop shelves, I've found Les Carlyon's *Gallipoli* extremely informative and readable.

The bulk of the stories and accounts of the campaign collected together here have long been unavailable to the general reader. Some have never been published before and some have been out of print since the 1920s. Needless to say, they have never before been published together in this way.

In compiling this collection I had two major priorities.

My first was to make the prose, and the verse, as accessible as possible to contemporary readers. Many of the unpublished and long-out-of-print stories were written in a style that can only be described as archaic.

There were some stories in which a wonderful central idea was obscured by poor or convoluted prose, or the writing was ponderous and longwinded by today's standards. In others a true sense of tragedy and passion, or humour and stoicism, was clouded by the inexperience. After all, many of these writers were soldiers with no writing background.

So, my first task was to treat many of the stories and verses as first drafts submitted for publication. I have edited heavily in order to produce what I feel is a coherent and readable collection. I make little apology for this. I wanted the feelings and ideas expressed by the various authors to be relatively easy to read and experience. It was also necessary to give some sort of flow and coherence to what is a collection of writings that vary enormously in style and literary quality.

I should hasten to say that there are also polished stories by experienced writers. Authors like Steele Rudd, Oliver Hogue and Frederick Loch hardly needed me to help structure their literary efforts! With these writers any editing was more to do with finding and using the relevant pieces of much longer stories and novels and, in some cases, making a new narrative from them.

My second priority was to give the collection some overall cohesion. With this in mind I arranged the stories in a sort of obvious chronological order.

The first section deals with enlistment and reactions to the news of war breaking out and the second section deals with the actual invasion of the peninsula and events on 25 April 1915. The Ottoman counter-attacks in May have a section of their own, as does the Allied offensive of August.

There is a section containing observations and reflections on the campaign and everyday life at Anzac, and another section covers the evacuation. The final section contains stories and accounts that look at the aftermath of the whole experience, both at the time and up until the present.

The variety of prose writers used in this collection, and the great differences in style and approach, posed a few dilemmas. I have attempted to place stories and verse in an order that not only is logical but also encourages a natural flow in reading and enables the collection to be read as a continuum.

Those prose writers who wrote while at Gallipoli fall into several categories.

Many Anzacs wrote letters home and quite a few also kept diaries. These documents reflect a stoicism and depth of character that is likely to amaze the modern reader.

An old friend of mine, Alan Murphy, who drew the maps which appear in this book, gave me a copy of his grandfather's diary from Gallipoli. Alan's grandfather was Sergeant Major Thomas Murphy, a cook with the 1st Battalion, and his diary is full of extraordinarily matter-of-fact observations and comments such as:

- 27/5/15 Wounded at Shrapnel Gully in the head. Shrapnel shell bursts over me while taking ammunition on mules up the gully. Mules play up and I am dragged down the hillside and badly bruised.
- 29/6/15 Leave Anzac for rest at Imbros.
- 6/7/15 Return to Gallipoli on SS *El Kahira*. Cooking resumes under heavy shellfire.
- 7/7/15 Receive letters and news of Mother's death. Send letters home. Turkish night attack; heavy losses on their side.
- 31/7/15 Aeroplane drops bomb on cookhouse; food spoilt, no one hurt.
- 7/8/15 Captain Shout and Pte. Keyzor earn V.C. Cookhouse shelled heavily. Wounded in right eye.
- 16/8/15 Sent to hospital ship *Rewa* in barge ... supplied with cocoa and food. Sleep on deck. Bullets fall on deck; shift bed to port side and go to bed.

I am in awe of Sergeant Major Murphy, and glad that he survived Gallipoli and went on to sire Alan's father!

Nevertheless, diary extracts and letters home do not always take the form of good stories, and this is a collection of stories. I have, then, avoided using diary and letter extracts except in one or two cases where they appear as part of a longer story. There have been many other books about the campaign which draw on letter and diary fragments to give historical accounts of the Gallipoli experience, and I didn't feel I needed to produce another such book.

A notable exception is Oliver Hogue, who wrote under the pseudonym of Trooper Bluegum and published a collection of letters home in 1916. *Love Letters of an Anzac* is a beautifully written

Oliver Hogue at Gallipoli

series of letters from Hogue to his wife at home in Sydney. There is only a thin veneer of fiction attempted and the letters are, in effect, a wonderful series of short stories which trace the course of the campaign.

Oliver Hogue was born and raised in Glebe, in inner Sydney. It is a sign of a different age that this inner-city dweller was an excellent horseman. He enlisted at the outbreak of war and served as an officer in the 2nd Light Horse Brigade and, later, in the famous Camel Corps in Palestine, where he attained the rank of major.

Hogue was a journalist in civilian life and an excellent writer with an eye for detail and mood. Tragically, having survived the war, he died of pneumonia in England in 1919 and never returned to his beloved 'Bonnie Jean', to whom he often signed his letters, 'Yours till the end of all things'. He also wrote and published another account of his experiences at Gallipoli, *Trooper Bluegum at The Dardanelles*, and stories from that collection appear in this volume as well.

There are also stories that rely on diaries kept at the time which were written up into fuller accounts at a later date. Writers such as Hogue, Hector Dinning, Joseph Beeston, General Birdwood, Hector Cavill and Eric Hanman fit into this category. All these men served at Gallipoli and wrote accounts of their experiences. Some of these accounts are quite prosaic and record everyday life in detail, others are far more reflective and literary.

Hector Cavill and Eric Hanman (known as 'Haystack' due to his size) both fought as privates and landed on 25 April. Their styles of writing differ enormously. Cavill is precise and formal; Hanman boisterous, energetic and almost childlike. Their grasp of the language and ability to communicate via the written word says a lot for the education system of the day.

Hector Dinning's writings make a real attempt to take his readers into the world of the campaign and I find that his descriptions of the Gallipoli landscape are second to none. His observations and reflections about a war being fought in a place of such natural beauty are poignant and thought-provoking. Dinning was a teacher from Brisbane and a clergyman's son. His background and classical knowledge give his writing a perspective and depth beyond the scope and focus of the campaign.

Birdwood and Beeston were well-educated, high-ranking officers. General William Birdwood was the overall Commander of the Anzac forces at Gallipoli. The Australian and New Zealand Divisions were commanded by Generals Bridges and Godley respectively. Unlike many of the British officers of high rank, Birdwood was generally liked and respected by the Anzacs forces and I wanted to include his account as it tells us much about the first day of the invasion and even more about the man. He was later knighted and promoted to Field Marshal.

Joseph Beeston was born in Newcastle in 1859. The son of the traffic manager on the recently opened Newcastle to Maitland Railway, he was educated in Newcastle and then went on to study medicine in London and later attended the Dublin College of Surgeons.

Beeston practised medicine in Newcastle and became president of the NSW British Medical Association and Honorary Surgeon at Newcastle Hospital. He was also president of the Newcastle School of Arts and the Newcastle Agricultural and Horticultural Society. In 1908 he was appointed a lifetime Liberal member to the NSW Parliamentary Upper House.

He served as Honorary Captain in the Army Medical Staff Corps from 1891 and enlisted on the outbreak of war in September 1914. As Lieutenant Colonel he was Officer in Charge of the 4th Field Ambulance at Gallipoli and was awarded the C.M.G. and V.D. He contracted malaria and was invalided to Wandsworth Hospital, London, and upon recovery served as Assistant Director of Medical Services to the 2nd Division. In 1916 he returned to Australia and wrote the book from which the pieces used here were taken, *Five Months At Anzac*, the same year. He died in 1921.

One of the most accomplished writers to serve at Gallipoli was Frederick Loch. A Gippsland grazier before the war, Loch served as an aide-de-camp to Lieutenant Colonel Johnson in the 2nd Field Artillery Brigade. He chronicled his experiences, thinly disguised, in a quite masterly novel, *The Straits Impregnable*, which he wrote under the pseudonym of 'Sydney de Loghe'. Loch appears as the central character 'Lake' in the novel.

Like Hogue, Loch was a writer by profession. A freelance journalist, he wrote several other novels, including *One Crowded Hour*. After the war Loch lived in Europe and worked with refugees for many years with his wife, the writer Joice Nankivell. Their life together is chronicled in her well-known autobiography, *A Fringe of Blue*.

The authors who didn't serve at Anzac, or in the war at all, tended to write more fictionalised accounts for obvious reasons. There are those like E. C. Buley whose writing was intended as a sort of 'Boy's Own Adventure' chronicle of the war based on first- and second-hand accounts. Buley, a writer of travel and adventure articles, wrote relatively accurate, though rather jingoistic and biased, accounts of the campaign for both adults and children.

The most notable Australian author to fictionalise the Anzac experience was Arthur Hoey Davis, the famous 'Steele Rudd'. Davis was born in 1868, in Drayton, near Toowoomba and worked as a horse breaker, stockman and drover before moving to Brisbane where he began to write poetry and draw sketches for local periodicals.

The first of his stories about selectors appeared in *The Bulletin* in 1895 and his many books typically portray life in the Darling Downs area of southern Queensland. His own family were poor selectors and his two main comic creations, Dad and Dave, are among the most famous in Australian literature. His fame was so great that he founded his own *Steele Rudd's Magazine*, in 1904. His son, Gower, enlisted in 1915 and much of the *Memoirs of Corporal Keeley*, from which the story included here is drawn, is based on Gower's reminiscences. Davis died in 1935.

Roy Bridges was a professional journalist with the Melbourne *Age* from 1909 and was also the author of over forty adventure novels, what might be called 'potboilers'. Bridges' series of character sketches and discontinuous narrative pieces about Gallipoli, *Immortal Dawn*, was published in 1917, while the war was still being fought. It contains some interesting literary mechanisms and character creations, but is very melodramatic in style. Bridges was the brother of the novelist Hilda Bridges, with whom he lived in Tasmania after his retirement in 1933.

By far the most enigmatic of the authors included in this volume is William Baylebridge. Born Charles William Blocksidge in 1883, the son of a Brisbane auctioneer and estate agent, he was educated at Brisbane Grammar School and had the classical scholar David Owen as a private tutor.

In 1908 Blocksidge went to London, determined, it seems, to become a poet. In London he self-published several volumes of poetry, copies of which were sent to the principal public libraries, but hardly any were sold to the public. He changed his name to William Baylebridge some time after 1923, and during his life wrote stories, philosophy, and much poetry.

Baylebridge returned to Queensland in 1919 after travelling extensively in Europe, Egypt and the Middle East. He is said to have been involved in 'special literary work' during the war and his familiarity with his subject material in *An Anzac Muster*, from which the stories in this collection are drawn, certainly suggests that he had personal experience at the front. There is no evidence, however, to show that he belonged to any of the fighting forces.

Both in his literary and private life Baylebridge was intriguing. A tall, good-looking man, he was a strong athlete and musician with an interest in the Stock Exchange. There is no suggestion of eccentricity, yet, while he was anxious for literary recognition, he adopted methods of publication which made this impossible. He was continually revising and rewriting his earlier work and always self-published his efforts in very small editions.

Some considered his work to be profound, innovative and unique, while others found it just plain dreadful. A review in *The Bulletin* in 1912, called him 'a new prophet, a new poet . . . or a new lunatic' and described his verse as 'astonishing in its gassy rhetoric and its foolishness'. In 1930, however, literary critic H. A. Kellow hailed Baylebridge as 'the greatest literary figure that Queensland has yet produced', and a 1939 collected edition of his earlier poems,

This Vital Flesh, was awarded the Australian Literature Society's gold medal for the most important volume of Australian poetry of its year.

An Anzac Muster was written in a very oddly stylised literary fashion to replicate Chaucer's *Canterbury Tales* and was issued in an edition of one hundred copies that are exceedingly rare. Baylebridge never married and lived the last twenty years of his life in Sydney, where he died in 1942.

The verse used in this collection comes from a varied and interesting bunch of poets and versifiers. Of many of these writers I know virtually nothing – except that they were at Gallipoli – as many have remained anonymous. Others wrote for the little magazines published behind the lines by the troops, or submitted their verse for the *Anzac Book* only to find there was no room for it and it was not used. We do, however, know quite a lot about two of them – Tom Skeyhill and Leon Gellert.

Tom Skeyhill was an interesting phenomenon. While at Gallipoli he wrote a large amount of rhymed verse that was popular at the time, but his fame was fleeting and his volumes of verse are now long forgotten. Skeyhill fought as a regimental signaller of the 2nd Infantry Brigade and was blinded at the second battle of Krithia on 8 May 1915.

He was hospitalised in Egypt, and later at the Base Hospital in Melbourne. His patriotic, stirring doggerel was published both here and in New York and he was something of a celebrity during and immediately after the war. Later he recovered his sight and lived into the 1930s.

Leon Gellert was a poet of a rather different kind. Born in 1892 and educated in Adelaide, he left school at seventeen and worked as a pupil-teacher until he enlisted as a private in the 10th AIF in October 1914.

Gellert landed on Anzac Beach at dawn on 25 April and survived nine weeks on Gallipoli before coming down with dysentery. He had to be evacuated to Malta, where he contracted typhoid and was sent to England to convalesce. This is where most of his volume of Anzac poems, *Songs of a Campaign*, were written.

After collapsing into a coma Gellert was discharged as medically unfit in June 1916. Amazingly, he re-enlisted in November, only to be discharged four days later when his medical record was uncovered.

Gellert continued to write and worked in Sydney as a journalist and literary editor with the *Daily Telegraph* and the *Sydney Morning Herald* until the death of his wife Kathleen in 1969. He then moved back to Adelaide where he remained until his death in 1977. Gellert was a truly gifted poet whose Anzac poetry and children's verse are much anthologised and remembered.

There are also short verses here from Henry Lawson and his friend Jim Grahame. These reflect the feeling of the time – the enormous pride and patriotism inspired in the general public by the Anzac landing.

Perhaps the most poignant tribute to the Anzacs is the poem written by English popular author Edgar Wallace. He wrote it in response to reading accounts of the landings and then, a little later, seeing the wounded Anzacs being shown all the sights around London.

Wallace was the illegitimate son of an actress. He was born in 1875, adopted by a Billingsgate fish-porter and grew up in the poorer streets of London. He went on to write more than 170 books, mostly thrillers, and also many plays and countless newspaper articles.

In the late 1890s he served in the Royal West Kent Regiment and the Medical Staff Corps and, as a war correspondent in South Africa for the *Daily Mail*, sent back reports that led Kitchener to ban him as a correspondent until World War I.

Wallace's novels featured sinister criminals and shadowy killers with numerous plot twists and secret passageways. More of his books have been made into films than any other twentieth-century writer.

At his peak he was selling five million books a year. This brought him a vast fortune, which he lost due to his extravagant lifestyle and obsessive gambling. When he died, in 1932, he was on his way to Hollywood to work on the screenplay of *King Kong*.

To my mind his tribute to the Anzacs is the best poetic tribute of them all:

... I see you go limping through town
In the faded old hospital blue,
And driving abroad – lying down,
And Lord! but I wish I were you!
... I'd count it the greatest reward
That ever a man could attain;
I'd sooner be 'Anzac' than 'lord',
I'd sooner be 'Anzac' than 'thane'.

*   *   *

It seemed a good idea to collect together these varied and disparate stories and verses about the Gallipoli experience. By focusing on the different writings that were inspired by the events and their aftermath, putting them side by side and reading them as a collection, I hoped to perhaps crystallise in my own mind what it is about the Anzac experience that makes it special and meaningful for Australians.

Having spent a year of my life finding, collecting and editing these accounts, in prose and verse, of an eight-month long military campaign that was over and done with ninety years ago, do I have any better insight into the importance of Gallipoli?

As far as the public importance of Anzac is concerned, I still can't explain it fully although I feel I am now in a much better position to do so.

At a personal level I understand my own feelings about nationhood and self-sacrifice much more clearly. Literature has always been a good way for me to discover my own feelings and make sense of the world.

I hope you will find, after reading these stories and verses, that the collection makes sense to you – that perhaps your notion of Anzac is a little clearer, and the exercise has been worthwhile.

Jim Haynes
April 2005

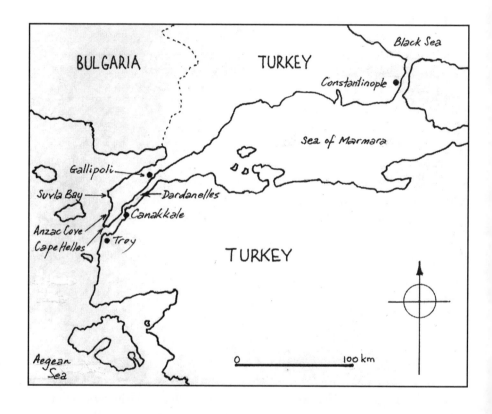

BRIEF HISTORY OF THE DARDANELLES CAMPAIGN

Jim Haynes

In order to appreciate the stories in this collection, readers may like to remind themselves of the basic history of the time.

After World War I began, the Ottoman Empire was lured into an alliance with the Central Powers, partly through the ruling committee's leader, Enver Pasha, having a German background and sympathies, and partly due to Russia being the Ottoman Empire's old and obvious enemy.

The Germans convinced the Ottomans to close the Dardanelles, the waterway between the Aegean Sea and the Black Sea, thereby blocking the sea route to southern Russia and preventing Allied arms and supplies being sent to the Eastern Front.

An appeal by the Russian Government to the British War Office and high command prompted the Allied decision to attack the Dardanelles.

Russian troops were being hard-pressed in the Caucasus and the Allies hoped that a British attack might cause the Ottomans to withdraw. They also hoped to open a supply route to Russia by forcing the Dardanelles.

It is generally acknowledged that the fall of Constantinople would have been a foregone conclusion had the Allied fleet passed through The Narrows.

French and British warships attacked Turkish forts at Cape Helles and along the Straits in February and March 1915. However, underwater mines, torpedoes and spirited defensive work by the Turkish forts along the shores of the Dardanelles at The Narrows, near the Turkish town of Canakkale, halted the assault.

On 18 March 1915 the British and French fleets attempting to force the Straits suffered a humiliating defeat, losing six battleships. British losses were the *Irresistible* and the *Ocean* sunk in The Narrows and the *Inflexible* crippled and run ashore at Tenedos. The French lost the *Bouvet*, sunk in The Narrows, the *Gaulois*, beached on a tiny island back towards Lemnos, and the *Suffren*, badly damaged and retired.

After a naval attack on the Dardanelles failed, the British military leader at Gallipoli, General Hamilton, conferred with the Sea Lords and Field Marshal Kitchener and it was decided that a naval action would not succeed without an invasion in force by infantry. Plans were immediately made for a massive invasion to try to seize the Gallipoli Peninsula.

At the time, the arrival at Gallipoli was the largest military landing in history. It involved about 75,000 men from the United Kingdom, France, Australia, New Zealand, Nepal and India. After several postponements due both to poor weather and to some of the supply ships being wrongly loaded and then having to be reloaded, the huge flotilla sailed from the Allied base on the island of Lemnos on 24 April 1915. The landings began to take place before dawn the following day.

The main Allied force, consisting of British and French troops, landed at five different locations at Cape Helles, on the tip of the peninsula.

*   *   *

The Australian and New Zealand Army Corps was a combined force of Australian and New Zealand volunteer soldiers. The corps was formed in Egypt during 1914 and was led by the British General William Birdwood. This force of about 30,000 men was to

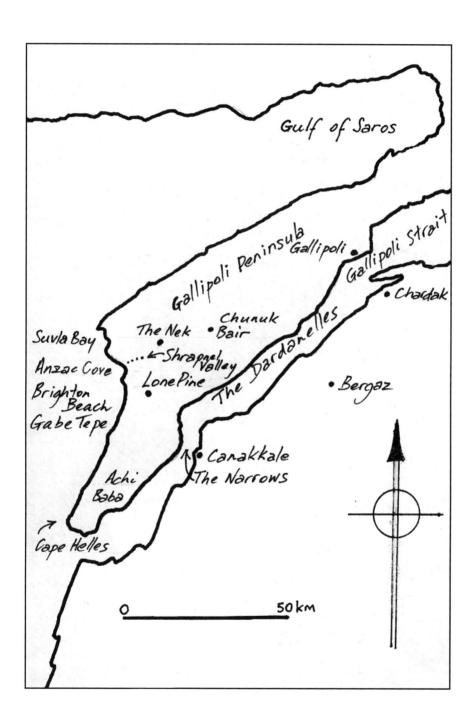

be landed at Gaba Tepe, more than sixteen kilometres north of Helles.

The Anzacs actually landed even further north, in an area later called Anzac Cove. On the first day, 16,000 Anzac troops went ashore, the majority of them going into battle for the first time.

The Allied forces suffered severe casualties during the landings. The Allied naval attacks in the area had alerted the Ottomans and their German commanders and they had strengthened their military defences on the peninsula.

Neither the British and French forces, nor the Anzacs further north, were ever able to penetrate more than a few kilometres inland.

The first day of the campaign saw the Anzacs fighting in small disjointed groups due to confusion caused by the landings not occurring where planned and the troops becoming separated from their officers and battalions.

They had been landed in a hilly, scrubby tangle of ravines and steep sandy gullies. Yet, amidst the confusion and poor leadership, groups of Anzacs attacked and briefly captured key points on the peaks of the range that commanded the centre of the narrow peninsula.

By the afternoon of the first day, with no supply lines opened and insufficient organised reinforcements, the Anzacs were unable to hold the positions they had gained. No covering artillery had been landed and the Anzacs were driven back and forced to dig in along a line that would become the firing line they would hold and defend for the entire campaign.

The geography of the region and the limited size of supporting forces available prevented the Allied troops from advancing beyond the positions they originally commanded both at Anzac and Helles.

The landings at the much better defended beaches at Helles resulted in heavy casualties and the British foothold there consisted of an area stretching approximately eight kilometres from the toe of the peninsula to the foot of a range of hills called Achi Baba, at a point where the peninsula is also about eight kilometres across.

Anzac Cove 1915

Efforts to take the hilltop failed time and again and many lives were wasted. Some Anzacs were sent to bolster the forces at Helles, the 2nd Australian Brigade and the 2nd New Zealand Brigade. They took part in the second battle of Krithia which consisted of charges across open ground into machine-gun-defended territory, being ordered on three successive days, 6, 7 and 8 May.

It was at the Battle of Krithia that Tom Skeyhill, whose verse appears throughout this collection, was blinded.

The Anzacs suffered incredible losses at Krithia. There is a photograph of some twenty-seven men who were all that were left standing of a brigade of over 700 after the Battle of Krithia. The hill was never taken and the campaign at Helles ground to a stalemate until forces were finally evacuated in January 1916. They were the last Allied troops to leave the peninsula. The battle-hardened 29th Division of the British Army fought bravely at Helles and over half their number were killed or wounded.

Having consolidated their hold on the narrow strip of beaches and hills at Anzac, the troops settled down to what really became a siege. The Ottoman forces controlled the heights and the key artillery positions on the shore. From the sea the British naval guns provided cover and protection for the Allied forces entrenched on the peninsula.

The infantry on both sides were entrenched along a front stretching for approximately five kilometres and curving in an arc from near Hell Spit up into the ranges and back down to North Beach. The distance between the Anzac and Ottoman trenches varied from a few metres to several hundred metres.

After the initial consolidation and digging in, the situation was stable for almost a month. Then, in mid-May, the Ottoman forces launched a fierce series of counter-attacks. On the night of 19 May, 40,000 Ottoman troops were thrown at the Anzac front line, which was made up of 12,000 men. The Anzacs held the line against overwhelming odds and the horrific losses on the Ottoman side led to a request for an armistice to bury the dead. This was granted on 24 May. Losses along the central area of the Anzac line were estimated as 160 Allied soldiers and over 4,000 Ottoman dead.

The next real development occurred in August when a new invasion was undertaken at Suvla Bay to the north of Anzac. This force of some 15,000 men was to land at Suvla on 6 August and advance across a dry salt lake and hilly open plain toward the Anafurta Range, Hill 971 and Chunuk Bair. Attacks by all forces on the peninsula were planned to divert Ottoman attention from the landing and enable this new force to become an important part of a pincer movement against the heights.

These invasion forces were made up of men who were newcomers to war and were poorly led. The command was given to Sir Frederick Stopford, who had been retired since 1909, was sixty-one years old, and had never commanded men in battle.

Whatever the reason – unclear orders, poor morale after a botched landing, heat and difficult terrain, heavy Turkish resistance, or simply poor and hesitant leadership – the forces which landed at Suvla on 6 and 7 August failed to advance as expected.

Meanwhile the Anzacs attacked according to plan. The Australians charged the Ottoman trenches at Lone Pine and

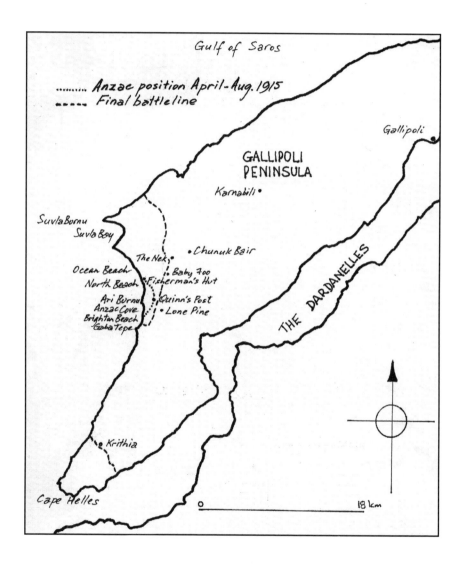

captured them, the Light Horse charged into the face of machine-gun fire and died at The Nek, and the New Zealanders charged up Rhododendron Ridge and took Chunuk Bair.

At Helles the 29th Division made yet another futile and tragic attack on Krithia.

Allied losses all round were devastating. Over 2,000 Australians died at Lone Pine alone. On the other side losses were even worse; 7,000 Ottoman troops died defending Lone Pine.

Ottoman troops under Mustafa Kemal recaptured the heights from the New Zealanders and Ghurkas on 10 August. The Anzacs held Lone Pine till the evacuation and the Allies effectively held most of the Suvla Bay area and Anafurta Plains after another concerted push with reinforcements finally allowed the forces at Anzac to link up with the forces at Suvla on 27 August.

After this time another stalemate eventuated; not one inch of territory was won or conceded by the Anzac forces from the end of August until they were evacuated in December.

By the end of August over eighty per cent of the Allied troops were suffering from dysentery. Winter brought snow and many soldiers died from exposure or suffered frostbite.

A long stalemate followed until the Allied troops at Anzac and Suvla were withdrawn in December 1915.

Unlike the landings and the eight-month siege campaign, the evacuation was a masterpiece of military strategy and coordination.

Troops were evacuated steadily from 11 December and the final 20,000 left furtively and completely undetected on 18 and 19 December.

A rearguard of 1,500 men occupied the trenches and fired rifles, made noises and set timers on guns and booby traps to make it appear that the trenches were occupied as normal.

On a given signal the rearguard ran to the deserted beach and were taken off under cover of darkness. Only two lives were lost during the whole process of evacuation.

*   *   *

Gallipoli established the fighting reputation of the Anzacs and passed into Australian legend.

A total of 5,833 Australian soldiers were killed in action during the Gallipoli campaign. A further 1,985 soldiers died of wounds, bringing Australian battle losses to 7,818. In all, 19,441 Australian soldiers were wounded. A total of 2,721 New Zealanders were killed and 4,752 were wounded.

Figures for the British were 21,255 dead and 52,230 wounded casualties. The French count wasn't accurate but was approximately 10,000 dead and 17,000 wounded.

Ottoman losses were 86,692 dead, 164,617 wounded and 20,000 who died from disease.

We have no accurate record of the numbers on the Allied side who died from disease but about 150 a day were evacuated with illness from June onwards.

It is safe to say over 150,000 men died during the Gallipoli campaign and twice that number were wounded. As the objective of the campaign was not realised it was a futile exercise for the Allies. The Ottoman Army lost over a quarter of a million men and eventually lost the war as well.

THE CALL

THE CALL*

Tom Skeyhill

Young and old, brave and bold, hark to the clarion call.
Over the rolling seas it comes,
With threat of death and muffled drums,
From fields afar, where shrapnel numbs,
War, War, War!

Big and small, short and tall, hark to the clarion call.
Stay not where the crowd hurrahs,
Speed ye straight to the fields of Mars,
Where red blood flows beneath the stars,
War, War, War!

Mother rare, sweetheart fair, hark to the clarion call.
Slain out there is the peaceful dove,
Rent and torn the heavens above,
Give to the flag the men you love,
War, War, War!

*extract

THE CALL

Frederick Loch ('Sydney de Loghe')

The afternoon was wearing out, and I began to think of home and tea. I stopped working, straightened my back, ran moist fingers through my hair, and sat down on the log. The axe went tumbling to the ground. 'Watch-and-pray' and 'Wait-and-see' got up from the fallen gum suckers, and trotted forward with waving tails and glistening, slippery tongues. I made haste to get rid of them. They began to play, biting ears and growling, but went back at last, laid keen black heads on narrow paws and watched me out of grave brown eyes.

To Gippsland spring had come. The day had been a day of spring until evening beckoned afternoon away. Now a little breeze – gentle, but rather cold – came out of the west and wandered through the tops of the gum suckers. The scent of eucalyptus came with it; and behind it followed the voices of countless rustling leaves. It moved among the wattle tops where they wound along the river; it moved across the rape crops and over the grassy flats beyond. It bent the sedges in the lagoons where the first black ducks were feeding, and where, on warmer nights, big eels bubbled below the sunken logs. I raised my forehead to the cool; and, lo! The breeze had gone!

Through the rape crop sheep were streaming. Anxious ewes pulled hurriedly at the broad green leaves or watched with care their frolicking youngsters. On the flats, round the salt trough, the bullocks chewed and meditated. Smoke climbed up by the river

'Call up poster.'

bend; and outside her cottage moved Mrs Pigg, bringing in the washing, pulling vegetables, feeding the fowls. Small and busy the distance showed her.

Behind me, and on either side, the suckers pushed up their heads. High over them leaned spectral trees: blackened, leafless, stripped of bark, weary with long waiting. About the ground great trees had fallen: grim logs – knotted logs – logs scarred with the breath of summer fires. Here and there showed feeding sheep; and this way and that way ran well-worn pads leading to the waterholes in the wattles. Over the hillside spread a faint green carpet where was shooting the young grass.

Out from hidden gullies floated cries of sheep. Mournfully they travelled across the hillside – now the voice of a ewe whose lamb had strayed, now a lamb hungry and alone. Other sights and sounds began to fill the evening. Small finches came hopping into the suckers, dodging and peeping and swinging through the boughs, and preening themselves between the leaves. Gay was the twittering as the hunt for supper went forward. Then a jackass swooped into a treetop, threw up its tail, raised high its head and pealed out frenzied laughter. Other treetops joined the madman chorus. Next a magpie hopped upon the big log and glinted an evil eye at me; and then forgot me to ruffle sombre shoulders, and join the evening hymn.

The sun was on the horizon, and shadows moved quickly across the lower lands. First they filled the reedy lagoons, the big wattle groves, the belts of scrub. They moved from bramble bush to grass tussock, from fallen log to waterhole. Faint wisps of fog rose about the river. It was late; I was hungry; it was time for home.

I put out a hand for my coat, picking up the axe as well; and 'Watch-and-pray' and 'Wait-and-see' sprang forward with glad barks. I pushed them off and got up.

'Hello there, Guv'nor,' a harsh voice shouted from the ruined gate, and old Scottie came through the gap on his ancient chestnut mare. The long sunbeams shone upon his weather-beaten face, with its broken yellow teeth and small hard beard. He wore an ulster, with a sugar-bag hanging out of the pocket. In the bag he had dived a horny hand, and now it came out filled with letters and papers. 'Here you are, Guv'nor,' he shouted again.

I went forward and took the packet, picking out all that belonged to me. What was left I handed back. 'There are one or two for the Piggs,' I said. 'You might take them over.'

'Right-o, sir,' he answered, and pulled the old mare round, and started away at a jog-trot. Through the suckers man and beast disappeared – an elderly man and a very elderly beast.

I leaned against the gateway and opened the letters. There was news from home, telling of weather five weeks old, and a garden party older yet. Still I read it all twice. An agent had written of some bullocks, and there was a third note about sheep. I pushed everything into my coat pocket, and picked up the papers. Four were there – I had not been to the township for a day or two. I opened the oldest of them, dated four days ago, and turned the pages in a hurry – I was hungry and thinking of tea.

But I forgot tea. Across the middle leaves ran staring headlines. Austria was at the throat of Serbia, and war was a matter of hours. All Europe was arming.

I opened another paper. Events had gone forward. Austria had begun the journey of chastisement. From East to West of Europe sounded the clamour of war. I scanned the pages, and threw the paper down. The next I opened, and again the next. No line of hope!

I leaned and read.

Dusk was deepening, and slow grey fogs wended across the flats. 'Watch-and-pray' and 'Wait-and-see' sat erect upon their haunches, peering up to know why I delayed. The evening had grown still again, birds and sheep alike were silent; but from the Piggs' cottage smoke climbed in cheerful wreaths. Pigg and his wife were at tea now, old Scottie no doubt with them; they were talking of war and ruin, though half a world lay between.

I picked up the fallen papers and put the axe upon my shoulder. 'Here, "Watch-and-pray", here, "Wait-and-see", we're off at last!'

I took the path through the ti-tree, though it was boggy still from the rains, and brought the dogs to heel as we passed beside the river through flocks of dozing sheep. Out of the calm skies first stars were coming. We reached the cattle-yards, and pushed a way through the loose barbed wire. The breath of honeysuckle was blown from Scottie's cottage, but the place was dark and empty. Scottie had not come back.

We left the yards to go along the path which crossed the hillside; then dipped into the gully and climbed the opposite bank. The horses stood under the pepper trees in a lazy, drowsy circle. I glanced into the buggy-shed to see that all was secure. I pulled open the garden gate. It was evening now, full evening, grey and a trifle chill; and among the grasses crickets shrilled and from the waterhole by the lightwood tree rose the voices of amorous frogs.

A score of perfumes met me at the garden gate. The peaches, pears, and apples were a-flower; and the lemon trees and oranges budded. When we came to the house, I reached down the dogs' meat from the shelf beside the window, and led the way to the kennels, which were among piles below the flooring. The dogs began to bark again, and ran to their places, sitting down to be chained up. I chained them, gave them their meat and a good-night pat, and went round to the back once more.

The house key came from its hiding place, and I unlocked the door and went inside. In the kitchen it was nearly dark; in the front room it was darker; but there were matches by the lamp on the table. Then I opened the front door and went on to the veranda. Roses had climbed all above it, all round it, all across it; and on either side the flowering peaches leaned for support. I pushed aside the rose branches and stepped down into the garden. The stars were shining and, across the creek, milking was over at the Browns', for a drowsy stream of cows returned to the paddock. I watched them a moment, and next went to the back of the house again. At the woodheap I picked up an armful of sticks to carry into the front room. Quite soon the fire was started, and it burned brightly. Then forwards and backwards I went into the kitchen, bringing the kettle to put on to the fire, carrying in plates and knives and forks, bread, butter. The table laid, out I went to the woodheap again, and this time chopped big logs. In the chill evening the axe blows sounded sharp and clear. It meant three journeys to the front room with the logs; but those made, I was ready for the night.

I took off boots and leggings, throwing the spurs into the corner. I went into the bedroom and washed, splashing water all over the place. Then I found the frying pan and lard, and began a dish of eggs and bacon. The kettle boiled for the tea. Soon the bacon was cooked and the eggs were ready; all was there, and the fire shining. I drew in a chair and began to eat. Presently out of a pocket the papers came, one by one to be read through. Long after I had finished eating, by the light of the lamp and the fire I sat reading on.

At last I got up. A kettle of water boiled, and I carried into the kitchen the supper things and washed up. In ten minutes the business was over. I made the bed ready, and put more wood on the fire. By this time it was eight o'clock. For a moment I waited by the mantelpiece, looking into the flames; but they were too hot, and drove me on to the veranda. Once more the perfume of countless blossoms met me in the dark.

There was no moon; it was all starlight, and on the right hand the Southern Cross swung round. At the garden end, the big waterhole glimmered through gaps in a broken fence, and from it came love-songs of a thousand frogs, while in the overhanging branches of the lightwood two cranes kept mournful watch. Each night they stood there at this hour, peering down into the reeds below.

The hill climbed up behind the house and fell away before me. All over it tall, barkless trees stood up – grimly some, some wearily – but each one a spectator of the endless procession of day and night. Across the ground other trees were lying. Bracken had closed round some and brambles had clambered over others. I heard the rippling of the river, and here and there caught the gleaming of waters: there beside the great white gums, there below the willows, there before the bridge; and farther off, upon the plains, showed there and there the farmhouse lights. Round all ran the distant hills. Now from afar a dog barked, now a bull bellowed; and ever, ever shrilled and croaked the crickets and the frogs.

The evening was cold enough for an overcoat, and, putting one on, I sat down on the veranda step. Most nights this was my custom before turning into bed. On and off, for two years, I had come out in the same way – on starry nights, on moonlit nights; on nights of cloud, on nights of rain; on nights of mist, of warmth, of cold. I had lain back on stifling nights when the mosquito alone seems abroad; and I had felt the breath of the frost come down and had fled beaten to the fireside. For two years I had watched the seasons come and go, and the stars swing round and round. Not a night but I could tell when the moon would sail up behind the hills. I had seen suns set in the west – and I had watched and watched until the east grew rosy.

Two years and I owned and lived upon these lands. I had challenged the wilderness, driving it ever back. I had known days of hope and days of uncertainty; but victory was within sight. Where scrub had waved, now was open country; where logs mouldered, now passed the plough. The fight had cost two years – but I had won.

Over the silent meadowlands I looked, where rape and oats were growing. 'Two years have you spent here,' they seemed to say, 'and this third year is to be the year of your hopes. We shall repay your labours; wait but a while.'

I looked to the gap in the hills where the moon would climb

forth, moving and mounting, presently to sail over lands where stalked sorrow and desolation.

A voice asked, 'Will you stay here for your payment? Or will you leave it – to follow the moon?'

'Aye, but why should I follow the moon?' said I. 'What hate have I to take me there? No; hard have I toiled; let me remain.'

'Stay with your plough, then,' said the voice. 'Muster your cattle and count your sheep. But never more shall you dwell alone. A stranger shall sit in your heart. A stranger shall abide with you to taunt you of your choice.'

The dogs woke me up. Footsteps came slowly along the path behind the house, and old Scottie went by on his way across the hill. Crowbar, shovel, and axe were on his back, and laden thus he passed away into the gloom of trees and suckers.

Through the wet winter we had pulled together fallen logs for burning; and before a giant heap Scottie stopped, and laid down tools. He rested a moment on the pile, to get breath no doubt; but quite soon started a search among the standing trees and bracken. He was looking for kindling. It was so dark – often I could not follow him. Presently he was back again at the heap; and a tender flame crept up, changing gloom into fairyland. An army of shadows were born, and leaped about the magic circle. Old Scottie was plainly now to be seen, even his stumpy beard; and the axe flashed when the flames danced on the blade.

The light grew broader and bolder, and flames licked through the gathered logs, while on all sides moved Scottie, like a priest at the altar – chopping, levering, and digging with axe, crowbar, or shovel. Now he would hurry away with burning sticks to another pile, so that furnaces grew out of half the hillside. With each breeze crossing the river, flames leaped and logs roared; and flights of sparks raced up into the night. The smoke coils were caught to the treetops, and the lofty, leafy boughs, drawn into the maelstrom, were dashed about. From furnace to furnace passed Scottie, tending their needs as a doctor watches his patients.

The night was ageing; all but one farmhouse light had gone out; but I did not think of sleep. I realised the cold and, rising, went inside. The fire still burned. The alarm clock on the mantelpiece said a quarter past ten. I went into the kitchen in search of cake, and next passed through the back door into the open, and took the track cut in the hillside, the track Scottie had taken. While I followed it, the light at the Smithsons' disappeared. As I came up, Scottie peered at me through the smoke.

'Hallo, Guv'nor,' he shouted. Then he shouted again, waving a hand at the fires. 'They're going well! Have you come to help? It wull take two tae shift some of these!'

I nodded. He picked up the crowbar, I bent down for the shovel; and for the next hour we made the rounds. By that time all the fires had taken good hold and could be left until morning. We were hot, dry, and tired and with one accord found seats on a log. I crossed hands on the shovel handle, laid my chin on them, and thus fell to watching the fog bands form over the river. I was surprised Scottie was so quiet: he stopped talking so seldom. Now he was content to spit and fill his pipe. This filling was slow of completion and only ended when he had blown and coughed and gurgled through the pipe stem.

'Guv'nor,' he said presently, and I stopped watching the river and looked round, 'the papers say there wull be a lot doing at home. We wull be fighting Germany in a day or two. Don't you say so, Guv'nor?'

'Yes,' I answered.

He smoked on, pressing a finger into the bowl of his pipe. 'If it's a big thing, men wull go frae this country. Don't you think so?'

'I expect so,' I said.

He cocked his head on one side. 'Maybe one or two frae down here wull be going.'

'I shall be going,' said I.

MALLEE

Roy Bridges

He rode the lean mare up the sandy track. The sun burnt his eyes and the black flies clouded about him. The sand clogged the mare's hooves as she bore him up the ridge; and to give her breath he paused upon the top.

The road went down the ridge like a ribbon of fire. The sandy paddocks, where the wheat had died in the spring, rolled mile beyond mile brick-red to the black pine clumps against the sky. At every swirl of hot wind the sand was blown up in yellow spirals merging into one ochre-coloured cloud, which crept down into the road.

But he saw none of this, taking in the mere impression of the Mallee around him, for his mind was elsewhere, visualising the lettering on the poster he had inspected back in town: 'Men needed for service overseas. Twenty thousand promised by the Commonwealth Government to England.'

In a good spring the wheat should have rolled miles out as a sea of green and gold under the sun. On the Mallee fringe the sheep would have cropped the grass. Now sand, shaped like the oncoming waves of the sea, made great banks where it met the scrub. The sand leaked through wire fences into the tracks like iron-coloured water. When the wind died the mirage appeared, a flickering fantasy to right and left with lagoons of silver merging into the grey smudges of pine and eucalypt, shadowy and mystical.

He was thinking of fellows he knew, excited, gathered in knots at the railway station, at the Post Office, before the pub. Recalling the khaki-clad figure of one chap on leave from Broadmeadows – the popular hero, one who had been previously known through the district as a waster, now straight and clean, slouching no longer. The same chap telling him he ought to go!

And he was going. He was sick of the Mallee. Only he knew the Old Man would not let him go; and he couldn't stand up to the Old Man. Never had been able to; couldn't now. He'd stop him from enlisting if he could. There was something about the Old Man!

He spurred the mare on down the track. He passed the old cocky's shack. Mud-brick and a shingle roof. The chap had got some straw left still; but his dam was drying. He was reduced to dipping the water into a bucket, and carrying it up to a rusty pot where a few fowls drank. Full of news of the war, he would have pulled in for a yarn.

The cocky's son was in khaki; and he wanted to know what his Old Man had thought, maybe get a hint from him how to deal with his own Old Man. But the black flies swarmed and a stinger shimmered, silver-winged, and the mare wouldn't stand, so he rode on.

Mum might work it; but then Mum wouldn't want him to go.

He pulled in by the gate a mile down. Leaning from the saddle, he pulled up the wire loop from the post, and dragged back the gate, two props and a few strands of barbed wire. He rode through and down the track between the dwarf gums and myall. Not a blade of grass, not a cicada piping, not a parrot chattering. Only the hard trees, a green mass above the brick-red sand.

The house lay a quarter of a mile back from the road. In 1911, the last good year, the Old Man had put up a new place, a weatherboard cottage, the paint now blistering pink upon it, iron roofs, with a couple of tanks under the chimney.

The black, mud-brick house, where they had lived before, stood a bit to the left. A few sugar gums shaded the yard. The garden had burnt up for want of water. The dam was holding out; but it was all wanted for the stock. Dead sticks and sand now – sand that drifted to the doors, and leaked inside.

Mum was standing out the front in the sun in her old blue print gown, print sunbonnet, and white apron. He pulled up by the gate as she came down to meet him, smiling to her smile. Mum might work it for him; but it would be horribly rough on her. She wouldn't want him to go any more than she had wanted him to go to town for a job. Though she had tried her hardest with the Old Man, and failed.

'Any mail?' she asked, smiling up at him.

'Only the paper,' he answered. 'Them Germans have cut the British up a bit – and Antwerp's gone. There weren't any letters. Where's Dad?'

'Cutting chaff,' she said, taking the paper. 'Put the mare in, and come for a cup of tea. Tell Dad. See anyone in the township?'

'Young Banks, that's all. Fancies himself no end! He's in khaki – up on leave.'

She caught the bitter inflexion; she gave him a look of apprehension, noting the discontent black on his face. She ventured: 'It'll make a man of him.'

'It's more'n I can stand,' he muttered, flicking off flies. 'To see that chap. War news is pretty bad, Mum ...' breaking off.

She said nothing for a while, her keen blue eyes estimating him – realising. Her eyes dimmed a little – the sun on the sand was glaring.

'You want to go?' she said at last.

'Of course I want to go, I want to get out of this Godforsaken hole.'

'Is that why?' she asked, her voice trembling a little.

He hesitated and would not meet her look. 'No – that isn't why! I don't want to leave you, Mum, stuck here!'

She said, 'I'm glad that's not the reason.'

'Only Dad won't ever let me go,' he muttered savagely. 'He wouldn't let me go to town to work. He wants me here to slave for him. Mum, if he won't ...' he paused, staring across the yard.

'You'll go? You'll go still?' she sighed, 'I shouldn't like you to go – that way.'

'Mum, can't you work it?'

She did not meet his eyes, but looked down on the sand.

'D'ye think you can work it with Dad? Think you can? Will you have a shot?'

She was scraping a semi-circle with the toe of her shoe. 'Go and put the mare up,' she said at last. 'I'll see ...'

After tea he lounged against the gatepost, smoking a fag.

The Old Man was sitting on the bench by the back door – the paper before him, puffing his clay pipe. He'd been grumpy at tea, wanting to know why his son had been loafing in town all the day when the sand needed scooping from the track.

The sun had dropped into the sand like a great live coal, another burning day tomorrow. Mosquitoes buzzed and he turned and slouched toward the door. He'd tell the Old Man straight out that he was going; and if he didn't like it, he could lump it.

Staying here; and the Germans burning through Belgium, murdering women and little kids! He would tell him straight – now! Mum had been yarning to him after tea: but the old chap said nothing, only sat down with his pipe and paper. His son slouched towards him, scowled and hesitated.

'Mum was sayin',' the Old Man suddenly growled, knocking the ashes from his pipe, and breaking off to blow through the stem. 'Mum was sayin', you wanted to go to the war.'

His son did not meet his eyes. 'Got to go, Dad.'

'Got to! Well, you got to do something. Ain't work on the place for two – not this year! Not a drop o' rain – nor a blade o' grass. I can't keep you. May as well be there as 'ere! Earnin' a bit for yourself ... doin' a bit for ... you know ...'

He blew hard into his pipe, and his son nodded and went past him.

Mum was sniffing a little to herself and putting away the dishes.

'Mum,' he asked a little huskily, 'how did you work it?'

'I didn't,' she sniffed, her back turned to him, 'I just started to tell him that he couldn't get along without you and he shouldn't let you go. Only ... only ... he said ... he said you should go ... every young chap should ... though he didn't want you to ... any more than me.'

A saucer slipped from her fingers and smashed on the floor.

She put her apron to her eyes.

RECRUITED AT THE TOWN HALL

E. F. Hanman ('Haystack')

Men lined up outside the recruitment office because our existence was threatened; because we were in danger, our homes, our wives, our children; because England needed us, because we were Britishers, and stood as one. 'Twas enough, 'twas the Call, the call to arms.

But it was at Lismore that the writer found himself on 18 September 1914. Having no home, no friends, no relations, what did it matter where he was? Nothing.

The town itself seemed deserted, save for a few rumbling, grumbling farmers' carts, groaning on their way to some distant little homestead in the bush.

Strolling down one of the sleepy, lazy-looking streets, he suddenly found himself one of a crowd, intent upon the same purpose – that of taking the oath to serve their 'King and Country till the termination of the War and four months after'.

In front of the recruiting hall was a quite respectable crowd consisting of nearly every class and profession. One could easily distinguish the lawyer, the bank clerk, the draper, and the labourer – mostly big, strapping fellows who looked as though they had every chance of becoming food for powder and shot.

In every face could be seen anxiety – anxiety that the owner was suffering from some complaint of which he was unaware – fearful lest he be found unfit. When a chap knows he is to be examined by a medical man, he becomes afraid, he imagines he has a weak heart,

'Waiting for the doctor ...' Recruitment Depot 1914

lung trouble, or any other of the too numerous diseases which afflict mankind. Assure him as fervently as you like to the contrary, and his brain will run to imaginary complaints until he does feel quite ill. Waiting for the doctor is nearly as bad as awaiting the word of command for a bayonet charge.

Thus every man is sizing up his neighbour and weighing him in the balance when the doctor puts in an appearance. What a relief! What are these chaps with such smart uniforms, such a magnificent martial bearing and such pretty little bits of red and gold spotted on their hats, shoulders, and sleeves? Surely they are Captains; but no, by their voice, and pompous manner, they must surely be no less than Generals! Wait, worried recruit. When you have been in the Army one little week, you will know, only too well, that they are after all only Sergeant Majors on the Instructional Staff.

''Tion, 'tion, 'tion! Look here, you chumps, fall in, fall in, we can't wait here all day, stand over there. No, come over here – that's right, no – damn it – that's wrong. Ah! now fall in.'

Some of us were beginning to think that we had fallen in right enough, but not in the way the drill instructor meant.

Then came the order to strip. What a funny sight!

The doors of the hall were wide open, and a rather fresh breeze blowing in, and there stand or sit in every self-conscious attitude about fifty fellows, all wondering what Adam did in cold weather!

One by one we were called to face the doctor, and it is not exaggeration to state that these same fellows were more frightened then than they were on that never-to-be-forgotten dawn of 25 April 1915.

At last the writer's own turn came. He hopped, jumped, stepped sideways, backwards, forwards, touched toes, waved his arms madly about, so much so that if a stranger appeared he would imagine he was beholding a Salome dance or a rehearsal for a 'corroboree.' He was tapped here, punched there, asked to cough – though that request is superfluous, because if by now you are not coughing, you ought to be. Twiddle round on your heels – very good – the recruit is brought to his senses by 'Halt, about turn'.

You walk forth a soldier whose battles have already commenced, for ten to one someone has admired the pattern of your shirt, and shown a preference for your socks.

BILL'S RELIGION

William Baylebridge

Among those questions put to men before we let them into our armed forces, the one that most troubles them is the question that bears upon their creed or religion.

To many men the beliefs of the various church conclaves and synods are dead things of which they know nothing. These men have their own creed, often kept well hidden and containing some strange articles. Some of these articles many a priest, perhaps, would set little store by.

This creed, the creed proper to Australians, we have not yet written down in books, thus, men are at times hard put to answer questions that bear upon their creed or religious beliefs.

There was a young bushman called Bill. He went early to join up for the Light Horse. Having passed the riding test, he was told, with others, to get stripped, and stand in a tent, and wait there till the tape Sergeant called on him. This he did. Seeing him there in his skin only, you could have marked that he was a lengthy lean fellow, broad of bone, with muscle sitting along it like bunched wire. The bush had done that.

Someone said: 'Step forward!' And he stepped up and on to the scale.

'Twelve seven,' said the Sergeant.

He then stood up to have the tape run across him.

'Five eleven and a half – forty – forty-four,' said the Sergeant again.

Then, when they were done with his age, his eyes, the colour of his hair, and the quaint marks, an officer said, looking up: 'What religion?'

Now, this man, because of the reason I have spoken of, could not well answer this.

'My kind,' he said, 'give little thought to that.'

The officer said, 'But, you must tell me this. We require an answer. What belief does your father hold to?'

'He kept it always inside his shirt,' said Bill, slowly, 'no one rightly knew.'

'How, then, was he buried?' asked the officer again, sharply. He did not care much for this man's manners. 'That will clear this thing up.'

'Well,' said Bill, 'the old man had the laugh on them there too, for he put that job through himself.'

'Himself! How so?'

'He dropped down a shaft,' Bill answered, 'and it fell in upon him. This we found out later and, as he was a dead man then, there was nothing left to do but to put the stone up.'

'A poor funeral!' the officer remarked.

'Well, he always said,' answered Bill, 'that he'd care most for a funeral that had little fuss about it.'

The officer, plainly, was losing his patience. 'Have you never heard tell of such things as the Thirty-nine Articles?' he asked, 'the Sermon on the Mount, and the Ten Commandments? Look, my man, don't you know what a Catholic is, and a Quaker? What a Wesleyan is, or a Seventh Day Saint? It might be, now, that you're an Anabaptist,' he said, 'or a Jew. But one of these things you must be. Speak up. The Sergeant has to fill this form in.'

'One of those things I might be,' Bill answered. 'But I can't tell that. I'm a plain man.'

The officer looked at him squarely and then said, with a hard lip, 'Tell me this – have you any religion in you at all?'

'That I can't swear to,' said Bill. 'But an old fellow up our way, who looked after us well as children and often chatted with us around the campfire, said he reckoned so.'

The officer smiled tartly, 'And this bushman had some articles of faith for this religion?'

'He did,' replied Bill.

'This ought to be looked into,' said the officer, 'it may be that he made up the decalogue for it, too.'

'In a manner of speaking he did,' answered Bill again.

'Indeed! And what, then, was that?'

Bill, taking his time about it, said: 'I got this off by heart. To give it in his own words it ran like this:

> Honour your country; put no fealty before this.
> Honour those who serve it.
> Honour yourself; for this is the beginning of all
>   honour.
> A mean heart is the starting place of evil.
> A clean heart is the dignity of life; keep your heart
>   clean.
> Think first; then labour.
> Lay to, so that your seed will stand up thick on the
>   earth.
> Possess your own soul.
> Thou shalt live ... and
> Thou shalt lay down thy life for more life.

'I think that was it,' he said. 'I can't go much into that swagger; but I guess that's about right. Now, if you'll put that question again, I think I could fix it.'

'What, then, is your religion?' asked the officer.

Glad at heart to have found his answer, Bill said, quickly, 'Australian, that's my religion.'

'Well,' said the officer, with a sour smile, 'that will do. Pass on to the doctor.'

On Bill's form, then, in the space against religion, he wrote this word – 'None'.

ENLISTED

Frederick Loch ('Sydney de Loghe')

Ted was driving me to the camp.

The wind had worked up into half a gale, and much of the way clouds of dust swept into our faces. The ponies faced the weather unwillingly, and Ted did not spare the whip. I crouched back in the buggy, with hat hard over my eyes, and for minutes together neither of us said a word, unless it was to curse our luck.

Sometimes the gale dropped, the dust lay down, the sun shone again; and then we found ourselves in grassy country, hilly and also flat. Up once more jumped the wind, and the dust sprang after it. It was damnable, nothing less.

At last, at a level crossing, we turned sharply to the right, and the buggy hood afforded some shelter. Between the dust storms, the camp was to be seen, ahead and to the left hand. Tents stretched over many acres. Also I caught a glimpse of paddocks filled with manoeuvring infantry and occasional artillery teams. Then we were passing a long row of pines. Opposite them were open paddocks, with Melbourne in the distance.

'It'll be somewhere about here,' Ted said, moving his head my way, and he pulled the horses into a slow trot.

The road began to fill up. Half-companies of infantry passed us in an opposite direction, made up of uniformed men and men in civilian dress. The whole moved to the shouts of sergeants and lesser fry. A gun team and an ammunition wagon rumbled by. The horses were awkward, the harness stiff, the drivers at sea. A mounted N.C.O. called the wrath of Heaven on the whole affair. We steadied to a walk, and the team ambled past.

'This must be the place,' Ted said again, and stopped the ponies. I pushed my head round the buggy hood to find us at an opening in the fence, with a sentry on guard there. The other side of the fence was a paddock filled with tents in rows, and between each row ran horse-lines. Between the tents and the road were drawn-up guns and ammunition wagons.

'Yes, this must be the place.'

Ted drew into the footpath while I got out. 'I'll wait somewhere about here,' he said, moving up on the road at a walk and calling back.

The sentry challenged me; but my pass let me in. I asked for the Colonel, and was directed straight ahead. Inside the lines, much was going on. Men ran, trotted, and walked; joked, argued, and shouted. Tents were going up, horses were being picketed; things were topsy-turvy. As for uniform, some men possessed military hats only, others had on military shirts, others military breeches; but the majority wore their civilian clothes.

Busy men were to be seen; but just as many loafed round. Outside the quartermaster's store, equipment of every sort was piled, all painfully new. A score of men lingered round it, and there seemed to be four or five unwilling sorters. In the middle stood the Q.M. with store lists in his hands.

I passed up a line of tents with horses picketed on the left hand, and at the top asked the way again of an individual balancing himself on a tent peg. He pointed to a large tent not far away, and stared hard after me when I left him.

Outside the big tent was a notice: 'HEADQUARTERS FIELD ARTILLERY BRIGADE'. An orderly stood in the doorway, lighting a cigarette. I asked for the Colonel. 'D'you want him?' the orderly said and he pushed up the flap of the tent. I stooped and went in.

The tent was furnished with a table and several chairs; at the table three officers sat. Table and chairs were covered with papers and books, and all three men were writing. Round the walls stood packing cases, filled to overflowing with strange instruments, odds and ends of harness, and signalling flags. I came to a full stop.

Two of the men went on with their work, but the third – the youngest of them, a Lieutenant about twenty – looked up, eyed me, and yawned. When he had finished, he picked up his pen again, and remarked casually, 'What do you want?'

When he spoke, the other men stopped writing and lifted their heads.

The centre man was a big man, and by cap and shoulder strap I knew him as the Colonel. The third man was small and sharp featured, by rank Captain – the adjutant, I guessed.

'I would like to see Colonel Jackson,' said I.

The big man put down his pen. 'I am Colonel Jackson.'

I looked him over as he spoke. He was a middle-aged man – nearly fifty, I thought, and rather handsome. His hair was turning grey, his complexion was high, and I warrant he knew how to enjoy life. He looked me straight in the face. A good soldier, I thought: a man worth following.

'Yesterday I received notice from the Commandant at Victoria Barracks to report to you,' I began. 'I volunteered, and have passed the medical examination.'

'What is your name?'

'Lake.'

'Have you had any military training?'

'I am sorry, none; but I can ride and shoot.' And I added, 'I hope this won't stand in my way. I am very anxious to get in.'

The Colonel drummed his fingers on the table a moment or two, and all the while looked at me. In the end he spoke gravely.

'You know, Lake, a soldier's life is a hard life, a very hard life – bad food, the ground for a bed, exposure to all weathers, work all hours. The officer is no better off than the man.'

'I have not rushed into it,' I said. 'I have thought it over and hope you will take me.' To this he answered nothing. 'I have some horses,' I went on, 'which would suit a gun team. I shall be glad to give them if they are of any use.'

He misunderstood me. 'Oh,' he said, 'we have enough now. In any case the Government does not give a high price. What do you want for them?'

'I don't want to sell,' I said. 'I make an offer of them. They are plough horses, and, should I go away, I shall not plough this year. I am glad to offer them.'

'Lake, I don't think there is any need for that. As long as a man gives his own services, it is all that can be expected. Keep your horses. If you join, when can you come into camp?'

'I can come now; but I should like first to go back to Gippsland. I have a place there.'

'That can be arranged.' He turned to the Lieutenant who first had spoken to me. 'Sands, take Lake to the doctor and afterwards swear him in.'

I noticed Sands got up rather hurriedly when the Colonel's eye reached him; but he recovered himself outside the tent. He pushed his hat on to the back of his head, stuffed both hands in his pockets and led the way all over the place.

The doctor was not in his tent and seemed to have died or deserted. We wandered about endlessly, without any obvious plan of campaign. Now and then Sands would stop someone and ask when the doctor had last been seen; and always he finished by swearing in a bored kind of way. Then off we moved again.

At last we found ourselves where we had started – outside the big tent. 'Stay there,' Sands said suddenly, and disappeared inside. He came out with a large printed paper, a book, a pen, and a bottle of ink. The bottle of ink he balanced on a post, the pen he put between his teeth. Next he began to open out the sheet; and the wind took hold of it, shook it and wrestled with it; and he bungled it, crumpled it, and finished by swearing again. But in the end he won, and we took up opposite positions and made a start on our business.

He asked endless questions, which I answered, and we came to the oath. 'Take off your hat,' he said. He became solemn in a moment with an ease entirely his own and took off his hat. Next he held out a Bible. I took it and we began the oath. The wind blew, Sands mumbled; and there was difficulty in following what he said. More than once he eyed me sternly, and repeated the sentence. But we came through it safely, the signatures were made, the ceremony was ended.

There was still the doctor's signature to get; but Sands was sick of me. He pushed the paper into my hand, waved in the direction of the doctor's tent, and departed.

I journeyed anew after the doctor, and this time found him in his tent. He was alone, reading a long letter and smiling over it. He asked what I wanted, told me to strip, and went on reading. He read still when I was ready; but presently put the letter away and started to tap me. He tried my teeth, tried my eyes, said I would do, and, while I dressed, he filled in the papers.

I took the papers to the Brigade Office, and gave them to Sands. The Colonel was there, talking to an officer I did not know. 'Captain Knight, I am giving Lake to you,' he said. 'He will be coming on Sunday or Monday; in the meantime he is going down to Gippsland. Make him out a railway pass, will you?'

The Captain swung round. He was a clean, rather well-dressed man, with a restless manner. 'Yes, sir,' he said, saluting. He told me to follow him, and marched off down a row of tents and across horse-lines, until we came to a tent with a notice board in front. A Sergeant Major and a couple of clerks were inside writing; sundry other fellows hung round the door. Knight bounced into the tent with me at his heels.

'This man has been given to us, Sergeant Major. He wants to get down to Gippsland tomorrow. Make a pass out, please.' He turned to me.

'When can you come, Lake?'

'Sunday or Monday,' I answered.

'Then come here Sunday morning. We have not much time, and you ought to get in all the drills you can. I can't wait. The Sergeant Major will give you your pass.' He went off at full speed.

I was given the railway pass, and left the tent with mixed feelings. There was no drawing back; but – yes – I was glad. I walked fast, guessing Ted would be bored, and in truth he was at the gate, passing time by cracking his whip. 'I'm in!' I called out. Ted grinned and drew the reins together.

DEVIL-MAY-CARE*

J. W. Gordon (Jim Grahame)

Devil-may-care is on the march, with ever their heads held high;
Theirs is a mighty sacrifice, cheer loud as they're passing by!
Give them a cheer to remember, give them a rousing hand;
Strong and fit, and they'll do their bit, the bravest men in the land.

Shearer's cook and rouseabout, hard-bitten tough of the 'Loo,
Have cobbered up with a parson's son and a freckle-faced
   jackeroo.
Cream of a nation's manhood, pride of a people's heart,
A Devil-may-care battalion eager to play their part.

Son of a city banker, son of a city slum,
Son of the boundless bushland, keen and alert they come.
Shoulder to shoulder they're marching, hard as steel and as true,
Devil-may-care and reckless – and ready to die or do.

A rollicking hardcase legion – see how the blighters grin!
Those are the kind that are needed, those are the men who'll win.
Swinging to war like their fathers, wiry and ready and game
The Devil-may-cares are marching – on to their deathless fame.

*extract

SAM AND ME*

Arthur Hoey Davis ('Steele Rudd')

I left home at seventeen.

It was drawing close to New Year when Sam Condle sent me word to get ready to go down the rivers with him and some other chaps.

I was ready to go anywhere with anyone, not because there wasn't plenty of work about, but because Connie Crutch had told me straight out one evening that she didn't want me coming to see her any longer. An' after all the conversation lollies I bought her, an' all the wood I chopped for her too! By cripes it made me furious.

'I'm off in the morning,' I sez to the Old Lady, 'an' might never come back to these parts again.'

'Frankie, if I was you I wouldn't,' she sez, with a terrible sad look on her. 'Me boy, you are not strong enough to shear beside men as old as your father. Wait till you get set and have more practice.'

When I think about how she coaxed and coaxed me to stay, it brings the tears to me eyes.

Of course, I didn't tell her about Connie, but I quoted Jackie Howe shearing his 300 a day to her, an' I reckoned if couldn't hack me way through a couple of hundred I'd eat me hat.

Next morning first thing I rolled me swag up an' strapped it on the packhorse along with a jackshay an' a pair of greenhide hobbles that I made on purpose about three months before.

Soon as breakfast was over I grabs me hat an' sez, 'Well, I got to meet the rest of the chaps at Hodgson's Creek in about an hour.'

Then the handshaking and the crying commenced, which was always the worst part of going away. Anyone who's never left a home in the bush don't know what that means.

No one, only me horse and the birds and the bears in the trees, heard the sobbing I broke into when I got away, and no one only them saw me wiping me eyes on me sleeve and swallowing me feelings when the banks of Hodgson's Creek came in sight.

There were seven of us, all in our teens except Tom Murray and Sam Condle, all sons of cockies and Darling Downs pioneers, an' wasn't we overjoyed an' happy an' agreeable to one another riding down Wyreena Lane like an army corps going to embark. The jingling of the billycans an' the quart pots an' hobble chains was keeping time to the horses, an' we had glimpses of the big brown plains starting to peep through the trees ahead of us.

The glories of the bush were beginning to reveal themselves to us already. Sam, feeling the influence of it, started reciting:

> It was merry mid the glowing morn, among the
>   gleaming grass,
> To wander as we wandered many a mile,
> And blow the cool tobacco cloud and watch the white
>   wreaths pass,
> Sitting loosely in the saddle all the while.
> Sitting loosely in the saddle all the while.

An' the effect his recitation had on the lot of us was wonderful. We couldn't help feeling it was wrote about us specially, an' those who hadn't their pipes alight started lighting 'em and blowing clouds right and left, and hanging their feet out of the irons.

Tom Murray said it was the best poetry he ever heard an' asked Sam who was the bloke that wrote it. Sam said he didn't know him, but a chap who he met the last time he was down the rivers wrote it out for him.

From that time forward for months an' for a year I followed Sam like a foal. Wherever we could get shearing to take on, we took it;

when we couldn't get it we took anything that offered, fencing, dam sinking an' horse breaking.

We worked our passage to Blackall, camping a night with Jimmy Power, the big shearer, at the Four Mile Gardens, belonging to a Chinaman, an' helped ourselves to some of his spuds.

From there to Isisford; to Barcaldine; down the Barcoo to Northampton Downs; then to Windorah and across to Adavale where we was heaping up big money when news come that war had broke out with Germany. I don't know how long it was coming but it seemed to have broke out a good while before it reached us.

From Adavale we cut into Charleville, intending to have a good spell there before arranging our next programme.

＊　　＊　　＊

We found Charleville full of nothing but talk and excitement about the war. From what some of them was saying you'd think the Germans had landed and were coming down by Cape York. According to the papers we saw they was all at it, hammer and tongs.

'Australia will be there,' blokes were singing in the street. 'The Empire calls every fit man to the colours' was printed on the walls, an' 'Your country needs your help' was staring at you in the bars.

Blokes was coming in from all parts of the country, selling their horses and belongings an' enlisting, an' some of 'em was blokes Sam an' me met at the sheds. Of course, we got talking to 'em.

'Yer can only get killed once,' they said. 'You got to die sometime, anyhow, an' you'll get a chance to see the blanky world before you do!'

Except for the tender-skinned toffs, who was more like girls than blokes, Sam an' me seemed to be the only two that wasn't enlisting. At intervals we used to take strolls up an' down the street thinking of it all an' saying nothing.

'We ain't been down to the Post Office yet,' said Sam, the second day we was there, 'to see if any letters come for us.'

Turning our heads around we went down there and the postman gave us a fistful of letters that was plastered all over with 'try

Blackall' an' 'try Adavale' an' 'try Isisford' an' goodness knows where else. They was just like the one in the poem that the bloke addressed in care of Conroy's sheep that went all over the country.

I seen the Old Lady's handwriting on one that I got an' stuffed the others in me shirt.

'I'm blowed!' Sam exclaimed, in the middle of one he got from his old man, 'Tom Murray and the other four got home six months ago, an' are going to the war!'

'Eh!?' I fairly squealed, 'to the war!'

'They're in camp in Brisbane,' Sam come in again. He was looking serious as a jew-lizard an' thinking hard to himself.

'Frankie,' he sez, hitching his pants up, 'I'm goin' to enlist; by God, I am!' An', from the look in his eye it would have been Lord help the German that happened to walk into the room at that moment!

'Goin' to enlist!' I said, starting to think. 'That's a dangerous game ain't it?'

'You've followed me into a good few tight places,' he went on, an' I brought you through 'em all right, but don't follow me any further unless you want to ... an' you think you ought to.'

'I don't know about following you there,' I said, 'but I'll think it over for all that.'

War was all right to hear about, but to make one to go into it was a different matter. The blooming idea of it made me start shaking all over, like a cove with the fever.

'Please yourself, old chap,' he answered, 'my mind's made up, anyway.'

I began to wish he hadn't mentioned the matter at all, an' asked him when he was going.

'I'll sell the nags here in Charleville,' he said, 'and buy that first-class ticket I always promised meself, then off down to Toowoomba an' enlist there.'

I didn't expect he had anything in his head so good as that!

'Oh, my oath,' I agreed, 'I'm with you in that, all right, an' when we get to Toowoomba I'll see about enlisting too.'

I never knew anyone look so pleased as Sam did when I told him I was goin' to enlist too.

'Good man!' he shouted, an' grabbed me by the hand. 'I knew you'd decide in the confirmative, a bloke like you couldn't do anything else!'

'Of course I couldn't,' I answered, 'I don't think there's much to be afraid of, anyway.'

All the same, I was forced to make a couple of swallers to get rid of a choking feeling that come up into me throat.

'Come on then,' sez Sam, an' up he jumps and led the way to the auctioneer.

* * *

'Two first-class tickets to Toowoomba,' Sam said to the stationmaster a week later.

'First-class, did yer say?' an' he looked out at the pair of us from under his gold-banded cap as if we was against regulations.

'If you have anything better than first we'll have it instead,' Sam said, an' he flashed a roll of notes.

The bloke looked us over again and kept quiet.

About two hours after that in come the iron horse from Cunnamulla way rushing along, as if it meant to smash into the platform, an' the blokes on the engine hanging out over the side ready to shove her off with their hands.

'Take yer seats, please!' the station official starts bellowing, almost before she'd stopped.

Sam and me ran up an' down for a bit, picking out the best, then into a bonzer first-class carriage we jumped and dropped down on beautiful soft leather cushions with springs under them, an' looking glasses above our heads.

'Lord, Frankie,' Sam laughed, 'this is all right!'

'My oath!' I said, jumping up and down on the cushions to get me money's worth outa them right from the commencement.

Seeing me at it, Sam started doing the same and a couple of times we fell onto the floor, an' a white-skinned old bloke at the other end, wearing gold rings on his fingers an' gold in his teeth, sings out, 'You seem to be enjoying yourselves.'

'By Cripes,' we said, 'we never struck anything like this before!'

Then Sam took a run like goin' off a high bank into a waterhole an' dived full length onto his cushion. I did the same onto mine and then we stood on our heads on 'em and fell over backwards, laughing joyously.

'Where do you blokes come from?' the swell says, when he got a chance to get a word in.

'I don't know where we come from,' Sam answered, 'but we're off to the blanky war.'

The bloke got a surprise. 'Well, you won't get any cushions to jump about on over there,' he said, grinning.

'An' we never got 'em to jump about on here until today,' Sam told him, and then asked him how long he thought the war was going on.

'Won't last three munce,' he grunted. 'England on sea can starve Germany to a shadder in a fortnight. On land, well, anyone knows that one British soldier is equal to ten Germans.'

'The Britishers must be a lot better than Australians,' Sam grinned, 'or else the Germans at home must be a lot worse than the ones we meet out here.'

'Not at all!' the swell snapped. 'I'm a Britisher and I know what we can do.'

'So was me old man a Britisher,' Sam said, 'an' I'm an Australian, but he couldn't knock me out, nor you couldn't either, not on your life. For all that, I wouldn't like to take on three Germans, to say nothing about ten. Would you, Frankie?' an' he drags me into it.

The swell runs his eye over me; I could feel he was sizing up me fighting qualities.

'Oh, I dunno,' I says, taking a seat opposite to him, 'I never found a German that could fight much!'

'Of course, you never!' An' the toff looked as if he'd have given me his daughter if he had one. 'Don't you reckon you would be good enough for a dozen of the mongrels?'

'For half a dozen, anyway,' I said, sub-editing him a bit so as not to be too hard on Sam.

'*What!*' An' Sam jumped to his feet an' fell back again to the motion of the train. 'With rifles in their hands?'

'Not with rifles,' I said, 'but with fists I could.'

'With fists!' Sam snorted. 'Who the hell's going to fight a war with fists!' Then he returned to the other end an', laying on his back, hung his two feet out the window.

The swell and me agreed on everything pretty well an' had a quiet yarn to ourselves.

'There'll be millions killed and blown to dust on both sides in this war,' he told me, in a sort of confidence.

'Killed and blown to dust?' I gasped, thinking of me and Sam.

'Look at the size of the armies,' he explained. 'The big battles of the past, when a hundred thousand or so used to fall on the field, were only a flea's bite to what's going to happen directly.'

'Cripes!' I said, looking across to Sam lying on the cushions and wondering if he oughtn't to be told about it before we went any further.

'The only thing that worries me,' an' the old swell lit a big cigar, but didn't ask me if I had a mouth, 'is that I'm too old to enlist.'

'That *worries* yer?' I repeated, wondering if he hadn't made a mistake or was losing his track.

'Certainly!' An' he blew a big cloud of smoke out the window like exploding a shell.

'But that oughtn't to worry yer,' I pointed out to him, 'not if they're goin' to be killed by the million.'

'There's nothing I'd like better than to die a soldier's death!' An' he knocked the ash of his cigar with his finger, as if it was the Kaiser's head he was disposing of.

'There ain't?' An' I looked at him wondering what sort of a bloke he was at all. An' I got up to see how Sam was getting on.

'If I had twenty sons I'd send them all to the front,' he said, before I went.

'How many have you got?'

'None, unfortunately!' An' he pulled a bonzer rug around himself.

'What have you been doing all the time?' I asked him, holding onto the side of the carriage to keep me legs.

The engine gave a loud whistle just then an' I didn't hear what he said.

Then I lurched across to join Sam again an' tell him what I'd heard about the war. But Sam was sound asleep with his two feet still hanging out the window, so I decided to let him rest.

*   *   *

The Toowoomba platform was crowded when me an' Sam arrived; an' how they all started an' gaped into our carriage as we come backing in.

'There must be a meeting of the Farmers' Union here today,' said Sam, 'look at all the blokes sporting wire whiskers!'

Then we started ducking an' shoving to get through the crowd.

Sam said, 'I never struck a mob like this here before.'

'So many girls reach the coming-out age every year in this place now,' I said, 'an' there being no place for them to go to see a bit of life except the platform ... it gets congested.'

'At that rate,' he considered, 'it'll have to be made a mile long in a couple of years.'

'All them that ain't Toowoomba girls or Farmers' Union,' I said, 'must be the travelling public.'

In the street, where there was nothing but cabmen watching us like hawks, we stood and put our heads together for a while and talked things over again.

'I think I'll go straight to the recruiting office and enlist before I change me mind,' Sam says.

Right,' I said, so into town we both goes an' marches up to the recruiting depot.

A lot of chaps same as ourselves was coming out an' goin' into the building when we arrived, most of them waving their hands an' talking about the war an' deciding how to win it.

Looking in the door we saw a couple of blokes in uniform, with stripes on their arms, sitting at a table covered with papers an' pens an' a empty water-bottle.

'There you are, in we go!' says Sam, giving me a shove.

Before I knew where I was the military blokes was pouring questions into me and writing me answers down like lightning.

'Into this room here,' says another in emu feathers and long-necked spurs, 'an' be examined by the doctor.'

In I stumbles, feeling sort of dazed by the imposing surroundings an' more like a bloke that was doomed to be executed before breakfast than a prospective soldier of the King. Cripes! I did get my eyes open all of a sudden, though. For a minute I thought I had got into the swimming baths, then I took it for a blooming asylum.

Here before me was about twenty blokes without a blooming stitch of clothes on, all of 'em naked as skinned kangaroos. Some was bucking round doing high kicks; some pretty old fossils, looking like plucked roosters, was sitting on a bench calmly philosophising on the appearance of the other chaps, an' some more was stalking about putting their chests out and admiring themselves like peacocks.

I looked round for Sam, but he had gone into a different room. So after thinking about it for a while, I started and took me togs off slowly; but not wanting to make a fool of meself altogether I kept me shirt on, an' even with it on I never in me life found meself in such an awkward predicament. A bloke couldn't help feeling downright ashamed of himself and that was all about it. Of course, I squatted on a bench as soon as I could an' pulled me shirt over me knees.

The doctor was putting 'em through one after the other, like a cove shearing with all the shed to himself, an' there was me waiting me turn like the poor old cobbler. Always having an active mind, of course, I got to thinking of the whole damn business again. 'I dunno,' I thought to meself, 'what the devil I wanted coming here for at all.'

'Your turn next,' a bloke sings out to me and disturbs me reflections.

'Oh!' I says, an' jumps up an' move across the room. Passing by a naked recruit he gives me a grin an' pulls up me shirt.

'Steady,' I says, 'none of that.' An' a lot of 'em started laughing.

'Think a bloke hasn't got a bit of respect for himself?' I says to the lot of 'em, an' they laughed more. But I let 'em laugh.

Soon as I face the doctor I began trembling all over an nearly choked meself pulling at me shirt to make it come down lower. He lifted his eyes from his writing pad an', without bidding a bloke good-day or asking how he was, snaps out, 'Take off your shirt!'

'What, right off?' I says, just to make sure what he meant.

'Yes, yes, what else?' an' he frowns like a burglar.

Back I creeps and chucks the shirt off, an' presents meself to him again with only me pants on.

'Dammit, man!' he blurts out, 'I want to see you with nothing at all on.'

'Oh!' I says, 'can't you examine some of a bloke at a time?'

'Are you married?' he says, an' thinking it was a comical sort of thing to ask a bloke, I grinned.

'Are you?' he barks, stamping his foot.

'Not yet,' I says, with another grin.

'And I don't think you ever will be,' he says.

Then, turning to the chap in the emu feathers and the long-necked spurs, he says, 'For God's sake, take the pants off this innocent abroad and let me get to my work!'

'Whip 'em off, everyone does it!' says the Captain or whatever he was, striding for me as if he meant to tear 'em off me.

'Oh, orright,' I says, 'if everyone does it I'll do it.'

Then, turning me back on 'em I lets down me pants an' was bending low getting me foot outa the leg, when that infernal Captain brought me the most terrific spank I ever heard, with his open hand! Cripes, I nearly hit the ceiling with me head!

'Oy, steady!' I says to him, 'I didn't come here for that sort of thing!'

When the doctor stopped laughing he steps over to me and says, 'Why, a man made like you ought to be only too proud to show yourself naked. You're the best built youngster I ever saw in my life.'

That changed me feelings an' me opinion of him in a second.

'Do you think so?' I says, forgetting the pain and me nakedness an' grinning proudly.

'I'm sure of it.'

Then he starts tapping me chest and putting his ear to me and pulling me about.

'Hmmm,' he says, an' looks into me mouth, as if I was a horse he was buying.

Then, to see if I ever went to school, he asks me to read the blooming ABC. Cripes, it was easy as snuff.

'Pass!' says the Captain.

'Wish we could get another hundred thousand like him,' says the doctor. Then, putting his hand on me shoulder, he says to me, 'Sound as a bell, me boy. Good luck to you, and see you come back with a V.C.'

Outside I found Sam waiting for me already, with a broad smile on him.

'How did you get on?' he asked.

'Good,' I answered, an' started laughing. Then he started laughing, an' we both went out the gate roaring laughing.

* * *

We went into camp at Enoggera, an' into dungarees an' a white rag hat and big boots that were a load to carry. Lord! Sam an' me did look a pair but one couldn't laugh at the other which was the only satisfaction about it.

For the first couple of days we thought it the maddest place we ever got into, an' the maddest lot of blokes we ever struck. The camp was all tents an' buildings an' sheds an' big holes in the ground an' trenches dug crooked an' big stumps half grubbed out. It looked like a goldfield.

Thousands of us blokes separated into different mobs was kept running about, on an' off, on an' off all day, drilling. When we wasn't drilling we was shooting at targets or digging, or anything else that wasn't of much use. An' talk about Colonels an' Lieutenant Colonels and Majors an' Captains an' Sergeants. That was the place to see those gentlemen. They was as plentiful as kangaroos was in the bush. Everywhere you turned you met two or three of 'em swinging canes, an' to hear 'em giving orders was better than listening to an auctioneer selling poor horses.

Cripes! I never knew what a small inconsequential bloke I was till I got into that camp. There was even a parson there that me an'

Sam run into once out at Blackall, stalking about in a uniform with leggings up to his knees.

'Well, I'm blowed,' says Sam the first time we saw him, 'surely he ain't goin' to the blooming war, too?' An' both of us burst out laughing.

'What's up with you fellows?' a Sergeant coming in for his dinner says.

We told him what the joke was and expected he'd join in it with us, but he didn't.

'That's Lieutenant Colonel Chaplain Brown-Smith,' he says, 'and he goes to the front with the next Division.'

'But we met that bloke once,' Sam told him, 'about forty miles out of Blackall, crawling along on a blessed old moke that you wouldn't give a feed to.'

'I don't care if you met him four mile outside of hell!' the Sergeant barked, 'you might meet him outside the trenches and be damn glad to, too! An' don't let me tell both of you again,' he added in his own interests, 'to salute your officers wherever you meet them.' An' suiting the word to the action he give us a demonstration.

Me an' Sam grinned an' give him one back, but by mistake lifted the wrong hand. Then he lifted his voice an' swore an' reckoned it was only wasting breath talking to blokes like us.

We shared a good tent along with some other recruits to camp in, but no bunks, so it was scratch the chips an' pebbles away an' sleep on the ground. But me an' Sam was used to that. When 'lights out' was sounded by the bugler we turned in as regular as clockwork, but we was there a long time before we could get into the habit of falling off to sleep.

Instead of the tinkle-tonkle of horse-bells an' the screaming of the curlews an' the howling of the dingoes, the voice of the officer drilling us kept ringing in our ears all night an' keeping us awake. An' though everything he said and explained to us in the day seemed to go in one ear all jumbled up and come out the other the same way, we could remember an' repeat every word of it when we was asleep. We could see him swinging his arms about an' demonstrating as plain as if he was standing inside the tent with the moon shining on him.

One evening we hadn't turned in long when Sam, leaving off snoring, yells out in his sleep, 'Order ... arms! Raise the rifle at the band and come to the order!'

Then he gives off a couple of small snores an' broke out afresh, 'Shoulder arms ... one. Give the rifle a jerk upwards with your hand in line with the elbow; at the same time slipping the right hand inside the guard, close your first and second fingers round the magazine!'

The other blokes in the tent sat up to listen an' one interrupted with, 'Close your mouth, we'll get enough of that termorrer!'

'Let him alone, he's asleep,' says another who was enjoying Sam.

Sam only groaned an', kicking the blankets off, commenced again, this time in a loud an' angry voice, 'Dammit, do it again! I'll keep the lot of yer here till yer do it! Now! Are you listening? Change arms ... one. Bring yer rifle to a perpendicular position! An' I said the right shoulder. Dammit, don't none of yer know yer RIGHT shoulder?'

Then all the other tent mates yelled like hell an' threw everything they could feel near them at Sam, most of which hit me.

'What's the matter?' Sam asks, waking up and gaping about in the dark.

They told him what the matter was an' he says, 'Arrr what are you giving us?' An' curling himself up in the blanket again, he was snoring in about a minute.

*　　*　　*

The route marches to the seaside agreed with us though. Sam an' me was pretty good at marching, we got plenty of practice at it going to the Barcoo, when we lost our horses which I didn't tell you about.

Some of the city blokes didn't take too kindly to marching though an' used to drop out along the road to have a spell. A great sight was the sea for the first time, Sam an' me couldn't take our eyes of it. Lord, it only wanted a bit of saltbush or a mulga tree sticking out of it here and there an' we would have reckoned we was on the edge of the Western Plains again.

'A bloke like you couldn't do anything else!' Embarkation march Hobart 1914

'That's where we'll be going pretty soon I suppose,' Sam says, 'right across there to blazes ... anywhere.' An' both of us folded our arms an' looked out as far as we could see to what seemed to be the end of the world. An' to many of those brave fellows shouting and romping there in the waves that day, it surely was.

'Hey, you there,' an officer called out an' disturbed our reflections, 'everyone in for a swim.'

'Right you are,' Sam answered, an' undressing ourselves we raced into the sea, churning it into foam like wild horses plunging through a lagoon.

When we got dressed I went with Sam an' about a hundred others over to a cocky's place an' made a great raid on a couple of acres of watermelons. Jee-roosalem, they was the biggest an' heaviest lot of melons ever I tackled in my life! Talk about eat! We did eat, an' kept running from one vine to another like blooming bees after honey.

When we had eaten all we could carry we thought of bringing some to the camp with us, but how to hump them was the trouble.

'We'll do it the way us blokes in the bush have to do when we haven't got bags to carry beef in,' says Sam, pulling off his pants. The others, who was mostly city bred, starts staring at him an' I does a bit of a laugh because I knew what was coming.

'Here, catch hold,' an' Sam hands me his pants all buttoned up again an' I held 'em while he stuffed a long thin melon into each leg an' a big round one into the seat. You should have heard them city blokes laughing, they reckoned Sam was a genius.

'Look here,' said one of 'em, 'you ought to be a General in this army.' Then every second one of 'em started whipping off their pants an' filling 'em with melons.

'Now,' Sam says, giving instructions, 'one bag of melons to every two blokes an' off we go. Fall in ... company take hold ... attention ... quick march!'

Lord it would have done your eyes good to see us marching outa that cocky's paddock in double file, one line of blokes without any pants an' the other line with pants on, an' in between us the melons.

The bugles were sounding like fury an' all the others had fallen into the ranks an' had their eyes right, dressing into file, when we come marching back to the beach all keeping step.

'What the hell's this?' the officer in command roars out as we paraded past him.

'Halt!' Sam yells. 'Drop melons ... dismiss!'

Then the officer couldn't help breaking into a laugh an' all the others broke ranks an' fought like hell for the melons.

The day we got our uniform, an' flung the dungarees an' old rag hat into a corner, was the day of our lives.

'Jeemimah!' Sam says, standing up in the tent, 'how the devil do I look in 'em, Frankie?'

'Holy war!' I says, 'you're all right. How do I look meself?' An' I marched around grinning at him.

'Cripes,' he says, 'if I look half as good as you I'm satisfied!'

I was six foot two, you know, an' a bit heavier than Sam.

'We must apply for home leave at once,' he says, 'an' go straight home an' show ourselves to everyone. Lord Nelson an' the Duke of Wellington was never in it with us, Frankie!'

I agreed with Sam on that count.

About a week later we got our leave an' off we goes without letting anyone know we was coming. But before we left we was told by the O.C. that we would be leaving for the front in eight days an' that we had to make our wills an' settle our private affairs.

That was a shock that was.

'Wills!' I gasped at Sam. 'Cripes!'

It took all the sport outa soldiering for me an' somehow I couldn't look forward to enjoying meself at home at all ... not after that.

'There's nothing in making your will, Frankie,' Sam said soothingly, 'everybody makes 'em whether they goes to the war or whether they doesn't.'

'Oh, I know that,' I answered, shrugging me shoulders an' trying to grin. But I nearly strangled meself trying to swaller the same infernal lump that was forever coming into me throat. 'I was just thinking it's hardly worth a bloke's while.'

Anyhow we got home all right an' didn't we cause a sensation!

© AWM H19500

'Leaving for the front.' Embarkation 1914

Four days we had of home leave an' a dance was held every night at some of the places in honour of Sam an' me. Wristlet watches was presented to the two of us an' three cheers was called for us, but I couldn't get the will business an' the thoughts of goin' to the front out of me head for a minute, they stuck there like bullets. An' when the morning came to leave I sat on the bed holding me uniform in me hands wondering for long enough if I ought to put it on again or not.

Lots gathered to see us off, an' they all shook hands with me, some of 'em more than once, an' others kissed me for the first time in their lives, an' Connie Crutch whispered into me ear, 'Be sure an' write often, Frankie, an' come back safe.'

An' then I ... I ... well, it don't matter what I did, now.

*   *   *

I was seasick nearly all the way round the coast an' took little interest in anything that went on, an' cared less. Leaving West Australia I stood on the deck beside Sam, a bit away from the rest of the soldiers, watching an' watching.

It was a strange feeling I had just then, an' it seemed to be shared by all the others. The cheering they gave us as we moved out died away, an' the cheering we gave 'em back died away. Hats an' handkerchiefs kept waving at intervals. The rays from the setting sun skimmed the top of the waves an' volumes of black smoke rolled from the funnels of the line of transports following behind an' melted into the sea.

Every man there seemed silent as the grave an' all kept watching for a last glimpse of their native land. Smaller an' smaller, dimmer an' dimmer the coast of Australia became; for a little while just a speck remained visible, an' then ...

'That's the last some of us will ever see of her,' I heard one soldier say. An' if he had run a knife into me heart he couldn't have dispirited me more than he did.

'It's seasickness, that's all it is, old chap,' Sam said, helping me down below an' seeing me into me bunk.

I was in that bunk pretty well all the way to Egypt, feeling down if ever a bloke was in this world. 'Damned if I can understand you at all,' the doctor said to me several times.

But I could understand meself well enough an' day after day I kept repeating the same useless reproach, 'Why did you enlist? Oh, why did you enlist?'

When we reached Alexandria I took Sam's advice an' pulled meself together an' did me best to forget what might or might not happen in the future. 'Who the hell cares?' I said to meself, fighting against it, an' when the sand of the desert got into me socks, an' me hair, an' me ears an' me eyes an' me mouth, I just laughed when the others was all swearing, an' went about whistling.

All the same, when we got to Cairo an' the pyramids an' all them places, I hadn't the desire for exploring an' sight-seeing that the others had. It wasn't that I hadn't plenty of money, either, because I had. But, whenever I was off duty, I put in me time writing to the old people, an' Connie Crutch, an' lying down just thinking an' thinking.

When we was finally leaving Egypt for Lemnos, an' Sam an' all the others was wildly excited about it, I sat down an' wrote what I thought would be me last letter home, telling 'em that our Division was on the move an' I didn't expect they'd ever see me again.

Mudros, when we arrived there, was alive with warships an' boats. On Mudros there was a lot of old houses, an' old gardens, an' what looked like a church, an' some wild flowers ... an' that's all I remember of what it looked like. But the cheer after cheer we got from the French ships an' the Tommies as we steamed into that harbour I will remember till the day I die.

'By God, Frankie,' said poor old Sam, 'that was worth coming all the way from Australia for, if nothing else was!'

*adapted from *Memoirs of Corporal Keeley*

THE LANDING

SONG OF THE DARDANELLES*

Henry Lawson

The wireless tells and the cable tells
How our boys behaved by the Dardanelles.
Some thought in their hearts, 'Will our boys make good?'
We knew them of old and we knew they would!
    Knew they would –
    Knew they would;
We were mates of old and we knew they would.

The sea was hell and the shore was hell,
With mine, entanglement, shrapnel and shell,
But they stormed the heights as Australians should,
And they fought and they died as we knew they would.
    Knew they would –
    Knew they would;
They fought and they died as we knew they would.

*extract

RED GALLIPOLI

H. W. Cavill

We were roused before 6 a.m. by the rattle of the anchor cable, and, by the time we had scrambled on deck, we were gliding down the placid waters of Mudros Bay. We could hardly believe our luck. After eight strenuous months' training, we were at last on the move and, before many hours, should realise to the full what war meant.

Winding our way through the throng of ships, we quickly approached the mouth of the Bay – passing, as we steamed out, the monster battleships *Queen Elizabeth*, *London*, *Prince of Wales* and *Queen*, while sleek, business-like destroyers darted hither and thither.

Passing the heads and the peaceful-looking little lighthouse, we steamed slowly round the island and dropped anchor again in a small cove on the opposite side. Here business began in earnest; iron rations were distributed; arms and equipment inspected; in fact, everything possible to secure success was attended to.

My! Didn't I grin when I saw the ship's grindstone. The boys were afraid their bayonets would not be sharp enough, so there they were, gathered around waiting eagerly their turn to get at the stone. By the time we left the ship it was gouged and worn to such an extent that it was fit for nothing but a kellick stone.

As I sit up here on the boat-deck writing these lines, it is hard to believe that within a few hours we shall be in the midst of slaughter and suffering. As I sit and look around, all is peace and beauty. The setting sun floods the dancing water and casts its rays over the

beautiful green hills of Lemnos, the quaint little windmills completing a sweet picture. But it is work that has to be accomplished, so we look to Him who has been our help in ages past.

The boys were entirely unconcerned; they lay about the decks absorbed in cards, reading, and so forth. Evening found them in the same good spirits, and a happy, rollicking time was spent. One thing, only, pointed to the fact that something unusual was happening. Before retiring, every man packed his valise with extra care; poised his rifle to an electric light and had a final squint through; then finally lay down, still in jocular mood.

I do not profess to know if it is the correct thing to sleep blissfully on the eve of a battle, especially such a battle as we were faced with, but this I do know, what within half an hour the ship was filled with the harmonious melody of a multitude of contented sleepers.

I was still enjoying that blissful period that comes on one just before fully waking. Events were taking shape in my mind; I had just become aware, by the even throb of the engines and the motion of the ship, that we were moving, when to my ears came a sound of distant thunder that swelled louder and louder, in a mighty crescendo, punctuated by terrific crashes as if the very heavens were falling.

You can easily guess I was fully awake by this time, and shouting 'We are there' I flew up the companion-way and on to deck. Already there were a few on deck, but there was little to be seen. The morning mist shrouded everything, and one could only judge the position of the land by the flash of the shore batteries as they returned the fire of the fleet.

Steadily we continued our way, passing battleships in action every few minutes. One after another they would loom up out of the impenetrable grey, deafen us with their mighty guns, and then, as we steamed on, disappear like phantom ships into the gloom. At last we dropped anchor close to two of our ships that could only be located by the flash of their guns.

Opposite page: 'We were at last on the move.' The convoy heads for Gallipoli.

It was a queer sight – on every hand these darting flames, followed by ear-splitting explosions, while every moment the leaden-coloured water would rise in a mighty column, like some magnificent fountain, as the shells from the shore plunged in.

Slowly the mist of the early morn lifted, and there before our eyes lay a scene such as I never dare hope to witness a second time in this life. I could hardly drag myself away to dress; but, at last, slipping into my clothes and putting the last touches to my equipment, I quickly got into a position where I could watch the mighty effort of the Fleet.

We occupied the extreme left of the position. Round about us lay scores of troopships, trawlers, destroyers, and warships. Standing out prominently among the latter was the old H.M.S *Euryalus*, so well known in Australia a few years ago as our navy's flagship. She was right inshore, and engaged at point-blank range the formidable Gaba Tepe battery, which had been doing serious damage, enfilading the beach.

The terrific duel that ensued made everything else appear trivial. The water about the *Euryalus* was churned into foam, and flew up in great columns, but the old ship doggedly hung to her position, while her gunners simply drove us into a frenzy of cheering, as, with marvellous exactness, they dropped shell after shell on to the position.

For over twenty minutes the scrap continued; till finally this piece of landscape lost all shape, the battery was silenced, and the forces no doubt retreated, for the guns were trained to throw the shells, first over the headland, then right up and over the first gradient.

One could hardly believe that at any moment the boys were under fire of the shore batteries. They filled the rigging and decks, and at every salvo from the warships a mighty cheer would rend the air, and then the ship would ring with laughter. No, there were no long faces, but rather a joyous, reckless fearlessness that boded ill for their foes.

The spasmodic crackle of rifle fire now grew into one continuous roll, like the beating of a thousand kettle drums; the 3rd Brigade were getting busy. But, hark!

'Fall in, A and B Companies.'

Swiftly, the eager waiters stepped into their places, and then just as quickly slipped over the ship's side and down the rope ladders, entirely forgetful of the seventy-odd pounds load of equipment they carried.

The crews of the destroyers on each side of the ship worked like Trojans, packing the men in like the proverbial sardines, while we of C and D Companies, who were to go by the second tow, wriggled out of portholes at the risk of cracking our necks, and shouted, 'Jack, I say, Jack, how'd things ashore? How did the boys go?'

Thus they rattled on in disjointed conversation, just as the pressure of business would allow.

At last, after what seemed an eternity, our turn came and with the eagerness of school children off for a picnic, we scrambled down the ladders and into the destroyer *Usk*. Scarcely had we left the *Derfflinger* than we heard a high whining noise.

'Down the rope ladders …'

A land battery had opened fire on her, and shell after shell came screaming overhead and plunged all round our recent home.

It was a nerve-trying time. Our destroyer raced toward the beach, escaping in a miraculous manner the storm of shrapnel. Within a few hundred yards of the shore the destroyer eased down; quickly we jumped into the ship's boats that were being towed alongside; and, with a hearty hurrah, gave way and rowed through the curtain of fire that enveloped the beach.

The question has been asked many times, 'What did you feel like when first under fire?'

I have already described our feelings when leaving the ship; but, as we drew nearer the shore, lips were set, faces grew stern and thoughtful, rifles were gripped more firmly, hands stole quietly round and loosened bayonets, and then – then nothing else to do, and being 'Real Australians', the lads once again joked and laughed, yes actually laughed.

As the keel of the boat grated on the rocky bottom, one and all jumped waist deep into the sea and waded ashore, still quite merry, in spite of the hail of shrapnel that bespattered the beach.

No sooner had we gained the shore than the first man was killed. Not five yards from where I stood a C Company man was struck in the head by a splinter of a shell that burst right in our midst; fortunately nobody else was hit.

We were now in the thick of business. Immediately the 1st, 2nd and 3rd Battalions were ordered to advance to support the covering party.

Dropping our packs, the 2nd Battalion rushed at once to the left flank, where a handful of the covering party were hotly engaged. Then came a toilsome scramble over the high bluffs, carrying, in addition to our equipment, picks, shovels, and boxes of ammunition.

Reaching the top of the first ridge, we came to a Turkish trench, in which lay those Turks who had stayed too long to dispute possession with the 3rd Brigade. Stooping low, we doubled across a plateau over which the sharp-nosed bullets flew, meowing like motherless kittens. A constant stream of wounded men – still quite cheerful – passed us on the way to the beach, saying, 'It's hot as hell up there' – and it was.

All down through Shrapnel Valley, thick with mines and pitfalls, infested with snipers, and torn with shrapnel – from whence it earned its name – hairbreadth escapes were now becoming so frequent that one scarcely stopped to notice them.

We commenced fighting our way up the third hill which, personally, I think was the worst of the lot. Never again do I expect to see such superhuman efforts. Dragging the ammunition and entrenching implements, the men struggled up this almost perpendicular, crumbling, scrub-covered cliff in the face of a withering fire.

One exposed knoll, which the snipers were paying particular attention to, we were compelled to rush over singly. As it came to my turn, I bolted, pick in one hand and rifle in the other, as hard as my legs would carry me. One had simply to claw one's way up the soft, yielding bank. No sooner had I reached the top than a dozen bullets kicked up the dirt all around me. An officer who followed me said, 'What's the matter, laddie?'

'Drop,' I shouted.

He did so, only just in time to miss a perfect fusillade of snipers' bullets.

Side by side we wriggled over the knoll, slid down the opposite side, regained our feet, and put up a record sprint to where the rugged hill afforded some little cover.

At the top of the hill we were in the full blast of the enemy's fire. It was a perfect inferno. A score of machine-guns filled the air with their rat-a-tat; just like a hundred noisy motor bicycles; while the Turkish artillery threw a curtain of shrapnel along the ridge that looked as if it would stop any further effort to advance. But, knowing that our only safety lay in victory, one had to forget self and fight like the very devil.

Many of the boys never passed that shrapnel-swept ridge. One wounded lad, who was bleeding badly over the shoulder, propped himself up as we passed, and grinning hideously with his shattered mouth, he wheezed, 'Got it where the chicken got the axe,' then fainted.

Right and left men were being hit, and a fellow had to just clench his teeth and keep going, with the vague thought somewhere in the back of your cranium that you might be the next. It was just here that my chum, Howard Proctor, was killed.

A shrapnel burst right in the midst of the platoon in front of me; it cut the haversack from the side of Corporal Turton, and splashed two or three others, but poor Proctor was struck with a piece of the shell, which inflicted a fatal wound. The lads close at hand, after shaking hands with him, offered a few words of cheer, and then had to advance.

A few minutes later, when my platoon advanced, I knelt by his side, but he was going fast; I tried to cheer him, but somehow I got a big lump in my throat, my eyes were dimmed, and after a few incoherent words I was silent. Then, in spite of the fact that he was paralysed by his wound, and almost at his last gasp, his face brightened, and with a smile he said, 'Don't worry about me, Cav; I feel quite satisfied; I feel I have done my bit; take my glasses and try and return them to my mother.' And so brave Proctor passed away.

Can you wonder, reader, that we old boys of the 1st Brigade reverence the very name of Anzac?

When we remember the number of our hero chums that sleep the long sleep on the bleak, forbidding hills above Anzac Cove, well have they been named 'The Glorious Dead.'

Can we ever forget the unselfish spirit of soldiers like Pte. W. Penton. Mortally wounded, face downward he lay. Yet, with his last effort, and his last breath, he raised himself, and turning to a mate, said, 'Good-bye, Warrington, old boy; I'm going; but tell Albert he will find plenty of cigarettes in my pack.'

Upon uttering those words, poor Penton fell forward and he was gone.

His parents weep and mourn, but we who knew him will ever cherish the memory of such a great, unselfish soul. No words are there more true than those of Souter, when he said:

We need no costly monument,
To keep their memory fast.

I trust I shall be forgiven if I tell of the heroism of yet another before I pick up the thread of my story.

It is the story of Sgt. Larkin, M.L.A. He lay wounded and dying and yet when the stretcher-bearers came to carry him in, he waved them on, saying, 'There's plenty worse than me out there.' Later, they found him – dead.

Can anyone feel surprised when we get in a rage at the sight of ham and beef shops branded 'ANZAC'?

The splendid courage of our officers compelled admiration. Separated from their own men – for in the wild fighting over the hills the 1st Brigade was quite mixed up – they gathered all the men in sight, and, with commendable courage, charged the enemy's position with the bayonet.

It was in this way that I was separated from my own Company, and fought throughout the day alongside of Major B. I. Swannell, who, with his Company, had got mixed up with our Battalion.

Never shall I forget the look on his face when we first got within striking distance of the enemy.

'Fix bayonets! Charge!' rang out his order.

There was a flash of steel, a wild hurrah, and the boys dashed straight at the wall of fire, heedless of the frightful slaughter. They were not to be stopped.

It was in this charge that Major Swannell was killed. He had seized a rifle, and with dauntless courage was leading his men, when a Turkish bullet, penetrating his forehead, ended his career, thus depriving the 1st Brigade of one of its bravest officers.

The few remaining hours of daylight were spent in such fierce, unequal fighting that I remembered little else until, about an hour before dusk, something hit me.

I thought at first that I had been struck by a shell. After picking myself up, and regaining a sitting position, I put my hand down to feel if my leg was still there; I was really scared to look, for fear it had gone. Feeling that that really useful member was still attached to my body, I started to discover the extent of the damage. Whipping off my puttee and slashing the seam of my breeches with my clasp knife, I reached my knee, to find a small, quite respectable looking puncture close alongside the knee-cap, from which oozed a thin stream of blood.

The bullet – for such it was – had gone right through, coming out behind the knee, severing, en route, some of the important nerves of the leg, thus paralysing the leg. This was temporarily useful, as it saved me any intense pain.

It was just at this stage that the Turks, heavily reinforced, counter-attacked, and compelled our sadly diminished force to fall back. I knew that if I jumped to my feet to retire I would only collapse, as my leg was as useless as though there was no bone in it.

The only thing to avoid capture was to crawl, and crawl pretty quickly.

So, on one knee and two hands, I started, faced with a three-mile journey over as rough country as it would be possible to find.

How I accomplished the distance safely I shall never know. At least a dozen snipers wasted a cartridge on me – the bullets clipping twigs in front of my nose, whistling through my hair, and kicking the dirt up in my face.

On one occasion a platoon of Australians passed on their way to the firing line. One man, dropping out, half carried me back about a hundred yards, and, with a sincere, 'Good luck, mate, I'm needed up above,' he raced away to assist the hard-pressed, exhausted men in the firing line.

So again I started off, crawling as hard as possible. While lying on my back, resting in one place, eight or nine shells burst in quick succession right over my head – one bursting so close that the black soot, like burnt powder, fell on my chest. The shrubs were torn and the earth scarred by the hail of shrapnel bullets, but again I got off without a scratch.

I came to the hurried conclusion, however, that there were many healthier places about, and made off again.

I had gone only a short distance when I came upon a touching spectacle. I was crossing a narrow road on the summit of a hill when I saw an officer sitting upright on the roadside, with his back to the shrubs that grew on either side.

I approached, but he did not speak or move, so I crawled up close, and found to my surprise that he was dead. He had just been in the act of writing when a bullet through the heart caused instantaneous death. He had never moved an inch; his notebook was still in the left hand; while the right still held a pencil poised in a natural position over the book. He was a Colonel, past middle age, grey-haired, and wearing a breast full of service ribbons.

In a shallow trench close by another pathetic incident occurred. Lying in a trench was an Australian, who had been badly hit. His eyes opened slowly, his lips moved, and faintly he murmured, 'Mafeesh', the Arabic for 'finished', and more slowly, 'Take money-belt – missus and kids – dirty swap dirty . . .' Then a strange thing happened. Dying, shattered beyond recognition, he rose to his knees and dragged his rifle to the parapet. With a weak finger he took shaky aim and fired his last shot, then collapsed in the bottom of the trench.

A little later I had another very narrow escape. I was crawling along, dragging a rifle which I had picked up in case I met any stray Turks, when right before me, at no distance, I spotted a rifle poking through a shrub, and behind it a New Zealander in the act of pulling trigger. 'Don't fire; I'm wounded,' I yelled and immediately a New Zealand officer jumped out from behind the bush. He was just rushing a company of infantry to reinforce the line.

'Where's the firing line?' he asked.

'Straight on, over a mile ahead of you,' I answered.

With a 'Sorry you're hurt, my boy!' he rushed his men on.

After escapes innumerable, and a struggle that I never expected to accomplish, I reached the ridge of the first hill in company with a New Zealander, who was also wounded. Together we hopped and stumbled, with our arms about one another's neck, finally rolling over the brow of the hill into a hole that afforded some little amount of shelter.

We settled down there for a short spell before continuing to the dressing station on the beach. The wounded still passed in apparently endless procession. They were wonderfully cheerful and full of information. But here our peace was short-lived.

Gradually the enemy's range lengthened, and shells crept nearer and nearer; machine-gun and rifle fire commenced to whisk about us again; then suddenly through the scrub broke the head remnant of the firing line.

Slowly they came, disputing every inch and reluctantly yielding the ground which they had so gloriously occupied during the earlier hours of the day.

The Turks evidently intended to drive them into the sea by sheer weight of numbers, but they were determined to die rather than surrender the position dearly won. Having retired some little distance in an orderly manner, they concentrated on the ring of hills commanding the beach, and, hastily entrenching, prepared to meet the massed infantry that were being hurled forward.

They had not long to wait, for very soon the whole ridge was black with Turks. On they came, evidently thinking that very soon they would sweep the remnant of our little force from their shores. But they were sadly mistaken.

When they were within easy range, a storm of rifle and machine-gun fire tore lanes through their massed ranks, while the *Queen Elizabeth*, which had been unable to support us during the afternoon, opened fire with her fifteen-inch guns, causing fearful losses.

The Turks were stunned by such a reception, and retired over the hill, giving the boys time to further consolidate the position; but they came again and again, meeting with the same withering fire each time.

Eventually they retired for the night, leaving the gallant survivors in peace, and in possession of the joyful thought that they had come through the severest fighting, and 'had done their bit.'

Thus ended the memorable 25 April 1915, 'The Day' ... on which 16,000 Anzacs won for Australasia an 'Imperishable Record' and a 'Name among all the Nations'.

THE FIRST DAY

Field Marshal Sir William Birdwood

At 3.30 a.m. the battleships hove to, and the tows went ahead. It was very dark, and the tows got a mile or so farther north than had been intended; and some tows crossed one another. The enemy, entrenched on the shore to the number of about 900, with machine-guns, did not suspect our approach till we were quite close, when they opened heavy fire on the boats and inflicted many casualties.

Meanwhile, as soon as this advance guard of 1,500 had started off, the remainder of the covering force trans-shipped from their transports into eight destroyers; these followed closely, until the men were taken off by returning tows. All this worked entirely 'according to plan'. The boy midshipmen in command of small boats earned, and ever afterwards retained, the deep admiration of all my Anzac men.

Hardly waiting for the keels to touch the shore, men leaped into the water and raced ashore, dashing straight with the bayonet upon the Turks and driving them through the thick undergrowth.

This landing farther north than was intended naturally caused some temporary difficulties; for these I must take the blame, for they were caused by my insistence on landing before daylight. But the error brought great compensations also. The original spot chosen for the landing was on fairly open ground not far from Gaba Tepe, and troops landing there must have suffered heavily from machine–gun and other fire from the trenches in that locality, which had clearly been dug and wired in anticipation of an attack thereabouts. But though, by this accident, our right avoided this danger, our left came in for bad trouble farther north, beyond Ari Burnu.

On the open beach near the fishermen's huts we suffered heavy losses; some boats drifted off full of dead with no one in control. The centre landing, in the neighbourhood of what was later known as Anzac Cove, was more fortunate. The country here was very broken and difficult, and the Turks had evidently not expected an attack, for they were only lightly entrenched and were soon driven off by the impetuous Australians.

But the crossing of the tows in the dark was to cause great confusion and, for a time, dismay. Battalions had got hopelessly mixed up, and for a considerable time it was impossible to sort them out. My extreme right was being badly enfiladed by machine-guns from Gaba Tepe, till the *Bacchante* (Captain Boyle) steamed right in, almost putting her bows on shore, and poured in welcome broadsides which silenced the enemy there – a gallant deed which the Australians never forgot.

Gradually the Turks were driven back through this very difficult country, which is covered with high scrub and in places quite precipitous. The day was very hot, and no water was available. It was a wonderful feat, therefore, that the Australians had performed – and they were nearly all young soldiers receiving their baptism of fire. Thanks to the first-rate naval arrangements, Bridges' entire Division (less guns) of 12,000 men was ashore by 10 a.m., and Godley's Division followed later.

As soon as I could, I went ashore to see the progress made, and clambered around as much as possible of the front line on the heights. Owing to the thick scrub I could see very little, but from a point later known as Walker's Top I got a fairly good idea of the situation, realising for the first time that a large valley separated the New Zealanders there from the Australians on a ridge to the east.

The men were naturally very exhausted after so hard a day – and inclined to be despondent, too. Small groups would tell me that they were all that was left of their respective battalions – 'all the others cut up'!

On such occasions I would promptly tell them not to be damned fools: that the rest of the battalion was not far distant, having simply been separated in the tows. This always had an encouraging effect, though I must confess that I might not yet have seen 'the rest'.

Another factor, which did much to restore our men's confidence, was the landing of the two Indian Mountain Batteries (Numbers 1 and 6) for which I had so earnestly petitioned Lord Kitchener. Thanks to their great handiness and mobility we were able to get them, but no other guns, ashore on the twenty-fifth. Before their landing, the infantry were naturally perturbed by the fact that they were being continuously shelled, while no reply could be sent from our side.

The very first shot from one of our mountain guns (very hurriedly rushed up on the ridge over the landing-place) had an electrifying effect upon our troops, who felt they could now hold their own.

The first brilliant advance was now checked, for the Turks had been able to bring up guns and there was a constant hail of shrapnel all the afternoon. In the scrub it was impossible to keep men together, and many stragglers found their way down gullies to the beach. Later we found that our casualties numbered some 5,000 all told: in round figures, 500 killed, 2,500 wounded and 2,000 missing, although many of the 'missing' came in later.

Some, I am sorry to say, had in their impetuosity, advanced so fast, and with so little regard for their supports or troops on their flanks, that they had disappeared right into the enemy's position.

The heavy rate of casualties gives some indication how bitter and unceasing the fighting had been. By the superb efforts of Neville Howse, my D.M.S., the wounded were got away to the ships as fast as they could be collected.

Nevertheless, the situation ashore seemed fairly satisfactory when, in the evening, I returned to my headquarters on the *Queen* after discussing matters with Bridges and Godley. I was therefore horrified, about an hour later, to receive a message from Bridges asking me to return at once, as the position was now critical.

I went ashore again and was met by Bridges and Godley, with several of their senior officers. They told me that their men were so exhausted after all they had gone through, and so unnerved by constant shellfire after their wonderfully gallant work, that they feared a fiasco if a heavy attack should be launched against us next morning.

I was told that numbers had already dribbled back through the scrub, and the two divisional commanders urged me most strongly to make immediate arrangements for re-embarkation.

At first I refused to take any action. I argued that Turkish demoralisation was in all probability considerably greater than ours, and that in any case I would rather die there in the morning than withdraw now.

But, on thinking things over, I felt myself bound to place the position before Sir Ian Hamilton, if only because every report I had sent him so far (and these reports had been largely based on what Bridges himself had told me) had been entirely optimistic.

Sir Ian had little idea of the extent of our casualties at Anzac, though we knew that the 29th Division had suffered very badly indeed at Helles. It struck me, therefore, that, in view of the losses sustained by both forces, he might consider it advisable to abandon one landing or the other and concentrate all his strength either at Helles or at Anzac.

His reply came as an almost incredible relief to me, telling us to 'hang on and dig' as we were now through the most difficult part of the business. He also gave us the cheering news that the Australian submarine *A.E.2* had got through the narrows and torpedoed a gunship – a feat which opened up a new vista in the problem of checking Turkish reinforcements.

And so ended a day which will always stand out in my life: a day of great strain and of sharply contrasting emotions. I recall my feelings of confidence but natural anxiety as the troops entered the tows at 2.30 a.m.; my elation and pride when I knew that great numbers of troops had landed on a broad front and with less opposition than we had feared; my growing satisfaction as cheering reports of progress continued to reach me; and then, at night, the sudden cold fear of threatened disaster.

But directly I got Sir Ian's reply, which accorded so well with my own wishes, I felt a load lifted from me. I longed for the daylight, so I could get round to the troops.

THE LANDING

E. F. Hanman ('Haystack')

It was Sunday morning, just before daybreak, when the first troops left their ships' side in small rowing boats. The 3rd Brigade, which had been given the post of honour, was headed for the shore.

All was still as death, the dim shore was quite peaceful, giving not the slightest sign of the lurking force, or of the terrible drama which was so soon to be enacted. The sea was calm as any rippling lake. Where the land met the sea was a long silver line, reflection of the dawn.

From our position on the transport, we had as it were 'front stall seats' at the show. The long lines of boats, looking no larger than as many ducks, the dark, looming coast, and the stillness of death over all. Nearer and yet nearer, drift those little boats, crowded with that gallant body of men, the 3rd Brigade.

The boats had been towed by steam pinnaces until they were fairly close in, then they turned them loose, knowing full well that they would drift ashore by themselves. Everything was so still – that made the situation worse. Imagine those men in the small craft, gradually drawing closer and closer to what? They did not know! The awful silence was worse than any fusillade. Had the enemy seen them? Where was the enemy?

Nearer and nearer looms the shore – still no sign.

'Hello!' say the men. 'Johnny Turk is not expecting us, we shall get ashore unnoticed. Look!'

'Those little boats, crowded with that gallant body of men.'

'All the boats have made the shore safely ...'

On the summit of one of the hills a bright light bursts into view. Is it a star? No, it can't be – no it isn't! It's a fire of warning to the foe, watching and waiting amongst those rugged, bush-covered hills. To our ears comes the faint music of British cheers, like foxhounds on the scent.

'Hurrah! Our boys are landing. Hark! Don't you hear them cheering? There they are again. Hurrah! Hurrah! Hurrah!'

The boats now are to be seen, rocking and tossing about at random, deserted. The cackle of rifle fire is carried to us on the cool morning air.

Crash! Boom! Boom! Boom! Our good friend, the Navy, is talking to the Turks. Flash, flash, flash! There the shells are bursting high up on the hills. Boom, boom, boom! Hurrah! The men-o'-war are covering our fellows' advance! The entire range of hills is dotted all over with golden flashing balls.

The sight was beautiful to behold, but we were anxious to see for ourselves what it was like under that appalling fire. Surely nothing living can survive under this awful cannonade. The noise! Boom, boom, boom! 'Look, something is catching it pretty hot over there! Hey! Pass me the glasses!'

The sun rose magnificent, tinting the dark hills and purple valleys a glorious golden hue. Shells appear now like snowballs. What is that funny-looking, sausage-shaped contrivance hanging in mid-air? The observation balloon. From here, the range is picked up and passed to the waiting gunners on the smoke-enveloped cruisers. The *London* was doing good work, firing in shot after shot.

If any living thing is up there, they had better retire to a more favourable position. The entire ridge is under fire. Shells dropping as evenly and regularly as raindrops off a dripping roof.

The bugler sounds breakfast. No notice whatever is taken. Eyes are glued to glasses, ears strained to catch the note of battle. This is no time for eating. Why, this is both food and drink! Is not this for what we have worked and slaved for the past months? Look at that! Phew! If they go on like this they will knock Gallipoli into fragments.

Some of our officers bring us the tidings that all the boats have made the shore safely. Hurrah! Hurrah! Hurrah! Enthusiasm knows no limit. We are wild with excitement, some fellows capering wild war dances on the decks. Other strings of boats can now be seen gliding towards that little bay – Gaba Tepe.

Hello! The Turkish forts are replying. See! A huge geyser of water is shot up into the air. A trooper draws back. Swish! There's another, and a large shell, too!

Cackle, cackle, cackle, the rifle fire, from the sound of it, must be pretty severe. Our fellows are at it now with a vengeance.

From a transport close by large bodies of men descend into boats and are towed towards the shore by the ever-busy steam pinnaces. Their cheering is frantic and catching. It is echoed by all. No fear of these fellows shirking their work!

Looking down, we see more pinnaces, ploughing towards us. In their wake are long strings of rowing boats filled with what? There is little or no sign of life in these – but what are those huddled figures? Why, they are the first batch of wounded. This sight brings home to us, more than anything else, the stern realities of life.

As the gallant fellows passed under us, we gave them three roaring cheers. One poor chap in his last agony stood on his feet, and tottering and swaying, shouted with his last breath, 'Use the bayonet, boys! Are we downhearted?'

As his comrades, wounded like himself, yelled 'No!' he fell back exhausted and done.

Other boatloads not so badly hit sang, 'Tipperary, and it's a hell of a long way to go' while they waved bandaged legs and arms.

'Are we downhearted?'

'No!'

'Oh! When will they give us a chance?'

'When shall we get off?'

The afternoon sun shone hot and sullen. The air was full of the smell of powder and flying, drifting smoke clouds. We were simply eating our hearts out to get away.

A wireless message stated that our men had advanced inland six miles, the 3rd Brigade, headed by the 9th, had taken trench after trench. Their bayonets had sent cold terror into the blood of the foe. They were fleeing from us. Utter panic reigned amongst them. Our boys had scaled those fearful heights. How had they done it? We could not realise it. We were wild with joy. We had not failed.

Our greatest hopes and ambitions were fulfilled. The foe was actually running before the onslaught of our cheering men.

Aeroplanes, or rather hydroplanes, rose from the water, and with much purring and throbbing of engines, went sailing over the hills. They were going to locate the position of both our troops and the enemy. When they sight the enemy trenches, they hover over them as a hawk hovers over its prey. The range-finders can then easily pick up the distance, with disastrous results to the enemy trenches and earthworks.

Two or three shells have fallen near us, rather too close for perfect peace of mind. Our skipper thought it wise to draw further off. The whole afternoon that cannonade continued, we had no idea what was happening onshore, or how the battle was going. Later, however, another wireless message came that our fellows had been forced to retire – they were badly in need of reinforcements. This news was not altogether so satisfactory, and rather depressed us, but we thought that surely now we should have our turn.

We were quite prepared. Every man was issued three iron rations, consisting of tin corned beef and hard biscuits, 250 rounds of ammunition, and a pile of firewood, which was to be carried on the top of our packs. The weight of this equipment was far from being light, and more than one of us decided to be free of it at the first opportunity.

Evening approached, and our officers told us to eat as much as possible, as it should probably be some days before we had a decent meal again. We acted on this advice, and never was a meal so much appreciated!

As we ate, we thought of what we should have to go through before we should all be comfortable and at ease again. We talked of what we were going to do, how we ought to act. Our rifles were taken and oiled, and well cared for, because they meant everything to us. They meant the difference between life and death. Dusk fell and still found us disgusted and grumbling aboard the transport.

We were weary from standing in our full equipment, sore at not being ordered ashore, and thoroughly discontented. It was then rumoured that we were not going ashore that day at all, but that we must wait for the morrow. Happily, this rumour was finally routed by the order to 'Stand to and prepare to disembark'.

The hour had come. We were to land. Men joked, men swore, men laughed, but all were fastening their equipment – having last looks at rifle bolts. All were ready and drawn up. Some there were who may have known fear, some there were who may have had qualms, some there were who may have thought with regret of home and laughter, but all were one in the determination to do or die.

Suddenly silence fell, men spoke in whispers, pals found one another. There was much silent handshaking, and whispered wishes for good luck.

Bang! What was that? Every man jumped and turned in the direction of the sound. Some unfortunate chap had accidentally discharged his rifle and scared the whole boat. Fortunately, no one was hurt, but the shock was great, coming at a time like that when nerves were strung so high.

There is heard a swishing of water and a destroyer glides into the circle of light thrown by the ship's portholes. A gangway was thrown down, and we began our descent to the pulsing, throbbing destroyer below.

Who will ever forget that memorable journey? When we were crammed together, so closely that it was an impossibility to send any more men down, a stentorian voice calls, 'Let go.' The water churned to a lather. Slowly, ever so slowly, we commence to turn. Now the transport stands out dark and clear against the sky, her few lights throwing an eerie, mystic glow over her. High on the bridge stands the solitary figure of the Captain. His cheery 'Good-bye, boys, and good luck!' is answered by three resounding deep-throated cheers, that awaken echoes in the darkness, and drift out to sea.

Our speedy craft is now ploughing its way towards the black shore. The water is inky black, all lights are out, absolute silence is essential. The sky, too, seems glum. Here and there shy stars peep from behind dark rolling clouds, and then bashfully hide their loveliness behind their protecting veil. It was a strange journey. None of us knew what was ahead of us. We could only surmise.

A man-o'-war's searchlight was playfully prying over the hills, illuminating gullies and valleys, making small objects stand out weird, fantastic. It flits restlessly about, here and there, never still, always searching like some gigantic will o' the wisp. In its wide circlings, it catches sight of us. We are blinded by its intense brilliancy, and crouch down to avoid its searching gaze. Apparently it is satisfied with our appearance and switches off once more to continue its vigil.

The destroyer stopped, two or three sharp orders rang out, bells tinkled, and we could discern the dim shapes of barge-like boats in the tow of a small steam pinnace. They had come from the shore to take us the remainder of our journey. The destroyer was rocking violently, and it was no easy task to jump from her decks to the deep bottoms of the lighters. To make a misjudged jump meant disaster. The unfortunate one would land in anything but a dignified position in the middle of a much-suffering comrade's chest. The language was blue, the air full of muttered curses and threats of dire vengeance.

We were crowded so tightly together that whatever position we fell in, we had to maintain. We were anything but comfortable. The Turks came in for a fair share of abuse. Then the boats were rocking and tumbling in a most sickening fashion, and as it was some time before we got under weigh, many of us were showing signs of seasickness. Roll, roll, toss, toss, this way and that, first one side would feel the pressure, then the other.

'Don't push!'

'Stop your shoving!'

'Oh! My leg!'

'Here! Get off my head!'

'I say! Lean on your own tea!'

Such were the exclamations on all sides. It was with heartfelt thanks that we at last glided away into the night. The sickening rocking was at last stopped. The night became still more gloomy, rain threatened; the sky, the coast, and the water merged into one black blur. Men's faces were not recognisable at arm's length.

At last the pinnace swung loose and we were free to get ashore the best way possible. The searchlight threw our landing place into bright prominence, and we could plainly see that we were still some distance from land, and it looked as though we were to be wet through before we should attain our goal.

The air was full of whirring noises. Here and there the water was thrown up in little jets. Even then we did not realise that they were bullets. 'Plonck, plonck, whizz!' How they did sing around us, yet not a man was hit. This did not surprise us. We should have been far more astonished if one had. Anyway, something had to be done, and that quickly. We could not remain here all night. With flying leaps we bounded from boat to boat, many falling, midst roars of laughter, into the water beneath.

At last! At last, dripping and chilled, we stood on the beach, the beach which, earlier in the day, had been the scene of violent action, of heroic death.

We were all lined up, the great hills towering before us. The sound of rifle fire was spasmodic and sharp, echoing and rolling in an eerie manner, all along the gullies. One of the 3rd Brigade, who was on the beach, met us and enquired who we were.

'Oh!' said he. 'We've been through hell. Nearly all my battalion are gone, God only knows where! Half our officers are dead, those who aren't are somewhere up there hanging on like grim death. All my pals are either dead or wounded. You chaps will have a taste of it before morning.'

Just then our company commander singled out the writer and told him to go and fetch up the other half battalion, which had come in boats just behind us. He was running along the water's edge, full of excitement, knowing nothing of war and its ways – was just passing some Indian mule drivers and their charges, when he heard a dull, sickening thud. One of the men was seen clutching at the air – he reeled, staggered – and fell face downwards, the water lapping his head. He had gone to Allah!

After this little incident, it was wiser to remain closer to the hills, as it seemed evident that someone was keeping up a continued fire along the water's edge.

'Hello! Are you the right half of the 15th? This way, then.'

We were all waiting, anxious, and, to tell the truth, feeling rather queer. The time passed slowly. It was worse waiting here than if were actually under fire. The night was cold, we were wet and damp, and our teeth were chattering.

A voice: 'This way, 15th! Come on quickly, you're wanted in a hurry. This way, double up, double up.'

We have at last commenced the ascent, our eyes have become accustomed to the dark surroundings, and we behold many grim evidences of the hard day's fighting. We stumbled, swore, fell, and cursed – on all sides were haversacks, rifles, packs, overcoats, bayonets, and other discarded equipment. The gullies were full of accoutrements. As we advanced – up, up, ever up, we stumbled over dead stiff bodies, and moaning, huddled, wounded khaki figures.

It was a funny sight to see us all bobbing and ducking as bullets whined harmlessly overhead. Some fellow, bent nearly double, would call out that it was no use ducking, if a bullet had your name on it, you were sure to stop it. Then he would burst into laughter as he became conscious of his own position. Invariably our heads went down, and our eyes turned up. The singing little missiles were a constant source of amusement.

Sections and pals kept close together. No one seemed to know where we were going. We were not even sure where the firing line lay. All we did actually know was that our Colonel was in front with the regimental Major, and that was good enough for us.

'We don't know where we are goin', but we'll get there.'

Up, up we go. Our packs drag at our shoulders, and become an awful weight. Perspiration drips from us, our cold wet clothes become warm and clammy, and the top of the range seems just as far off as at first.

The firing sounds nearer though, and it is growing in intensity. Somewhere, our line is being attacked.

'Hurry up, 15th! Reinforcements, this way!'

Somehow or other in the darkness we became broken up and separated. Little parties of men, followed their own non-commissioned officers or section leaders. We stumbled, climbed and swore, following always the direction of the firing. It did not seem real – no, not the slightest bit. Could we really be going into action? Certainly we could hear firing, but that was nothing new – we had often listened to the same music on the desert. Those dark, hunched-up looking objects were men, but it was very difficult to realise that they were dead ones, and that they had been shot by the enemy.

Where was the enemy? None of our boys, so far, had been hit! It seemed no worse than a night on the desert. Soon, however, we were to realise in full the awful horrors of war. Soon we were to learn what it was like to be face to face with an enemy bent on our utter annihilation, our destruction.

A small party of us, about twelve in all, was blindly groping about, wondering where we were going, and where lay our firing line. One of the party tripped over a wounded man, who began to groan and curse. We must be somewhere near the firing line now.

Suddenly, out of the darkness, dark figures sprang into being, our bayonets flashed, we prepared for instant action.

'Halt! You men! Where do you come from? Who are you?'

'Halt! You men!' cries an officer's voice, and we knew that we had fallen amongst friends.

'Fifteenth!'

'Very good! By the way, have you fellows been under fire before? It's quite simple. Rifle bullets whine, and some crack, machine-gun bullets go sizz, sizz, sizz. Oh, there's nothing to worry about! Just keep your heads well down and lie still. Remember, too, that there are about 200 of your comrades lying killed in front of us. You know your work – do it. Follow me.'

He led us where we could just make out the dim figures of men stretched out full length. They seemed utterly weary, completely worn out. Three of us threw ourselves down together, bullets flying regularly, their whining notes spelling death and desolation. Down we flopped in double quick time. Next to us was a very young officer, as game a boy as any one of us, who had changed Australian shores for those of Gallipoli. He was lying stiff and inert, being wounded both in the arm and leg – he had lost much blood and looked both weak and done. The only part of him that seemed alive was his brilliant pair of determined flashing eyes.

'Welcome to Turkey!' he said in a laughing, boyish voice. One of us offered to take him to the rear, but he would not hear of such a thing – said he was not going to leave his boys. 'No fear!' he said, 'Would one of you chaps mind digging me a bit of shelter?'

So we dug him a small trench and lifted him into it. Then, smiling, he told us to get well under ourselves, as he expected we should have 'some more damned fireworks in the morning'.

'And,' he added, 'mind you jump straight up and go for the "Unspeakable" if he deigns to pay us a visit.'

'Rightoh!' called out our Corporal, 'Cockney Bill'. He was a short, sturdy chap with one leg a little shorter than its mate and a twisted humorous mouth covered by the inevitable little black moustache, branding him, as he was – a true 'Tommy Atkins'. He neither knew fatigue nor bad humour and was the life and soul of the battalion. He took a mighty pride in his handful of men and 'mothered' us with the fondness of a hen for its chicks.

Even now, he was stealthily passing us loose cigarettes and an extra supply of tobacco in case we became separated. How he ever had these commodities passed our comprehension, but have them he did. His bluff, Cockney voice could be heard in all times of stress. He was a peacemaker, yet a bulldog fighter. He could swear like any of his calibre, grumbling he had brought to a fine art, yet still, when he was wanted, he was there, always ready, always willing. His boisterous Cockney ditties had wiled many a weary hour away. His honest curses and openhearted generosity had kept us in our places.

''Ere, you there, get a wriggle on!'

'What? Goin' to sleep?'

'Dig in, yer flamin' idjit – yer will 'ave a 'ell of a long sleep tomorrow if yer don't.'

We acted on this advice. Out came our entrenching tools, instruments with a small shovel one side, and a pick the other, and we dug and scraped for dear life, taking good care to keep our heads well down. Ping, ping! The bullets were neatly severing the tops of the low bushes around us. Ping!

'By jove, that's 'ot! Who ever would 'ave fort it!' said Bill, as a bullet knocked a cloud of dust down his neck.

It began to rain now, and the earth became muddy and sticky. It stuck to our tools and hindered our work. Off came our packs. They made very serviceable head protection indeed, and we were more than pleased that we had carried them so far.

Something was going to happen. The Turks were approaching.

'Fix bayonets!' rang out the order.

It goes muttering down the line and is followed by hundreds of significant clicks as the bright steel is affixed to the right end of the rifle. We could hear the Turks coming, shouting their peculiar sing-song war cry of 'Allah! Allah! Allah!' Nearer and nearer they come. We are like sprinters ready for the race.

Suddenly a terrific fusillade is opened on our right. The Turks are enfiladed, their approach is cut off, we are saved the trouble of meeting them. They are, judging from their noise, retiring in disorder.

The rain, which by now had rendered us wet through, cleared off. The dense veil of cloud began to break, bright rifts showed us the clear velvet sky beyond. Our vigil ceased not for one moment. Never must we turn our gaze from the country ahead!

We could see nothing save the top of a small hill just in front, the bushes on it standing out black and clear against the clearing Heavens. We must watch and wait. How we longed for daylight. Our ears were strained to catch the slightest noise of a lurking foe. It was possible for them to crawl right on us without our perceiving them.

Several times we thought they were charging – they were, too – but their advance was stopped by the withering fire of our friends on the right. Time after time we were on the verge of rising to the attack. More than once we thought we should be forced to test the quality of our steel. It appeared that the authorities were doubtful of our capability of holding our present positions. In fact boats had been despatched to bring us off, should the occasion arise. However, matters must have brightened considerably, for the order was brought us that on no account were we to retire from the position we now occupied.

'Retire!' said one boy. 'Retire! What the devil do they think we are? Do they think we are goin' to leave our little 'omes? Not we! Why damn 'em, we've taken three parts of the night to scratch 'em out. No, no! We're staying right here.'

Such was the unanimous opinion of the men that night. The night passed very quickly, our every sense was strained to its highest pitch, nothing escaped us, not the smallest sound or movement.

So far, where we lay, we had not fired a single shot, we were told to work silently, and to use the bayonet on every possible occasion.

'Stick it into 'em, lads! Give 'em the steel!' said our Lieutenant.

We meant to obey – the steel it should be.

That first night, lying wet and cold, out under a dark sky on a damp rain-soaked ground, was a queer experience. We did not know the country, and we were blissfully ignorant of our whereabouts. We were watching and waiting, digging and digging, never resting, dig and watch.

Every third man kept vigil, while his comrades dug under the ground, like so many human moles, or rather, wombats. Moles, as a rule, are clean-coated little creatures, whereas we were now covered with thick layers of brick-red mud, our hands and arms completely caked with the slimy stuff. Ears and hair were full, it gritted between our teeth, and still we worked with the frenzy of gold discoverers.

Well for us that we did!

SAM AND ME – POSTSCRIPT

Arthur Hoey Davis ('Steele Rudd')

In the middle of the night we left Mudros for Gallipoli.

I was lying in me bunk an' listening to the throbbing of the engines an' thinking, as usual, what was to be the end of it all, when who comes along to see me, with a smile on his face, but Lieutenant Colonel Chaplain Brown-Smith. I never thought to ask him about it later, but I was pretty sure it was Sam who sent him.

He started telling me things about the big wars an' heroes of olden times an' was just beginning a yarn about something that happened on the plains of Troy, when I asked him what did he ever do with the old moke that he was riding when me an' Sam met him on the plains outside of Blackall.

Lord! I never saw anyone look so surprised. He stopped dead an' stared at me an' I had to tell him when it was, an' the very exact spot, an' the time of day, an' exactly what the old moke was like.

'Well, well, well,' he says, an' then he laughed an' got to telling me all about his experiences in the west until both of us nearly forgot that we had to get off at Gallipoli. Then he shook hands an' went up on deck where most of the soldiers was gathered, an' where the moon was shining, an' millions of stars twinkling like the eyes of angels looking down on us from Heaven.

Just after that we were all ordered on deck an' then they lowered us into the open boats with packs on our backs an' rifles in our hands. As the boats moved off Sam felt for me with his hand. 'Don't worry, Frankie,' he said, 'I'm here, old chap, we'll come through this flying.'

I didn't speak because I couldn't.

Then rifles started cracking on the land, an' bullets hummed over us an' past us like bees.

'Go like hell!' someone called.

'Take to the water!' from someone else.

An' into the water they plunged, an' I followed, up to me waist, an' Sam was dragging me along after him, an' that's about all I recall of the landing.

All that day, an' days an' days, an' weeks an' weeks, we spent digging in an' digging in. Every moment waiting to be attacked an' waiting for the order to attack. At least the others was waiting for it, I wasn't. I lived in constant an' indescribable dread of it.

Twice I was numbered among those told to stand ready to jump out, but I was never ready for a moment. Whether I could have jumped out if the order had come, God only knows.

'Sam,' I would often moan, sitting there cramped up in them damn trenches, 'this was a hell of a place to come to, a hell of a place.'

'Never mind, Frankie,' he'd say, 'we'll have these Turks walloped in no time an' be back home in Australia for Christmas.'

There was never any despondency about Sam, an' it was always 'home for Christmas'.

Then, one day about four o'clock, we suddenly got a warning. Hardly had we got a grip on our rifles an' stood to when over the parapets an' down on top of us came the Turks, shouting an' yelling. There was no time for thinking then.

'Frankie!' Sam shouted, an' then I heard nothing but oaths an' the clashing of bayonets and rifle barrels. I saw nothing but red, red, red!

God! I fought an' lunged an' struck at anything in a strange uniform an' above it all at intervals I heard Sam shouting, 'Frankie!'

An' I shouted back, 'Sam!'

I fought till I couldn't see a face or a uniform but a friendly one.

Then I called, 'Sam!' again an' again, but he didn't answer.

I tried to see the faces of the men I was walking over as I looked for him.

I found him lying across a heap of Turks an' lifting his head onto me knee I shouted, 'Water!'

When I spoke to him he just murmured, 'We won, Frankie.'

An' then his head fell back an' I put him down.

HEROES OF GALLIPOLI

Oliver Hogue ('Trooper Bluegum')

'No troops in the whole world could possibly have done better than those magnificent Australian infantry. They performed the impossible. In the face of exploding mines and withering fire from machine-guns, shrapnel and rifles, they stormed the hills and, with bloody bayonets, routed the Turks and Germans.'

That was a tribute all the more valuable because it was not an Australian who spoke, neither was it an Englishman ... it was a Frenchman.

It was the remark of a French naval officer who watched the landing of the Australian Division on Gallipoli. And when the whole tale was told the world saw how rightly our boys deserved all that was said of them.

What a terribly expensive business it was all to be! How many brave Australians and New Zealanders – yes, and Englishmen, Frenchmen and Indians – were yet to be sacrificed!

It is well that the Great Ruler over all, Who holds us in the hollow of His hands, does not permit poor mortals to see into the future. The 'forcing of the Dardanelles', the words were on the lips of all of us and were printed in newspapers all over the world. It seemed only a matter of a little while, and then ...

Great is the British Navy, magnificent are its officers and men, but hellish was the work of 'forcing the Dardanelles'. You remember how the *Goliath* and the *Irresistible* went down. You remember how a great French ship – the *Bouvet* – was sunk. You remember the mines that came down the waters, and the shore torpedoes, and the strength of the Turkish forts, the power of the Turkish guns, erected and manned by German officers.

The Navy could not force the Dardanelles alone! It was necessary to have the cooperation of land forces. Perhaps the operations should never have been begun until the Army was ready to cooperate. I do not know; it is not for me to judge.

General Sir Ian Hamilton first visited the Dardanelles and carried out a reconnaissance on one of the warships and then came to Egypt – a lightning visit – and our forces began to move. Australia, for the first time, was right up against the Hun! South Africa was a picnic to it.

There were spies everywhere. There were spies in the transports, spies amongst the interpreters, spies in the supply depots. The Turks, or rather their German officers, were kept informed of every move the Allies made.

They knew exactly the hour of disembarkation and the places of landing. They learned all the Australian bugle calls and used them with telling effect. The French landed and formed up as if on parade, and then, with beautiful precision, marched on and drove the enemy before them.

The British, despite the fusillade which greeted them on landing, were steady as veterans and there was no hope of withstanding their landing. The 29th Division were magnificent.

But there was an electric quality about the charge of the Australians that inspired panic in the Turkish trenches. Angry at the loss of several of their officers, they charged so fiercely that they looked like getting out of hand.

Scorning cover, they also scorned rifle fire. They scaled the steel-lined heights like demons. It was the bayonet all the time. One huge farmer actually bayoneted a Turk through the chest and pitchforked him over his shoulder. The man who performed this feat was a huge Queenslander. Sergeant Burne, of the 9th Battalion, who was afterwards wounded and returned to his Australian home, is a man whose modesty is as great as his size.

We smiled at first when we heard the story, and people in England and Australia read of it with amazement. But Sergeant Burne, standing over six feet high, and massively proportioned, looks quite capable of the feat.

He himself tells the story in these words: 'It is not a case for me to take any credit at all. I was in the platoon that landed first on the right. Our Lieutenant was the first on the right. Our Lieutenant was the first man to get ashore – and as game a man as ever faced fire. I followed him. I was ordered to take in hand a line of Turkish sharp-shooters who were causing a lot of trouble. There was also a machine-gun on the hill. Somebody had to stop it. Myself and two lads went up, and we stopped it.

'That's all. There were ten Turks there. We got the Turks and we got the machine-gun, but I lost my two lads. They were only boys, but let me tell you the Australians are the best fighters in the world. One of the lads "fixed" the German officer who was working the machine-gun. The Turks were higher up than we were, and I suppose that is how I was able to throw one of them over my shoulder. It's an old trick that is taught in the Guards.'

Sergeant Burne once served in the Irish Guards, and he carries a scar on his forehead, the result of a blow from the butt-end of a rifle at Rhenosterkop, during the South African war. He had been living in Australia for about six years when the Great War broke out, and he was one of the first to answer the Empire's call. His stay on Gallipoli was short, for on the same day as that on which he performed the feat of which I have written he received a bullet in the shoulder.

'It was a very short experience,' he said, 'but I'll be back there again.'

And that was, and is, the spirit of them all. It is sad to think that so many senior officers lost their lives right at the outset of the fighting in the Dardanelles. Australia could ill afford to lose men like Colonel Onslow Thompson, Colonel MacLaurin, Major F. D. Irvine and Colonel Braund. Colonel MacLaurin was in the act of warning soldiers to be certain to keep behind cover when he was shot in the head. He was hurriedly conveyed to the rear, but only lingered half an hour. Curiously enough, he had a presentiment that he would be killed, and mentioned it to one of our Light Horse officers just before leaving for the Dardanelles.

It was a wicked trick that resulted in the slaughter of so many gallant men of the 1st (NSW) Battalion. They had been holding the line splendidly, despite shrapnel and maxim fire and rifles, and had repulsed several attacks by the enemy. Then a message was passed down the line for the Battalion to attack and capture the guns in front. Not doubting the genuineness of the order, the Battalion charged, only to be met with a withering fire, which immediately told them that a trap had been set.

Their leader, Colonel Onslow Thompson, was killed instantaneously by a cannon shot which struck him in the head. He was one of the first to volunteer in Sydney when war broke out. Colonel Arnott knew that Colonel Onslow Thompson was a splendid Light Horse officer, and begged of him to wait for a mounted regiment. 'No,' he replied, 'I'm going, and I'll take the first chance that offers.'

The casualties among the officers were tremendous – brave men who led Australia's soldiers in that awful charge! And among the bravest of them were the young officers from the Duntroon Military College that stands amid delightful country surroundings near the capital of Federated Australia that is now in the making in the Mother State of New South Wales.

These young fellows fought in a way that showed their native courage and the excellence of their training. Only the year before, when Sir Ian Hamilton, as Inspector General of the Overseas Forces, visited Australia and inspected these lads who where training for the army at Duntroon, as the representative of the *Sydney Morning Herald* I remember seeing them laugh and cheer when Sir Ian, on leaving Duntroon, jokingly wished them 'plenty of wars and rapid promotion'.

It seems only a few days since we were dancing and flirting in a Cairo ballroom. Now many of them lie sorely wounded at the base hospital, and several will never again hear the *reveille*. But the College will not forget its first fruits offered up so gladly for Empire.

Officers and men, it was all the same – they went to their death with a cheer for King and Country.

I heard an Imperial officer, newly returned from Flanders, say that the 3rd Australian Infantry Brigade was the finest brigade of infantry in the whole of the allied armies. In physique they were far superior to any of the British, French, or Belgian troops. Whether this be true or not, there is no doubt that the sturdy 3rds under Colonel Maclagan fought like Trojans on the Gallipoli Peninsula, and covered themselves with glory. Incidentally, I might mention, some of them never fired a shot during the fierce fighting of 25 April. They simply trusted to the cold steel, and flung themselves at the Turkish trenches.

The 1st Brigade (Colonel MacLaurin), the 2nd (Colonel McCay), and the rest of the Australians and New Zealanders fought with equal valour, but the brunt of the attack was borne by the 3rds. So many hundred gallant lives was a heavy price to pay for a footing in Gallipoli, but those impetuous charges, absolutely irresistible in their fury, would, we knew, bear rich fruit, for the Turks could never again withstand a bayonet charge by the Australians.

It was noteworthy that only a few thousand prisoners were taken. I asked one of the 1st Battalion boys (Lieutenant-Colonel Dobbin's command) why that was. He replied: 'How could 12,000 of us take prisoners when we were up against 35,000?'

And through it all our Army Medical Corps did yeoman service. Several stretcher-bearers were shot, for they dashed forward too soon to succour the wounded. The doctors were right up in the firing line all the while. Colonel Ryan and some other doctors were attending to serious cases on the beach, where the landing was effected, and snipers shot two orderlies who were assisting, one on each side of the Colonel.

I doubt if there was a single branch of the service that did not suffer and share in the glory of that charge.

General Bridges, before he was killed, handled his gallant Australians with consummate skill. He seemed to anticipate the Turkish attacks. His dispositions for defence were brilliant. Then

General Godley and his New Zealanders landed and threw themselves into the fray. General Birdwood came and took charge of the Australian and New Zealand Army Corps ... ANZAC!

From the fateful day, 25 April, Anzac has been a name to conjure with.

MAKING HEADWAY

Joseph L. Beeston

At midnight we left Cairo and arrived at daybreak at Alexandria, the train running right on to the wharf, alongside which was the transport to convey us to Gallipoli – the Dardanelles we called it then.

Loading started almost immediately and I found that I – who in ordinary life am a peaceful citizen and a surgeon by profession – had to direct operations by which our wagons were to be removed from the railway trucks on to the wharf and thence to the ship's hold. Men with some knowledge of the mysteries of steam winches had to be specially selected and instructed in these duties, and I was as innocent of their details as the unborn babe.

However, everyone went at it, and the transport was loaded soon after dinner. We had the New Zealand Battery of Artillery, Battery Ammunition Column, 14th Battalion Transport and Army Service Corps with us, the whole numbering 560 men and 480 horses.

The next day saw us under weigh for the front. The voyage was quite uneventful, the sea beautifully calm, and the various islands in the Aegean Sea most picturesque. Three days later we arrived at Lemnos, and found the harbour (which is of considerable size) packed with warships and transports. I counted twenty warships of various sizes and nationalities.

The *Agamemnon* was just opposite us, showing signs of the damage she had received in the bombardment of the Turkish forts a couple of months before. We stayed here a week, and every day practised going ashore in boats, each man in full marching order leaving the ship by the pilot ladder.

It is extraordinary how one adapts oneself to circumstances. For years it has been almost painful to me to look down from a height; as for going down a ladder, in ordinary times I could not do it. However, here there was no help for it; a commanding officer cannot order his men to do what he will not do himself, so up and down we went in full marching order. Stretcher-bearer work was carried out among the stony hills which surround the harbour.

Finally, on 24 April, the whole armada got under weigh, headed by the *Queen Elizabeth*, or as the men affectionately term her, 'Lizzie.' We had been under steam for only about four hours when a case of smallpox was reported on board.

As the Captain informed me he had time to spare, we returned to Lemnos and landed the man, afterwards proceeding on our journey. At night the ship was darkened. Our ship carried eight horse-boats, which were to be used by the 29th Division in their landing at Cape Helles.

Just about dawn on Sunday 25 April I came on deck and could see the forms of a number of warships in close proximity to us, with destroyers here and there and numbers of transports.

Suddenly one ship fired a gun, then they were all at it, the Turks replying in quick time from the forts on Seddul Bah, as well as from those on the Asiatic side. None of our ships appeared to be hit, but great clouds of dust were thrown up in the forts opposite us.

Meanwhile destroyers were passing us loaded with troops, and barges filled with grim and determined-looking men were being towed towards the shore. One could not help wondering how many of them would be alive in an hour's time. Slowly they neared the cliffs; as the first barge appeared to ground, a burst of fire broke out along the beach, alternately rifles and machine-guns.

The men leaped out of the barges – almost at once the firing on the beach ceased, and more came from halfway up the cliff. The troops had obviously landed, and were driving the Turks back. After a couple of hours the top of the cliff was gained; there the troops became exposed to a very heavy fire from some batteries of artillery placed well in the rear, to which the warships attended as soon as they could locate them.

The *Queen Elizabeth* was close by us, apparently watching a village just under the fort. Evidently some guns were placed there. She loosed off her two fifteen-inch guns, and after the dust had cleared away we could see that new streets had been made for the inhabitants. Meanwhile the British had gained the top and were making headway, but losing a lot of men – one could see them falling everywhere.

The horse-boats having been got overboard, we continued our voyage towards what is now known as Anzac.

Troops – Australians and New Zealanders – were being taken ashore in barges. Warships were firing apparently as fast as they could load, the Turks replying with equal cordiality. In fact, as Captain Dawson remarked to me, it was quite the most 'willing' Sunday he had ever seen.

Our troops were ascending the hills through a dwarf scrub, just low enough to let us see the men's heads, though sometimes we could only locate them by the glint of the bayonets in the sunshine. Everywhere they were pushing on in extended order, but many falling.

The Turks appeared to have the range pretty accurately. About midday our men seemed to be held up, the Turkish shrapnel appearing to be too much for them.

It was now that there occurred what I think one of the finest incidents of the campaign. This was the landing of the Australian Artillery. They got two of their guns ashore, and over very rough country dragged them up the hills with what looked like a hundred men to each. Up they went, through a wheat-field, covered and plastered with shrapnel, but with never a stop until the crest of the hill on the right was reached. Very little time was wasted in getting into action, and from this time it became evident that we were there to stay.

The practice of the naval guns was simply perfect. They lodged shell after shell just in front of the foremost rank of our men; in response to a message asking them to clear one of the gullies, one ship placed shell after shell up that gully, each about a hundred yards apart, and in as straight a line as if they were ploughing the ground for Johnny Turk, instead of making the place too hot to hold him.

The Turks now began to try for this warship, and in their endeavours almost succeeded in getting the vessel we were on, as a shell burst right overhead.

The wounded now began to come back, and the one hospital ship there was filled in a very short time. Every available transport was then utilised for the reception of casualties, and as each was filled she steamed off to the base at Alexandria.

As night came on we appeared to have a good hold of the place, and orders came for our stretcher-bearer division to land. They took with them three days' 'iron' rations, which consisted of a tin of bully beef, a bag of small biscuits, and some tea and sugar, dixies, a tent, medical comforts, and (for firewood) all the empty cases we could scrape up in the ship.

Each squad had a set of splints, and every man carried a tourniquet and two roller bandages in his pouch. Orders were issued that the men were to make the contents of their water-bottles last three days, as no water was available on shore.

The following evening the remainder of the Ambulance, less the transport, was ordered ashore. We embarked in a trawler, and steamed towards the shore in the growing dusk as far as the depth of water would allow. The night was bitterly cold, it was raining, and all felt this was real soldiering.

None of us could understand what occasioned the noise we heard at times, of something hitting the iron deck houses behind us; at last one of the men exclaimed, 'Those are bullets, sir,' so that we were having our baptism of fire. It was marvellous that no one was hit, for they were fairly frequent, and we all stood closely packed.

Finally the skipper of the trawler, Captain Hubbard, told me he did not think we could be taken off that night, and therefore intended to drop anchor. He invited Major Meikle and myself to the cabin, where the cook served out hot tea to all hands. I have drunk a considerable number of cups of tea in my time, but that mug was very, very nice. The night was spent dozing where we stood, Paddy being very disturbed with the noise of the guns.

At daylight a barge was towed out and, after placing all our equipment on board, we started for the beach. As soon as the barge grounded, we jumped out into the water (which was about waist deep) and got to dry land.

Colonel Manders was there, and directed us up a gully where we were to stay in reserve for the time being, meantime to take on looking after lightly wounded cases. One tent was pitched and dug-outs made for both men and patients, the Turks supplying shrapnel pretty freely.

Our position happened to be in rear of a mountain battery, whose guns the Turks appeared very anxious to silence, and any shells the battery did not want came over to us. As soon as we were settled down I had time to look round. Down on the beach the 1st Casualty Clearing Station and the Ambulance of the Royal Marine Light Infantry were at work.

'Many stragglers found their way down gullies to the beach.' Anzac Cove on the evening of 25 April 1915.

There were scores of casualties awaiting treatment, some of them horribly knocked about. It was my first experience of such a number of cases. In civil practice, if an accident took place in which three or four men were injured, the occurrence would be deemed out of the ordinary; but here there were almost as many hundreds, and all the flower of Australia.

It made one feel really that, in the words of General Sherman, 'War is hell', and it seemed damnable that it should be in the power of one man, even if he be the German Emperor, to decree that all these men should be mutilated or killed. The great majority were just coming into manhood with all their life before them.

The stoicism and fortitude with which they bore their pain was truly remarkable. Every one of them was cheery and optimistic; there was not a murmur; the only requests were for a cigarette or a drink of water.

One felt very proud of these Australians, each waiting his turn to be dressed without complaining. It really quite unnerved me for a time. However, it was no time to allow the sentimental side of one's nature to come uppermost.

I watched the pinnaces towing the barges in. Each pinnace belonged to a warship and was in charge of a midshipman – dubbed by his shipmates a 'snotty.' This name originates from the days of Trafalgar. The little chaps appear to have suffered from chronic colds in the head, with the usual accompaniment of a copious flow from the nasal organs. Before addressing an officer the boys would clean their faces by drawing the sleeve of their jacket across the nose and I understand that this practice so incensed Lord Nelson that he ordered three brass buttons to be sewn on the wristbands of the boys' jackets.

However, this is by the way. These boys, of all ages from fourteen to sixteen, were steering their pinnaces with supreme indifference to the shrapnel falling about, disdaining any cover and as cool as if there was no such thing as war.

I spoke to one, remarking that they were having a great time. He was a bright, chubby, sunny-faced little chap, and with a smile said: 'Isn't it beautiful, sir? When we started there were sixteen of us, and now there are only six!' This is the class of man they make officers out of in Britain's navy, and while this is so there need be no fear of the result of any encounter with the Germans.

Another boy, bringing a barge full of men ashore, directed them to lie down and take all the cover they could, he meanwhile steering the pinnace and standing quite unconcernedly with one foot on the boat's rail.

ADVANCE, AUSTRALIANS*

Roy Bridges

We were all standing to arms. Some of the fellows were tightening up their equipment and sharpening their bayonets with bits of stone.

We had left Lemnos on Friday night, 23 April, and were now off the peninsula. We had been steaming very slowly with British and Russian gunboats for escort.

At two o'clock on the Sunday morning we were served a hot meal, the last decent meal that we had for many weeks. In the case of some poor boys who went down there on that first day at Anzac, the very last meal, poor chaps!

We were taken in small boats at about six thirty in the morning. We'd known the attack had begun, by the gunfire and by the rattle of musketry, when the 3rd Brigade landed. So, we got ready to start off in the boats. Every man had seized his rifle and sprung to his place. It was a beautiful clear morning, not a cloud in the sky. Eagerly we waited our turn to go.

All this time we could hear the big guns. Their fire was intermittent, not very quick, I should say about three or four minutes between each shell. Some of us, as we waited, were looking rather tense and excited. Other men were laughing and joking amongst themselves and talking about what they would do with their bayonets, when they got at the Turks. I saw one man in particular keep putting his bayonet on his rifle, to see that it wouldn't fall off.

We got ashore at about ten minutes to seven in the morning.

We went ashore in little ship's boats, a steam pinnace pulling about six or seven of them, one tied after the other. As we came close in the pinnace pulled us around into line with the shore and left us to row to the beach. There were about forty men in each boat. Lieutenant Campbell was in command of ours.

The boat we went ashore in had brought off a load of wounded and there was a lot of blood on the seats in the centre. You could see the men, as they stepped in, take a half circle round to the other seats and look at the blood out of the corners of their eyes. No remark was passed, only wherever those bloodstains reddened the seats they sat away from them. Others pretended to ignore the blood, but every man was looking at it.

I was in charge of a section and, seeing their faces as we went ashore, my impression was that our men were going to do well. They did do well. No men could have done better.

The Turks' shrapnel was bursting over us and you could hear the bullets dropping into the water like hailstones. There were five men wounded in our boat as we rowed in. One chap who was hit started to swear at his luck.

'After training for nine months and coming all those thousands of miles,' he said, 'here I am hit before I get a shot at the cows!' Just like an Australian, that was his thought, not the pain, but to have lost out on the fun of it all.

The fire was now intense and we were in direct line from machine-guns and shrapnel at times as we rowed in. I reckon it took us half an hour to get into the shallows, and then we had to jump into the water, and we landed in it breast-high.

We dashed out of the water and across the sand and formed up under the cliffs. After all of the 6th Battalion had landed we went single file up a gully and formed up again under a rise. We unloaded our packs there and, may I say, we never saw 'em again. Mine went with my safety razor and everything I had in it.

We next advanced by platoons in open order and we came under very heavy fire when we came to the top of Dead Man's Gully.

You could see down the ridge into another gully and up another from the top of which the Turks were firing. So we charged down the gully and up the ridge and chased them out of there.

We didn't get into reach of 'em with our bayonets. When we got to the top of the second ridge we came up with the 3rd Brigade, whom we were reinforcing. Here the fighting became one of isolated groups of men, not always under the command of an officer, firing and advancing in rushes.

It was here that the spirit of the Australians, to my mind, stood out at its best. The men who were wounded sang out, 'Go on, boys! Don't mind us!' And the men who were still standing ran on with renewed courage. Every man of them, though they had not been in the firing line before, showed the same grit and courage of the highest order.

On the second ridge beyond Dead Man's Gully I was wounded in the shoulder by a Turkish sniper from behind me. The bullet lodged under my shoulder blade.

I held on till about three thirty in the afternoon and then I had to return to the beach to get the bullet out. Not that it was giving me much pain but, you see, I was getting a bit weak from loss of blood and the business at hand wanted every ounce of a chap's strength.

Colonel Ryan took the bullet out and bandaged me and gave me a ticket to go on a transport, which I strongly resented as, barring a little stiffness in my shoulder, I felt perfectly fit.

So I said to Colonel Ryan, 'Would there be any danger to my wound if I went back to the firing line?'

He laughed and said, 'Do you want to go?'

I said, 'Sure I do!'

'Well, if you let a doctor see that shoulder every twenty-four hours,' he said, 'you can run the risk.'

So I went back to the firing line up Shrapnel Valley and I remained in the trenches until 5 May. Every man was wanted to do his bit, you see. We were short of men and short of supplies. We had nothing except what we disembarked with.

On Friday, 30 April, word came down our trench that we were going to have a rest in the rear. It had been a tough time holding the line against the Turks and the idea of a rest was much appreciated by us.

The men were much disgusted, when we got to our rest camp, to find that the rest meant making roads up Shrapnel Valley to facilitate bringing up artillery. While thus engaged we were in more danger than we had faced in the firing line, the danger being from spent bullets.

I remarked to the Captain in charge of the road-making that, if this was the rest, I wanted to get back to work in the trenches. His answer was, 'We must take everything as it comes.' And we took everything as it came.

On Sunday, 2 May we went back into the firing line and on Wednesday, 5 May we were informed that we had been selected to go round to Cape Helles to reinforce the 29th Division of the British. Whether rightly or wrongly we took this as a compliment to our fighting powers.

We were marched down to the beach and issued with another two days' iron rations. At twelve o'clock that night we were taken aboard mine sweepers and sent to Helles. We arrived there on Thursday morning.

It was a steep place to land. It was where Commander Unwin had run the *River Clyde* aground, with the Dublins and Munsters, on the morning of 25 April. We pulled alongside her and got ashore. We were marched a mile and a half inland and there we dug in.

It was an open plain we were on and we were not under fire except for an odd shell. We remained there until Saturday morning, 8 May, and then the order came for us to advance.

The men sprang up with glee for they didn't know what we were involved in. It was the famous charge of Achi Baba. We went up a gully under fire and 500 yards behind the line of British trenches we were debouched from the gully to the right, in a line parallel to the trenches.

In short rushes we arrived in the Tommies' trenches, where we were welcomed by the Munsters and the Dublin Fusiliers. But, I can tell you, we lost a lot of men in that 200 yards rush.

'Before we got 300 yards I only had two men from my section and myself left standing ... out of sixteen.' Bodies at Krithia, 8 May 1915.

Twenty-seven men who were all that were left standing of a brigade of over 700 after the Battle of Krithia.

The 6th and 7th Battalions led the charge under Colonel McNicholl. The Brigade was commanded by Brigadier General McCay. My platoon was Number 9 of the 6th Battalion.

By five thirty it was clear evening. After only a few minutes' breathing space in the British trenches, the order came.

'Advance, Australians!'

I will say here that I couldn't believe my ears, when I heard the order. Being an old soldier, I couldn't believe the Brigadier General was going to rush us up those steep inclines in front of the trenches.

When that order came again – 'Advance, Australians!' – I said to an Irish Corporal, 'Give me a hand up, Mick.' He held out his hand and I put my foot in it and he hoisted me out onto the parapet. My men were out a few seconds ahead of me and were looking for me for the word of command.

I stood up on the parapet and we advanced, trying to get the line as straight as possible. But, before we got 300 yards I only had two men from my section and myself left standing ... out of sixteen.

Shells were not very numerous at first, but the Turks were just beginning to find their range, and the bullets were zipping around us like hailstones.

The next thing I remember is hearing a shell burst somewhere behind us and feeling a sensation like being hit with a hot iron bar fair in the neck. I struck the ground head down.

It was only after I fell that I realised I was wounded. A shrapnel bullet had got me in and had come out at my mouth, breaking my jaw and nine teeth. I remember like a bad dream spitting out those teeth.

That ended my fighting. I lay there between the trenches until the following Sunday morning. I was down and out of it. I don't remember it all and I'm thankful I don't.

On coming to, I found that some kind-hearted Australian, in the face of all that awful fire, had knelt down and bandaged me.

Some time on that Sunday morning Dr James Black, commonly known among the boys as Jimmy, turned me over and said, 'Hello, so you've got it a second time. I'd better take you out of this and give you a chance!'

He lifted me up and carried me on his back over the open space, swept by machine-gun fire, until we came to the top of the gully. Then he asked me if I could get along by myself but I couldn't. Fortunately, the cook from my own Division came along and took charge of me and helped me down to the dressing station.

I would like to say here that Dr Jimmy Black deserves the V.C. if ever any man did. I have never met him since and I don't know him personally, but if it's ever in my power to do him a service – I will!

I was taken down to the dressing station and from there I was carried down to the clearing station and transferred in a wagon to the beach. I was out into a tender there with thirty other very badly wounded men. I found it very difficult to make the orderlies understand what I wanted as my wound made it impossible for me to speak or to swallow anything.

Somehow I didn't get on board the hospital ship until 15 May, a week after I was wounded. What happened until then remains a complete blank. I have no recollection of going on board the hospital ship and I believe I was fed with milk through a tube. I woke up on board, being attended by a swarthy Indian with very bright black eyes.

It strikes me, as a career veteran and one who was not born in Australia myself, that the Australians were the ideal soldiers to tackle the invasion at Gallipoli. If they had only been trained and disciplined as normal soldiers they wouldn't have done half so well. But, you see, Australians maintain their own initiative and, even if there was no officer to hand, there was always an N.C.O. or a private to realise the position and initiate action.

I will tell you one thing that struck me as rather typical. Up until 27 April we occupied a trench that turned at right angles near the mouth of a communication trench. The Turks kept up a strenuous hail of fire on this corner, in the hope of hitting the men coming from the communication trench.

I had a young bloke on sentry go and, at about two thirty in the morning, I passed behind this chap and remarked, 'They seem pretty busy.'

He turned to me without any trace of a smile and said, 'If them fellows don't stop soon, Sergeant, they'll be hurtin' somebody.'

It was the one spirit right through, the spirit that got us to Gallipoli, and kept us there.

*This is the story of a Sergeant of the 7th Battalion who took part in the Anzac landing on 25 April and also the attack on Krithia on 8 May 1915 and lost 795, killed and wounded, out of a total of 1,110 men. Irish by birth and Australian by temperament, he had served in the South African War with the Royal Dublin Fusiliers in 1901–02. After that war ended he had returned home but, restless and out of work, emigrated, first to New Zealand in 1904 and then to Victoria in 1910. He enlisted on 6 August 1914 as he felt '... the Empire needed trained men to set an example for the untrained.'

THE RED CROSS NURSE

Tom Skeyhill

When you're lying in your bed, with a buzzing in your head,
And a pain across your chest that's far from nice,
She moves about the place, with a sweet angelic grace,
That makes you think the dingy ward is paradise.

She's dressed in red and grey, and she doesn't get much pay,
Yet she never seems to worry or complain.
She's Australian through and through, with a heart that's big and
    true,
And when she's near, the deepest wound forgets to pain.

With her hand upon your head, she remains beside your bed,
Until your worries and your pains begin to go,
Then with fingers true and light, she will bind your wounds up tight,
And when she leaves you're sleeping fast and breathing low.

When the ward is sleeping sound, she begins her nightly round,
With eyes that share your sorrows and your joys.
With a heart so full of love, she beseeches Him above
To watch and care for all her darling soldier boys.

There is something in her face, that can hold your tongue in place,
When you'd curse because your wounds refuse to heal.
But if once you get her cross, you will find out to your loss,
The velvet scabbard holds the tempered sword of steel.

When you're once again yourself, and they pull you off the shelf,
And send you back again to do the fighting trick,
You'll just grip her by the hand, with a look she'll understand.
Outside you stand and curse your wound for healing quick.

Though she hasn't got a gun and she hasn't killed a Hun,
Still she fights as hard as veterans at the front.
When the Allies start to drive and the wounded boys arrive,
It's always she who has to bear the battle's brunt.

She's a queen without a throne, and her sceptre is her own
True woman's smile and sympathy so sweet.
So when guns no longer shoot, I'll spring to the salute
Every time I pass a sister in the street.

THE ANZAC WOUNDED

Unknown British Female Correspondent
Egyptian Times, 29 May 1915

When, under the auspices of the Red Cross, I was admitted to the list of hospital visitors I must admit that my craven heart fairly failed me.

I had visions of myself attempting the role of ministering angel to most unresponsive patients, forcing my conversation upon those whose only desire was to be left to themselves. I imagined myself arousing suspicion as to the real reasons for my visits, seeing sights and maybe hearing things that would be inexpressibly painful to a susceptible nature such as I was certain of possessing.

My first visit, undertaken with many tremors, was, however, an agreeable surprise. Since then I have become so thoroughly interested in the cases all round me that I have extended my visits to various other hospitals in Cairo. Practically every afternoon in the week is occupied in one direction or other, while the hours devoted to such visits have become protracted till long after dark.

Numerically, in most of the hospitals thus visited, the Australasian patients exceed the Britishers almost in the proportion of three to one, and therein is conversation made easy; for besides being splendidly plucky, these magnificent Colonials are born talkers. They are never so happy as when exploiting the country of their birth, even at the expense of the 'old country' to whose defence they are sacrificing their lives and fortunes.

At times they do 'flap their wings' somewhat (and who indeed can blame them), but they are the most sociable, friendly souls imaginable, and their sociability and friendliness is combined with so much proven pluck and endurance that one does not know which to appreciate the most.

Life in these hospitals is necessarily deprived of luxury. The food is not over plentiful and, in many cases, is not particularly palatable. Yet it is rarely one hears a grumble, unless on the score of flies or the heat, and then it is more as an excuse for a joke. Murmurs over the pain these men are enduring are practically non-existent.

Like Peter Pan, the boy who never grew up, they treat life mostly as one great joke – we know one bed over which hangs the inscription 'The naughty boy of the family'.

It is only when one gets talking confidentially that one hears of the little details of home life, their concerns as to the fate of brothers and pals, the frightful tales of all they have seen and undergone, the horrors of war. Very little of their talk is of the actual pain they are so heroically undergoing.

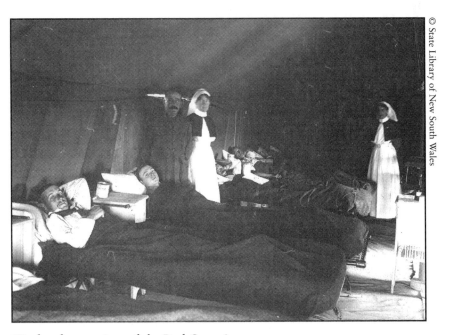

'*Under the auspices of the Red Cross.*'

'I'm all right, Miss, doing fine,' is their almost invariable reply to questions about their own condition.

'Yes, I'm going out in a few days, in a fortnight I hope to be at the front again, and getting a bit of my own back ...'

'You see, it was like this ...'

'How you would have laughed to hear us yell "Yalla imshi" as we rushed that hill.'

'Of course it was Hell, but you must remember we had been on that transport more or less for weeks; we were ripe for any sort of action. We would have been painting Cairo pink if we had been there, so we painted Gallipoli scarlet instead ...'

'What, the bayonet charge? My, but it was fine, real bonza ...'

'Lady, I want to write to Mother, but I can't let her know I am wounded and in hospital, so what had I better do?' (And then one suggests that the Alexandria postmark might sound more healthy and that a covering letter to the port might save the situation.)

'Cards? Yes, thank you ever so much; I am practically alone, and many an afternoon I've spent sitting on a log playing patience – never got it out for days on end sometimes ...'

'What's this?' I asked one badly wounded man as, from beneath a pillow, I saw sticking out a corner of a little testament.

'Not mine,' was the disclaimer, 'for I don't seem to have much use for these things, but I picked it up on the beach, and it has the name and address of some poor English lad inside, so I am keeping it till I can get outside to send back to his family.' (The thought seemed to me to have a virtue high above any protestation I could offer.)

'Socks, Miss, why I can knit them myself a fair treat. Three purl, one plain, decrease down the back seam, etc. I got a first prize at the Arts and Craft Exhibition in India for knitting a lady's petticoat.' (And after the tedium of lying idle in bed he fell to work on a chance ball of wool as eagerly as a dog given an unexpected bone.)

Oh, they are a very cheery human crowd, these wounded men. They are extraordinarily thoughtful to their fellows, though they will scrap like fury sometimes, extraordinarily appreciative of their nursing sisters and visitors and extraordinarily content with their surroundings, even though they lack much in the way of creature comforts.

One watches the distribution of enormous hunks of bread and butter smeared with jam for tea, served on the pillow or little table or any other old place, where they are hurriedly covered over with a fragment of mosquito netting or none-too-clean towel. But few complaints are ever heard as to the quality of the fare. Frequently the hospital diet will be reinforced by dainties handed round by generous visitors and often the passage through the wards by a popular figure or a pretty child will take on the nature of a triumphal procession and be followed by a thousand words of interest and approval.

In spite of the rough association and upbringing of a number of these wounded, and the tedium and boredom of their life in hospital, their politeness and courtesy to their visitors is quite extraordinary. They will talk freely, though never rudely, and never forget to voice their thanks, and hope that the visit may be repeated. Quite a number of them are really musical, and, oh, the pleasure that is afforded them by an unexpected concert would soften the heart of many an amateur musician if he or she would only realise it.

The beds are frequently being emptied and re-occupied, for numbers of patients are being turned out day by day, to take their place in convalescent homes or to become the guests of private hospitality. Fatal cases have been, thank goodness, comparatively few in number as far as the Cairo hospitals are concerned. Many have been serious cases, but maybe seventy per cent are on the high road to recovery, and will doubtless face the music again with their hardihood undiminished.

One fears, though, that their future actions in the front line will never quite have the same spontaneity of ignorance which served them so magnificently in their earlier exploits at Gallipoli. Those landing operations and their aftermath will live for countless generations among the thrilling incidents of the war. They formed an epic, one of the most heroic in history; please God that the troops engaged therein will never have to face their like again.

ANZACS

Edgar Wallace

The children unborn shall acclaim
The standard the Anzacs unfurled,
When they made Australasia's fame
The wonder and pride of the world.

Some of you got a V.C.,
Some 'the Gallipoli trot',
Some had a grave by the sea,
And all of you got it damned hot,
And I see you go limping through town
In the faded old hospital blue,
And driving abroad – lying down,
And Lord! but I wish I were you!

I envy you beggars I meet,
From the dirty old hats on your head
To the rusty old boots on your feet –
I envy you living or dead.
A knighthood is fine in its way,
A peerage gives splendour and fame,
But I'd rather have tacked any day
That word to the end of my name.

I'd count it the greatest reward
That ever a man could attain;
I'd sooner be 'Anzac' than 'lord',
I'd sooner be 'Anzac' than 'thane'.
Here's a bar to the medal you'll wear,
There's word that will glitter and glow,
And an honour a king cannot share
When you're back in the cities you know.

The children unborn shall acclaim
The standard the Anzacs unfurled,
When they made Australasia's fame
The wonder and pride of the world.

HOLDING THE LINE

THE HOLDING OF THE LINE

Tom Skeyhill

You have heard about the landing and our deeds of gallantry,
Of how we proved our British breed out on Gallipoli.
We charged the cruel bayonets, we faced the cannons' roar;
We flinched not from the bullets, as through the air they tore.
The storming of the hillside like the brightest stars will shine,
But the grandest feat of all of them was The Holding of the Line.

The foe, like demons, countered and the bullets poured like rain;
But our orders were to 'hold on' or be numbered with the slain.
When hot Australian temper could stand the strain no more,
We leapt out from the trenches and drove the foe before.
And now, when in Australia you hear this soldier's rhyme,
We know you'll give us credit for The Holding of the Line.

AN ENGAGEMENT IN MAY

E. F. Hanman ('Haystack')

About two o'clock one afternoon the foe opened fire on us again. By now, we knew his music only too well, but, thanks to our trenches, which we were ever improving, none of us were hit. We simply crouched well down, awaiting a happier mood.

Two or three times the enemy could be seen advancing in numbers. Our machine-gun, and several others along the line, was a continual source of nuisance to them. They evidently spotted where ours was concealed, for the gunner put his hand to his head and slid gently down to the bottom of the trench. We placed him up behind us and left him until a burial party should make his last bed.

Shell after shell whizzed close to us. They were not shrapnel, but small high explosive missiles. One of them hit the machine-gun square, knocked the gun section off their feet, took the parapet clean away, and continued on its way. Strange to relate, it did not explode. The men who had been taken off their feet jumped up, laughing boisterously. They thoroughly enjoyed the fun, and as they were in no way injured, the affair was a huge joke. A new gun was quickly mounted, and as quickly in action.

The afternoon dragged slowly away, the shells were still screaming and hissing overhead, but we had become callous. Let them shoot away at us as much as they desired!

We were not very hungry, though we had not eaten a meal for two whole days, but our officer advised us to make the most of our time and take something to eat, as we might not now be feeling hungry, but we should become faint later on and unable to continue our duties, if we did not do as he asked us. So we opened beef tins and jam tins, and set to work on our ample supply of biscuits. More water was smuggled up to us, so we were perfectly content with our lot.

The sun shone down, bright and hot. We were very sleepy, but it was impossible to think of that, as every man might be required at a moment's notice. We did think that perhaps we might be able to snatch a wink at night, but we little knew what was before us Tuesday evening.

Darkness visited the earth, accompanied by rain. By this time we presented a sorry picture. Knees and elbows were worn through. We were covered with dust; it was down our necks, in our hair, in our ears. We were all unshaven and unwashed. The rain fell gently and lightly, turning the caked dust and dirt on us into slimy mud. It was all we could manage to keep our weapons in good working order. The mud clogged in the rifle bolts and prevented them from sliding freely.

We were dog-tired. How sleepy we were, no one would ever realise! Our heads ached and swam – our senses were dulled. It was a horrible nightmare. Nothing seemed real. As we gazed with heavy stupid eyes in front of us, the earth seemed to swim around us. We found our heads nodding, and as we were just on the point of falling to the ground, our senses would reassert themselves with a sickening, sudden jar.

This was awful; it could not last, if something did not happen to excite us and keep us at fever heat. We longed for the Turks to attack. Let us charge! Let them charge! Anything would be preferable to this state of affairs!

Of course, sentries were posted, and they stood the picture of forlorn desolation, the folds of their overcoats wrapped round their rifles to protect them from the cold, drizzling rain. Their uniforms were stained a red patchy colour where they had been in contact with the slimy sodden soil. Boots were wet, feet became numb and frozen, ears tingled, teeth chattered, and we stood and shivered, thinking of soft pillows and warm dry beds.

Lack of water is bad, but lack of sleep is worse. It renders us gloomy, miserable – it renders us beasts, savages. We snarled and snapped, cursing war, cursing everything, cursing ourselves, and cursing our comrades. We were not responsible for our words, or our actions. Bosom pals swore and staggered one against the other in their mad endeavours to remain awake. Some wet their eyes with their moistened finger, vainly hoping to drive away the ceaseless, tantalising attacks of Morpheus. Others gazed with dim, unseeing eyes, straight in front, still as statues, graven images, plain suffering written on their mud-stained faces. And all the while, the rain trickled down, augmenting our abject misery. Oh! For something to happen!

What was that?

To our right front, a bright light bursts into view. What is it?

Dim figures, jet black and weird, could be seen flitting about and around the lurid red flame. Evidently, it was some sort of a signalling apparatus the enemy was employing. It looked a very clumsy affair. The machine-gunners chuckled and turned their gun in that direction. It was laughable to see that light disappear so quickly, and cries of 'Allah! Allah!' reached our ears.

We were wide awake now. Surely an attack was meditated. Yes! The enemy was advancing in mass formation. Our fellows had received orders to allow the Turks to come within ten paces, and then to pour the lead into them. Our rifles hold eleven cartridges, and are, in every way, very formidable little weapons.

'Allah! Allah! Allah!'

They are coming with leaps and bounds, their dismal, howling cry rending the night. Closer and closer, they are almost upon us! 'Fire!' yells an officer.

We comply willingly; rifles crack and rattle all down our line, the high-pitched music of machine-guns being audible above the din.

What a withering hail of lead met those dusky warriors. They hesitate, rally, and then, throwing courage to the winds, they turned and fled, trampling under foot their dead and dying. The air is filled with moans and cries. 'Allah! Allah! Allah!'

A bugle sounds a long-drawn, dreary note. They are coming again. 'Allah! Allah! Allah!' We can easily distinguish their officers' voices, haranguing them, encouraging.

With a very determined rush, they come again. The darkness is illuminated by thousands of tiny spitting flashes – the rattle and roar is terrific. Our dark-hued foe melts before our well-directed fire. They stagger, stumble and fall like so many skittles. Then, again, they eventually turn and flee, as if possessed.

Again, and again, they came at us, determined to dishearten and dislodge us. We had come to stay. Undaunted, the wounded were removed, all the while under a veritable rain of shot. We turned to face them once more.

The Turk wearied first. He gave up the attempt as hopeless that night. He had learnt a lesson. The scrubby hills were littered with dark huddled forms. The cries and groans of the terrified wounded wretches were appalling. We, too, had not escaped unscathed. There were many sad vacancies. We had witnessed our comrades' heads severed from their bodies, huge gaping wounds had appeared about our pals' limbs. They had been dragged away, cursing and crying to be allowed to remain to deal sudden death to the oncoming wave of Turks.

Others, too badly hurt for speech, were limp and inert, lying white and bloodstained, clawing at the ground. Others writhed in their death agony, calling upon us in piteous tones to shoot them and put an end to their sufferings. The din of battle never diminished. Oaths and curses could be heard on all sides. Faces and figures stood out distinct and red, red, like labouring demons, habitants of the lower regions. They disappeared and reappeared as the rifles flashed and flickered.

The enemy thought to trick us. They tried to blow our charge, thinking thus to draw us from our lair. We knew, though, that we had no bugles with us. All our orders were given by whistle. They played every call they knew – some of them we could not distinguish at all, but when the strains of 'Cook-house door' went echoing through the hills, we all roared with laughter. It was too ludicrous! 'Cook-house door'!! In the midst of all this butchering and slaughter! It is not necessary to relate that this ruse was not successful.

At last we could breathe, at last we could with safety throw ourselves down and rest, even though sleep was not allowed us. In fact, we no longer wished to sleep; we were too busy discussing the result of the attacks. Dawn found us still watching and waiting. How bitterly cold it was! A fierce, piercing wind was blowing, the icy-cold rain had penetrated our clothing, and we were wet through.

It was rumoured that we were to be relieved shortly. We became, all at once, jubilant and delighted. We had glorious visions of hot coffee and steaming stew. What a blessing would be a warm, dry shirt, and a good wash!

The relieving party crawled up without being perceived by the enemy. The morning was dull, and the light bad, so this was no wonderful feat. Out we scrambled, stiff and stumbling from being so many hours in awkward positions.

We made our way as quickly as circumstances permitted, past our reserve trenches. Here we saw lines of grinning, joking men, asking us what we thought of the night's attack. Snipers were exceptionally busy. Little spurts of mud close at our feet warned us that we had better hurry. Down the ranges we went, taking flying leaps, being torn by brambles, tripping and falling over stumps and holes in the half-light.

'Crack, crack, crack!'

'Run for it, boys! Come on!'

Round bends, over ridges, through slimy puddles, we kept to our mad pace. The beach presented a very inviting appearance. There were hundreds of men, all war-worn and battered, muffled up to their eyes in coats and scarves, sitting round little smokeless fires, cooking hot sizzling rashers of bacon. Its smell was to us famished chaps, simply heavenly. Then we felt safe, we had a respite. It did not take us long to make up more fires and do likewise.

How we did enjoy that early morning meal! When we had satisfied our appetites, we lay down in little groups and awaited the rising of the sun. Up he rose, bright and golden, despite the cold, damp night, it gave every promise of being a hot day.

Our hopes were fulfilled, it became very warm. The next best thing to do would be to have a wash. Here was the gently rolling ocean, water to spare, why not have a bathe? Bullets kept falling, making plopping sounds as they sent up little spouts of water. No one seemed to take any notice of these. It was well worth the risk to have a clean skin.

One of our section, who like ourselves, had come through the awful night safely, was stripped, and just in the act of diving into foam. A dull, resounding thud made us turn in his direction. We were just in time to see him reel and pitch face forward, blood issuing from his mouth. In less than a minute, we were forced to cover his face, and there he lay, a grim warning to others. There were nearly as many casualties down on the beach as in the first line of trenches.

The roll was called. We noticed the many silences as name after name remained unanswered. Every battalion was collected and drawn up in the usual manner. There were many who would never again call 'Here!' as his name was read from the roll. We said nothing, but we felt the loss of every man. Every silence was like a knife. Not till now had we realised how much our comrades were to us! We had lived with them, eaten with them, slept with them, fought with them! Now we knew their worth, now we were cognisant of the fact that they were gone. It could not be realised. Why, only yesterday, even this morning, early, we had spoken with them!

As our Company Commander listened, tears filled his eyes. He was, for several moments, unable to speak. We could see him swallowing hard, and we turned away so as not to embarrass him.

As he parted his lips to address us, we could not help thinking how much he was to us. Standing very little over five feet, this tiny chap, with those sad, solemn eyes, that firm but gentle mouth, the high intellectual forehead, the long sensitive nose and small well-knit frame, how much he was to us!

Never once had he lost control of his well-balanced temper. Defaulters he had chided, and pointed out their errors. Faithfulness to duty he had always applauded. With words of encouragement, he had consoled us. He never sent a man where he himself dared not go. He was consideration itself, as cool and thoughtful during the hottest engagement, as when on parade.

He always addressed us as 'lads'. 'Now, lads, play the game' from him worked wonders. Where he went, we would follow. Yes, our Captain was the essence of an officer; like Nelson, as gentle as a lamb, as brave as a lion. He was of necessity a gentleman, but we, who knew him, can pay him far greater homage by saying, with Shakespeare, 'Nature will rise up and say to all the world – this was a Man!'

A little incident, which may throw more light on the character of our little skipper, might be of interest. We had been keeping up a fairly rapid fire for some hours and the Captain declined to take proper cover, though the bullets were flying freely. All the while he kept saying to us, 'Keep down, lads, steady, lads! It's all for your own good!'

While attempting to observe the tactics of the enemy, he was wounded in the hand. At the time he was holding a hard biscuit, well plastered with jam. The blood poured down on to it and, with a rueful smile, he threw it away, saying, 'There goes my breakfast!'

With these words he stepped back and accidentally trod on a man lying prostrate behind him. With his usual courtesy he apologised, and asked the man's pardon. The soldier, of course, granted it without hesitation. The Captain's hand was then bound up, and he continued his observations.

THE LIGHT HORSE WAITS

Oliver Hogue ('Trooper Bluegum')

Some of the Australians and New Zealanders had already got the call, but we of the Light Horse still waited at Mena Camp outside Cairo – growing more and more impatient every day.

It was the arrival of our Australian wounded back from the Dardanelles that settled it. It was a wrench to leave our horses behind – the dear old horses that we petted and loved, the horses that were a very part of us – but it had to be done.

When we saw our fellows coming back with their wounds upon them – when we heard of what they had been through – when we listened to their story of that wonderful landing on Gallipoli on 25 April, and of the wild charge they made up the frowning hill – all of us, to a man, begged to be sent to the front as infantry, but it didn't matter – we were soldiers of the King!

I saw the Red Crescent train as it steamed in loaded with the wounded, and I went to the base hospital to see and chat with the men who knew now what war was – the men who had clamoured so impatiently for so many weeks to be sent where 'the fighting' was, and then came back again to be nursed in an Egyptian hospital!

Yet they were happy. They had 'done their bit.' They smoked cigarettes and yarned about their experiences. I watched the slightly wounded ones marching from the train to the hospital – an unforgettable sight. Most of them were shot about the arms or scalp. Their uniforms had dried blood all over them, and were torn about where the field doctors had ripped off sleeves or other parts to get at the wounds.

As they marched irregularly along, one young fellow with his arm in a sling and a flesh wound in the leg limped behind and shouted out, 'Hey, you chaps, don't make it a welter!'

I visited the wounded men and chatted to one soldier of the 3rd Brigade who had landed in the first wave.

'Bah!' he exclaimed as he lit his cigarette. 'The Turks can't shoot for nuts! But the German machine-guns are the devil, and the shrapnel is no picnic!'

His arm was in a sling, and his leg was bandaged from hip to ankle. But he was cheerful as could be, as proud as Punch, and as chirpy as a gamecock. For he was one of the band of Australian heroes, wounded and back from the front. And we who listened to the deathless story of the wild charge they made could not help wishing we had shared in the glories of that fight.

'We fought them for three days after landing,' said a big bushman in the 2nd Brigade, 'and they made about a dozen counter-attacks. But when we had a chance of sitting down and letting them charge us it was dead easy – just like money from home. They never got near enough to sample the bayonets again. But on the twenty-seventh they tried to get all over us. They let the artillery work overtime, and we suffered a bit from the shrapnel. The noise was deafening. Suddenly it ceased, and a new Turkish division was launched at us. This was just before breakfast.

'There is no doubt about the bravery of the Turks. But we were comfortably entrenched, and it was their turn to advance in the open. We pumped lead into them till our rifles were too hot to hold. Time and again they came on, and each time we sent them about their business. At three o'clock we got tired of slaughtering them that way, so we left our little home in the trench and went after them again with the bayonet.'

'Say, what do you think of "Big Lizzie?"' asked another Cornstalk.

It is necessary to explain that this was the affectionate way our fellows alluded to the super-Dreadnought *Queen Elizabeth*. The soldier continued: 'All the while our transports were landing, "Big Lizzie" just glided up and down like an old hen watching her chickens. Every now and then Turkish destroyers from Nagara tried to cut in and smash up the transports. But the moment "Lizzie" got a move on they skedaddled. One ship was just a bit slow. Didn't know that "Big Liz" could hit ten miles off. Shell landed fair amidships, and it was "good-night nurse".'

One of the 9th Battalion (Queenslanders, under Colonel Lee) chipped in here, 'Ever tried wading through barbed wire and water with maxims zipping all round you?'

This pertinent question explained the severe losses of the 3rd Brigade. The landing was effected simultaneously at several points on the peninsula, but one spot was a hornet's nest and they started to sting when the Australians reached the beach. A couple of boats were upset and several sailors killed. Others dashing into the shallow water were caught in the barbed wire.

'My legs are tattooed prettier than a picture,' added the Queenslander, 'and I've a bit of shrapnel shell here for a keepsake, somewhere under my shoulder.'

'Fancy 10,000 miles and eight months' training all for nix,' said a disgusted Corporal. 'Landed at 4 a.m. Shot at three seconds past four. Back on the boat at 5 a.m.'

And so on.

To have gone through all they had gone through, and then to treat it all so lightly, seemed an extraordinary thing. All the doctors and nurses commented on the amazing fortitude and cheerfulness of the Australian wounded. I used to think the desire to be in the thick of things, that I had so often heard expressed, was make-believe, but I know better now.

I used to say myself that I 'wanted to be there' (and *sotto voce* I used to add 'I don't think'); and now, in my heart-searchings, I began to wonder if I didn't really mean it, after all.

I used to strike an attitude and quote 'One crowded hour of glorious life is worth an age without a name', whilst all the time I felt in my heart that I would prefer a crowded age of inglorious life to an hour of fame. Now I began to wonder whether in my heart's core, in my very heart of hearts, I did not agree with the poet. The proper study of mankind is Oneself. And what was I doing there, anyway?

Yes, it was extraordinary – not a doubt of it. Doctors and nurses said they never saw anything like it in the world. Those soldiers back from the Dardanelles, many of them sorely wounded, were laughing and joking all day, chatting cheerfully about their terrible experiences, and itching to get back again.

'Nurse,' said one of them with a shattered leg, as he raised himself with difficulty, 'will you write a little note for me?'

She came over and sat on the side of the bed, paper and pencil in hand.

'"My dear Mother and Father, I hope this letter finds you as well as it leaves me at present." How's that for a beginning, nurse?' he said with a smile.

I heard of another man who sent a letter from the Dardanelles. It ran: 'Dear Aunt, This war is a fair cow. Your affectionate nephew.'

Just that, and nothing more. The Censor, I have no doubt, would think it a pity to cut anything out of it.

I heard of another, and at the risk of an intrusion into the private affairs of any of our soldiers, I make bold to give it. It was just this: 'My darling Helen, I would rather be spending the evening with you than with two dead Turks in this trench. Still it might be worse, I suppose.'

Those cheerful Australians!

Can you wonder that the Light Horse wanted to get a move on and make a start for the front? Can you wonder that when we heard of the terrible list of casualties which were the price of victory, and when we saw our men coming back, many of them old friends, with their battle scars upon them, we fretted and fumed impatiently?

We had a church parade, and the chaplain, Captain Keith Miller, preached from the text, 'Let us run with patience the race that is set before us,' and it only made us angry. There was only one text that appealed us, and that was, 'How long, O Lord, how long?'

We could stand it no longer. Our boys needed reinforcements, and that was all we cared about. They must have reinforcements. It would be some days before men could arrive from England and France. Sir Ian Hamilton wanted men to push home the attack and ensure the victory.

We knew that no cavalry could go for a couple of weeks, and our fellows were just 'spoiling for a fight'. They were sick and tired of the endless waiting, with wild rumours of moving every second day. Men from all the troops and squadrons went to their officers and volunteered to go as infantry, if only they could go at once. B Squadron, 6th Regiment, volunteered *en masse*.

Colonel Ryrie, accurately gauging the temper of the men, summoned the regimental commanders, Lieutenant Colonel Cox, Lieutenant Colonel Harris and Lieutenant Colonel Arnott. What happened at this little Council of War we don't know. But we guess. Word was sent on to the General that the whole Brigade would leave for the front within an hour, on foot if necessary.

A similar offer had just been made by the 1st Light Horse Brigade (Colonel Chauvel) and the 1st Brigade of New Zealand Mounted Rifles.

What it cost these gallant horsemen to volunteer and leave their horses behind only horsemen can guess. Colonel Ryrie's Brigade was said to be the best-horsed Brigade in Egypt. Scores of men had brought their own horses. After eight months of soldiering we were deeply attached to our chargers.

Fighting on foot was not our forte. We were far more at home in the saddle. But Colonel Ryrie expressed the dominant thought of the men when he said, 'My Brigade are mostly bushmen, and they never expected to go gravel-crushing, but if necessary the whole Brigade will start tomorrow on foot, even if we have to tramp the whole way from Constantinople to Berlin.'

* * *

There came a day when there was sudden movement in the camp.

General Birdwood had arrived back from Gallipoli, with a wonderful string of medals and decorations, and there were other 'signs of the zodiac' pointing to our early departure.

When at last Colonel Ryrie announced to us of the 2nd Light Horse that we were to make ready, you could have heard the cheering miles away. The residents of Ma'adi, when they heard it, thought peace had been declared!

Men who had of late been swearing at the heat and dust and the flies and the desert suddenly became jovial again. At dinner they passed the joke along, sang songs, and cheered everybody, from Kitchener to Andy Fisher, and the brigadier down to the cooks and the trumpeters.

So we are off at last, after weary months of waiting – on foot. Blistered heels and trenches ahead; but it's better than sticking here in the desert doing nothing.

THE BATTLE OF THE WAZZA*

Oliver Hogue ('Trooper Bluegum')

I remember the riot.

The Light Horse and many other troops waited still, outside Cairo. Men were keen to be off to the front, waiting is not a good thing for soldiers. It seemed that something must be done to stir the authorities up; and some of the 'hot heads' got up a riot in Cairo.

They went into Cairo singing 'There'll be a hot time in the old town tonight'; and sure enough there was. It was not meant to be quite as hot as it turned out. Things have a way of shaping themselves sometimes.

Nobody could tell afterwards exactly how it all happened; but before the night was spent some houses had been burned down, some shots had been fired and some men had been wounded.

There were some Australians, some New Zealanders, some Maoris and a few Territorials in it. And it all happened so simply. Some publicans and other sinners presumed to treat the Maoris as 'niggers'. This was too much for the New Zealanders, and they began to pull some of the furniture out of a public house, and to make a bonfire of it in the street, while the Maoris danced a war dance round it.

One or two other bonfires were started. The native police rolled up and kept the crowd back, one of the police inspectors remarking that it would be a good thing for Cairo if a few more of the 'dens' were burned down. 'I've been wishing for a fire among these rotten tenements for a long time,' he said, 'and now the fire-engines are coming, and it looks as if they'll be saved again!'

The fire-engine came clattering up the street. The soldiers attacked it. In self-defence the firemen repelled the attack with the fire-hose. The soldiers renewed the attack and, reinforcements having arrived, captured the hose and turned it on the firemen, completely routing them. Then they cut the hose up – and the Maoris went on their 'haka'.

But in the end, of course, law and order had to prevail. Other engines came upon the scene, escorted by a squadron of Territorial Dragoons. The soldiers cooled down. The fires were put out.

Not creditable behaviour, of course. Not quite the sort of thing we had been sent there for. But human nature is human nature, and a crowd of soldiers is a crowd of soldiers.

Bad grog will make the best of soldiers bad, especially in Cairo; and the evil that's in men must come out of them as well as the good. Hence to call the Maoris 'niggers' – well, who can blame the New Zealanders for resenting it, and who can blame the Australians for siding with the New Zealanders, or the Territorials for assisting their overseas brethren?

We have Mr Asquith's own word for it that 'Who touches them touches us'. Not creditable behaviour then, but human nature and British brotherhood. And high spirits, and the chafing under the monotony of camp life in Egypt!

Trooper Bluegum, at all events, long ago forgave them. Nothing came from the official enquiries.

The same men were among those who were to create for themselves and their country, in the words of General Ian Hamilton, 'An imperishable record of military virtue'. Many of them are no more. Maoris and all have given their lives cheerfully for their Empire and the sacred cause of Right. Let us remember their virtues and forget their faults.

* The Wazza (also known as Wassa, Wazzer, Wazzir) was the red-light district of Cairo where two riots occurred on 2 April and 31 July, 1915. An official enquiry came to no conclusion about the reason for these events.

THE SAPPERS

E. F. Hanman ('Haystack')

Much amusement is to be gained from watching the manoeuvres of men as they pass some sniper-covered spot.

These snipers were always a pest. Just when one had boiled the billy, had warmed the stew or fried some bacon, one of these gentry would, with a deadly accuracy, send billycan, fire and food, skidding through space. How we cursed them. But it was no use – just when it was least expected, a bullet would spurt close to one's feet. It was wise to move.

We saw our comrades throw up their hands and roll on their faces, we saw our best pals pass away in agony. We cursed, we swore, we gnashed our teeth and took shots at the suspected hiding place of the foe. There was, too, the humorous side. One chap was hit in the thigh. He grimaced and said, 'Thank Heaven! Now I shall get a clean shirt!' We saw the last of him hobbling for the beach.

The snipers were excellent shots and extremely cunning. Several were captured, most of them having short shrift, but one was taken prisoner and photographed as a curiosity. His hands and face were painted green, his rifle was also the same colour. He was entirely covered by a bush, which was fastened to his person. This disguise was wonderful. When still, he looked like a common or garden bush. It would take a very keen pair of eyes to detect anything human about it.

The Indians excelled in finding and despatching snipers. They knew the art of concealment and stealth, and could meet the Turk with his own weapon.

After we spent some time in the firing line the next two days were spent 'resting' – that is, digging reserve trenches, tunnelling and sap making. There were innumerable fatigue parties, water to be carried, ammunition to be taken to the firing line, provisions and stores to fetch. It was work, work, work.

Once, just as a party of us were turning in for the night, crouched up in our little earthen holes, a Sergeant Major came along and called upon us to come out. It appeared that the engineers and sappers were dead beat; they required help – it didn't matter how they obtained it, or where they obtained it – they must have it. We happened to be nearest to hand, and we were accordingly sent to their assistance.

Growling and swearing, we were marched up, up those towering hills. In places it was so steep that it was necessary to ascend by means of a rope, hand over hand. The hillside was a mass of white

© AWM G0377A

'He was entirely covered by a bush, which was fastened to his person.'
Captured Turkish sniper.

shifting sand – there was no foothold, to lose the rope was to tumble, rolling, bouncing to the bottom below. It was a laborious climb, and we were not sorry when we found ourselves, puffing and blowing, at the top.

We were then sent off in pairs, to work in different parts of the line. The saps, which we were to continue, were a few yards in front of our firing line. It was pitch dark, and the feeling of being entirely alone grew upon one as one toiled.

The sap was only sufficiently wide to allow for the entrance of one man at a time. To enter, it was necessary to go on hands and knees, as the Turkish lines were about ten yards away, and if one so much as showed a finger, a shot would ring out and be very close to adding another wooden cross to the already great numbers at the beach cemeteries.

To keep this huddled position was very tiring, and the work was slow. Every time the pick appeared over the top of the sap, a bullet would ping past and bury itself in the loose soil thrown up, and send showers of it down on to the worker. The Turks, too, were tunnelling towards us. It was a race, a race with death. We were bent upon blowing them to perdition and they were bent upon blowing us to perdition. They were equally determined to best us. Who was going to win?

Just to add spice to matters, the Turks would roll bombs towards us. They would glide, unnoticed in the darkness, right into the sap, behind the man who was digging. The trench was too narrow to turn around; if one wished to retrace one's step it was compulsory to crawl backwards like a huge crab. Several times bombs came rolling in, the only sign they gave of their presence would be the burning smell of the fuse.

The moments before the bomb would be picked up and thrown back seemed an eternity. While one of us worked away at the sap, our comrade would amuse himself by sniping the enemy. They would do likewise.

'Rotten shot, you cows, try again!'

'Here, you shot out of your turn, it's my go now! Take that, you swine, and that!'

'Look out! A bomb – quick, quick, pitch it back.'

Bang! It had burst in mid-air, just above the Turkish trench. It was a case of the biter bit.

For many hours we sweated and toiled, alternately digging and watching. The foe could be heard plainly picking his way towards us. Thud, thud, thud. They are only a few feet from us. When we stopped working, they did also. At any moment now we could expect to meet. When we did, there would be trouble for someone. We two chaps, however, were destined not to see the final lap of the race – two others, New Zealanders, came to take our place.

We crawled back, back, back, until we were once more in the front line of trenches, then down the communication trench, out into the open. A bayonet was thrust forward under our noses.

'Where the hell do you come from?'

'Sappers, fatigue party, 15th.'

The sentry, being satisfied, let us pass, and we found ourselves under the stars, standing in the midst of a large number of recumbent figures, snoring and breathing heavily, rifles at their sides. It was the 4th Brigade, at least part of it, the colours of the 13th, 15th, and 16th were visible. We were behind the firing line, behind Quinn's Post, overlooking Shrapnel Valley.

A row of still, stiff figures caught our eye, their feet and faces were turned to the sky. Their limbs looked twisted and stiff. Over their faces had been thrown handkerchiefs and rags. They were the dead, awaiting burial that night, or on the morrow.

Others, who had been sapping, joined us and we were quite ready and willing to throw ourselves down where we stood. No sooner had our heads hit the ground than we slept. It seemed a few moments only – in reality, it was hours – when we heard the Major shouting 'Stand to!' It was dawn.

We were not required that morning, however, as the fighting was not heavy – the Turks were not attacking. The Marines, young boys, mere youths, were in the trenches, so we were at liberty to rest a little longer before we should be called upon to relieve them.

The day was hot and fierce, dug-outs were hot and sweltering. Flies were a pest and the smell of the dead was in our nostrils. We passed the morning away frying bacon and making tea. While we had a chance we took good care to take a meal, a full one, too.

At rare times like that you have a chance to think and reflect. How calm and peaceful the sea looks this afternoon! Why are we at war? What is it all for?

Musings and wonderings are brought to a sudden and violent finish. With yells and shouts, the Turks are attacking. Bombs are falling like rain on the Marines in the trenches. The smoke and stench is over-powering, explosions shake the earth. Wounded are being dragged down the communication trenches. Poor, mangled fellows, crying in delirium.

The attack seems fierce and lasting. We are all on our feet, bayonets fixed, rifles in hand, awaiting the order to rush to the rescue. The trenches are full and will hold no more of our men.

'Heavens!' The enemy is in, he is driving the overpowered, fighting Marines before him. Out pour the unfortunate boys, horror written on their faces. At the time, the General was standing conversing with the Major. Now he turns to us and in a stentorian voice calls loudly: 'Come on, 4th Brigade! Show yourselves Australians! At them, boys, at them!'

With a responding roar, we charged, up over the back of the trenches, over the sandbags, up the communication trenches, right in and upon those yelling, exulting Turks.

Their joy was short-lived. With resounding cheers, our steel meets theirs. They turn and attempt to evacuate the position. No use, our blood is up, we are mad, not one of these shall escape us. Thrust, shoot, butt, they melt away before us.

The position, Quinn's Post, was re-won, was ours! We meant to hold it, to regain it; many gallant lives had been sacrificed.

The Turks were making another desperate effort to dislodge us. Their short success had encouraged them. On they came, launching bombs upon us.

The General, standing calmly and coolly, under a terrible fire, exposed to snipers, exposed to everything, directed us in low clear-toned notes. He saw our predicament, and sent word for bombs to be passed on to us.

Now we could give the foe some of his own medicine. The Turk fought desperately and bravely, but we showered him with missiles, blew him to pieces, and he fell back before our onslaught.

We had won! Hurrah! Hurrah! Hurrah!

THE BATTLE OF QUINN'S POST

E. C. Buley

General Liman von Sanders declared he would drive the Australasians off the face of the Gallipoli Peninsula into the sea. The result of his attempt was a slaughter of Turks that has not been equalled in the Dardanelles fighting. If any boasting is to be done, the proper time is after the event.

At least 30,000 Turks took part in that frontal attack, and on a conservative estimate, one-third of them were put out of action. The wounded were sent back to Constantinople literally by the thousands, and the sight of them spread panic and dismay far and wide through that city.

The preparations made by von Sanders for his great attack upon the Australasians were long and elaborate. For days beforehand he was busy organising the transport of great stores of ammunition to the neighbourhood of Maidos, a town on the neck of the peninsula, opposite Gaba Tepe. Five fresh regiments were brought from Constantinople to stiffen the attacking force; they were chosen from the very 'elite' of the Turkish army. He also detached heavy reinforcement from the main body of defenders, who were holding back the Allies at Achi Baba. He was determined to do the thing very thoroughly.

The attack was launched on 18 May, with von Sanders himself in charge of the operations. Shortly before midnight all the batteries concealed in the hills around set up a hideous din, swollen by the roar of the machine-guns, and the cracking of countless rifles. In the shelling, twelve-inch guns, nine-inch guns, and huge howitzers were employed, as well as artillery of smaller calibre.

Naturally every Australian and New Zealander was on the lookout; and word was sent to every post to be prepared for the frontal attack it was assumed would follow. The assumption was a correct one; for soon countless Turks poured over the ridges and made for the centre of the Australasian line.

This line is a rough semi-circle. The left, or northern wing is on high ground where Walker's Ridge, named after Brigadier General Walker, faces north-east. To the right is Pope's Hill and then the great central gully or valley, first known as Shrapnel Valley by the Australian soldiers, but now called Monash Gully, after General Monash. Then the line continues south in an arc past Lone Pine and back down to the beach opposite Gaba Tepe.

The Turkish trenches, which are some 250 yards distant at the extreme left and right of the line, continue to get closer to those of the Australasians in the middle of the semi-circle. At Quinn's Post, named after a gallant Major from Queensland who died fighting there, the lines are less than twenty yards apart.

The trenches at Quinn's Post, right in the middle of the Australasian semi-circle and just to the right of Monash Gully, faced Dead Man's Ridge and it was here that the Turks attacked in huge numbers.

Stationed at Quinn's Post was the 4th Infantry Brigade, which comprised the bulk of the 2nd Australian Contingent. They had landed in early May and were commanded by General Monash. These men were put to the supreme test early on the morning of 19 May.

Heavy bombardment from Hill 700, and from the top of the ridge where enemy artillery and machine-guns were concentrated, kept Australian heads down. Then the Turks dashed bravely through the scrub, heedless of the field guns and howitzers of the Australians which were concentrated on them with deadly effect.

Many Turks got right up to the edge of the trenches, and were shot down at point-blank range, yet still they came out of their cover, massing in every thicket and advancing under pressure of those behind.

The first light of early morning revealed to the waiting Australians a dense mass of the enemy, exposed and within easy range. Then the Australian rifles rang out, and as fast as each man could pull the trigger, a Turk fell under that deadly fusillade. Yet, still they poured over the ridges, their officers driving them on from behind with loaded revolvers, as the slaughter went on.

It was discriminate slaughter, for each Australian, before he fired, marked his man and made sure of him. It was no time for sentimental considerations of mercy. Besides, the Australians were fierce with the anger of men who had been sniped at for three weeks and had seen their mates fall as they drove on in the face of shrapnel and machine-gun fire.

Now it was their turn, and they fired until the barrels of their rifles were too hot to be touched. 'It was like killing rabbits with a stick,' said one soldier, who was in the hottest part of the fray.

All along the line from Quinn's Post to Courtney's Post the dead were piled in heaps; and still they came on. Some died grasping the barbed wire protections in front of the trenches, others fell dead into the trenches, stopped only by a bullet they met on the parapet.

From daylight till ten o'clock that morning the bombardment and frontal attack continued; then, just after ten, the Turks fell back, and as they did so a heavy shrapnel bombardment began.

The Turks sheltered for hours in their trenches while the heavy cannonade continued. In the middle of the afternoon their officers made another attempt to drive them forward, but it was a half-hearted response that was elicited. Once more they faced that deadly accurate rifle fire of the men from the south, and before it their resolve crumpled and they fled again for shelter.

All night there was incessant fire from the enemy trenches, but in the morning it died away into nothingness. General Liman von Sanders had made the most expensive mistake yet made on the peninsula of Gallipoli.

The enemy had attacked in massive numbers, with the support of all the guns von Sanders had been able to muster. His huge store of ammunition was expended in trying to drive the Australians into the sea. But not a man budged from his post, no Turks had entered an Australian trench except dead Turks and not a yard of ground had been gained in any direction.

From Quinn's Post to Courtney's, the ground was piled with the dead and dying. 'Eight acres of dead bodies,' estimated one bushman, after close scrutiny of the field of battle through a periscope. Another tried to count the bodies in sight from his trench and stopped at an estimate of 4,000.

'The Colonials were ready to meet the strain when it came,' writes one who took part in the slaughter. 'The sight of seemingly endless masses of the enemy advancing upon them might well have shaken the nerve of the already severely-tried troops. Our machine-guns and artillery mowed down the attackers in hundreds, but still the advancing wall swept on. Not till the wave was at point-blank range from the nimble trigger-fingers did it break and spend itself amongst our barbed-wire entanglements.

'Turks were shot in the act of jumping into our trenches. Corpses lay with their heads and arms hanging over our parapets. It was sickening to behold the slaughter our fire made amongst the massed battalions as they issued from concealment into the open spaces. The unfortunate Turks scrambled along towards us over piles of dead bodies.'

The Australians coolly and methodically took the chance sent them by von Sanders and every bullet was sent home in memory of comrades they had lost. They had previously displayed bravery, hardihood, and resource beyond imagination; the qualities shown at the battle of Quinn's Post were steadiness, accurate shooting, and reasoned discipline.

After being sent forward over open country against fields of barbed wire and machine-gun fire, it was a sheer luxury to lie in the trenches and let the other fellow do a bit of self-immolation.

The Australians also knew that they had struck a deadly blow at German prestige with the Turks. General Birdwood told them so when he inspected their defences after the fight was over.

Two days later the Turks craved an armistice to bury their thousands of slain.

A FLAG OF TRUCE

Frederick Loch ('Sydney de Loghe')

There was a routine on Gallipoli.

With the morning rounds completed, the Colonel I served as aide returned to Headquarters, where I saw no more of him for an hour or two. That time was my own, when I crawled under the wretched awning of my funk-hole, and settled down to grill through the heat of the day.

Every afternoon, at four o'clock sometimes, sometimes at five o'clock, sometimes later even, we had our evening battle.

By three or four o'clock invariably the Colonel came to life again, arriving in the open to stretch and collect periscope and glasses. Then he would call out, 'Come on, Lake!' and we'd tread again the little path up the hill to the valley head.

Sometimes we took the left-hand trenches, where there was an observing station in Sand's charge; but more often at the B Battery observing station the fight had birth.

Every evening we asked for trouble, put in a round here and a round there until we got it. There seemed little need to do it; but maybe the Army would have lost hope if nothing like this happened.

Through much of the day – when even the flies fell exhausted into the tea – the snipers of either army lost heart to snipe, and the gunners lay by their guns wondering how it was they could not die. But as the sun climbed down his ladder, and a flagging breeze puffed off the sea, we rose again to our feet, picked up periscopes and telephones, and goaded ourselves into another evening of hate.

At this time – late spring or early summer – the Turkish army had lately made a mighty effort to drive us into the sea. 'Purging the beach of our presence' they called it in their newspapers. The old knowledge was reproven – it is hopeless to attack well-armed, well-entrenched troops.

At the end of several fierce hours the attempt was spent, and the enemy reeled back to his trenches leaving on a few acres of ground between three and four thousand dead. Everywhere you looked the dead men lay, and hours later you might see an arm move or a leg rise, where some poor fellow cried on Death not to delay.

In time the breath of decay searched you out the length of Shrapnel Valley, and when the wind veered in the trenches it caught you by the throat. I marvelled how the men there got down their dinners.

One evening, on the heels of the big attack, we had a pretty little battle. The Colonel observed from B Battery station, and I carried orders to the telephonist a few yards away.

The Major had not turned up, and Mr Hay was in charge. B Battery was dusting up one of the usual targets, and the other batteries banged away elsewhere with more than daily hate. A great many snipers were to work too on either side. We had all woken up this afternoon.

The great heat of the day had passed, indeed there were one or two signs of evening. The sun was three parts of the way down the sky, and shadows started to grow at the bottom of every bush. The high noon haze was no more, and you could see with great clearness over all the desolate country. Our shells burst in sudden white clouds on the great hill in the distance; and here and there appeared the puff of the enemy's return fire. And nearer at hand, you could follow the Turkish trenches by the vicious, short-lived dust spurts of our bullets.

Where the Colonel took his stand they were tunnelling out a machine-gun position and every few moments men came out of the earth with freshly filled sandbags on their shoulders. They crowded the narrow passage, blocking me every time I hurried to Mr Hay or the telephonist.

The Colonel stood on a platform, head just under the parapet, periscope just above. His size caused him to crouch, and his legs were wide apart. The brisker grew the battle, the more engrossed he became; so that now he never moved his head, but stayed bent forward staring into the glass. His exclamations made to himself were to be heard. 'That's a good one! Very good! Right on the target! That's pretty shooting! Green's into 'em now! Oh damn! Now they're off! Hay had got off! Are you there, Lake?'

I stood just below watching for the least sign, for when he grew interested often a movement of the hand was all his signal, and at best he would jerk out an abrupt word or two. Now I answered, 'Yes, sir,' and stood ready. 'Tell Mr Hay to come over more. Two degrees more right. That's better, that's better! Still he can come over more. Two degrees more right, tell him!'

Away I went. Mr Hay was at the periscope and nodded to show he had heard. As I moved off again, he called out, 'Tell the Colonel they seem to be waving flags over there. They seem to want to

'... *picking up a periscope and seeing all there was too see.*'

attract attention. They were doing it before, and now they have started again.'

I told the Colonel what he said, but got no answer for my pains. I would have looked myself had there been time.

'That's better, that's better!' the Colonel started to say. 'Now he is short! Damn it, he's short! Lake, tell him to add fifty. Say he wants fifty or a hundred.' I took the message and came back again, finding time to sit down.

The action went on, losing little or nothing of its briskness. Then came word down the line, passed in a mysterious, unofficial way that something was happening on the other side; the enemy was waving flags and looking over the parapets, as if to attract attention. But it seemed no more was to come of it, as the fire went on and the moment's excitement was spent. Yet five minutes later it had grown again, and I thought something must happen now.

I itched to see how matters went, but I must not leave the spot. The firing lost heart, becoming a number of sharp explosions in place of an unbroken roll. Again the word came along.

The Colonel took interest finally and stopped a passing officer to inquire, and next looked again at the opposite trenches. Finally he gave word for the batteries to cease fire, and stepped down onto the floor of the trench. Our part in the battle was over. I lost no time picking up a periscope and seeing all there was to see. It was little enough worth the bother.

The enemy must have given up their idea, for not one flag flew, gaze as I would. I soon tired and sat down on a ledge belonging to some machine-gunners who lived around here. It was their habit to sleep through the day and come out at evening. Each man had a recess of his own, with a blanket hung before it to cheat the sun. Their legs only were left in sight. It came about that I knew them better by their feet than their faces.

When I sat down, the Colonel disappeared. Maybe he went to pass the time of day with an Infantry Colonel whose dug-out was a few steps down the path. Commonly he did this, leaving me in the trench to call him if need be. Just now were several sets of legs showing beyond the blankets, and a half-hearted argument went forward.

'I joined fer the six bob of course. What else'd a bloke do it fer?'

'I joined 'cos I 'ad a row with the old woman. I went out in a 'urry and joined right away, and I blasted well wish I 'adn't.'

'What did you join fer, Darkie? Was it the six bob, or a row with yer tart, or was the police after yer?' Darkie made no answer. 'Wot was it, Darkie?'

'I joined 'cos I thought a bloke ought ter join.'

It was like the bursting of an 8.25 shell. Nobody said anything. Nobody moved at all. I looked around for a museum in which to put such a sentiment.

I sat where I was, hearing the noise of brisk musketry fire and yet not hearing it. The sun had stepped another rung down his ladder, a few shadows spread about, and there was even a suggestion of evening cool. I don't know what I thought of, nothing probably, for the place had power to destroy one mentally and morally. Then without warning there woke again the former interest.

'They're waving the flags,' came down from the right. 'There's something doing! There's something up!'

I got up with a yawn and went to the parapet, and poked up the periscope, and interest came with a vengeance. Straight before me was a big white flag charged with a red crescent, moving slowly forwards and backwards over the enemy parapet, and while I watched a second one rose up on our right and at odd intervals appeared other streamers which might have been small flags and might have been rags.

Round me all who by hook or by crook could get hold of a periscope were on the platforms finding out what was happening, and this must have taken place over a great deal of the line, as presently the musketry became completely broken up and on the point of cessation.

I had taken stand among the B Battery men, beside their periscope, where the parapet was quite low, and it needed no effort to look over the top. I fell to debating whether to take the risk and see first-hand how matters went, and while yet I stayed uncertain something happened to decide me on the moment.

There was a movement in the enemy's trench beside the largest flag, and a man climbed over the parapet and dropped down on to the open ground. He stood still a moment in uneasy fashion, next took into his hands the big white flag with the red crescent, held it overhead, and came forward.

I felt like crying out my admiration. Our snipers shot yet in scores, in hundreds may be; and any moment a stray shot or the aimed shot of a fool might tumble him over where he stood. And no one knew the danger better than himself, for he bowed his head and upper body as does a man advancing in the teeth of a great wind, and came forward with deliberate steps, moving his wide flag in wider semi-circles. To the devil with caution, said I, and stood right up and looked across the open. 'By Jove!' I exclaimed out loud. 'By Jove!' Beside me was Mr Hay, and he looked round to know had I gone mad.

News had travelled everywhere that something special was on hand, for cries went up and down: 'Cease fire there! Cease fire!' And the firing did die away, though unwillingly, lessening and returning again in gusts, like an April wind or a woman's last word in an argument. Even when you might say the musketry had stopped, there was still a splutter and a cracking here and here, for there are ever fools who cannot help themselves.

But all this while the man of peace continued on his way, at the same stride and in the same bent attitude. Maybe before starting on the journey he had delivered his soul into Allah's safekeeping, for no shot touched him, and no quick fear turned him from the path. There was something that moved me deep down as I looked on his unhurried pace and the slow waving of his flag.

It plucked my heartstrings to see him alone there, his life not worth a smoked-out cigarette. I stood right up, all my upper body above the parapet, so that the countryside was bared before me, and a draught of evening wind born of wide spaces came a-knocking at my nostrils. All my heart cried out to him. 'My salute, friend, my salute! Do you hear me over there? It is Gunner Lake who calls. A brave man's heart is crying out to a brave man! My salute, friend! In all honour I offer my salute!'

When the man of peace had advanced halfway, the musketry fire of both sides was nearly silent, and there was a stir of uncertainty in our ranks. You heard some crying 'Cease fire' and others calling out against it, shouting there was no order, and what the devil was everyone about. But the firing did not start again, or only in short-lived bursts, and the men hung by the loopholes, waiting what might befall.

There was a stir on our side now, near Clayton's trench it seemed from here, and soon an officer came into the open, with a handkerchief tied on to a stick or rifle, I did not notice which. At the same time a couple of Turks hopped from their trenches, and another of our men went forward; and it seemed they would hold a parley then and there. While I looked to see, I found the Colonel at my shoulder.

'Get the interpreter, Lake,' he said quickly. 'Get Bargi and bring him here. He may be wanted.'

Over I went to the telephonist and sent down word, then back again I came and told the Colonel, and next up I jumped once more to look over the country.

The little company had come together and were in parley. The distance was a matter of hundreds of yards, so there was little enough to see and nothing to be heard. I hoped when Bargi came the Colonel would go over there, and I grew eager for his coming.

I had become impatient, and cursed him for his fatness, when a second big flag was put up to our right hand, and two men jumped into the open and came towards our trenches, one empty-handed and one bearing the standard. The Colonel looked round sharply, and made as if to go over there, then of a sudden he turned to me.

'Where's Bargi, Lake? Where's Bargi?'

'He's on the way, sir.'

'Meet him and hurry him up. Say I want him at once!'

I pushed towards the trench mouth as speedily as could be managed, not the least eager for the run down the hill and back again. But at the turn I met Bargi puffing with his exertions and a look, half-pleased, half-scared, on his sweating face.

He was a little Italian who spoke and wrote a dozen languages. By trade he had been an art photographer, traveller for a firm of jewellers, and one or two other things as best I could make out. War was declared, times grew hard, and he made up his mind to go a-soldiering. 'My disposition is very nervous,' he said to me once. 'I am too sensitive.' And he shrugged his shoulders deprecatingly. 'Sensitive,' thought I. 'Good friend, we call it by another name.'

He got on badly with other men, and I was sorry for him, and on the whole liked him well enough. Now I pulled him up, and he panted and asked what was wanted. 'The Colonel wants you in a hurry. He is waiting for you a few yards up the trench.'

No more was said. Bargi went on without more speech, and I turned to follow. But Lewis pulled at my sleeve and asked what was happening. He had been Bargi's guide up here. 'There's a bit of an armistice on,' I called out as I turned. 'Have a look for yourself. I have to get after the Colonel.'

The couple of seconds' delay had lost me Bargi, and I did my best to catch him before he met the Colonel and both disappeared. Fortunately, I saw their heels rounding a traverse, and caught up with them quite soon.

The trench was rather empty, and the Colonel moved in a great hurry, so that fat little Bargi, who had not found his breath, was hard put to it to keep up. We dodged round one turning and then another, nobody speaking all the way. Sometimes Bargi threw glances over a shoulder at me, for it was his first trench journey, and truly he was receiving a brusque introduction.

Presently the press of men grew again, curbing us to a slower rate; and next we met a crossway, which brought us to a standstill. Someone put us on to the right road, and we started anew to elbow forward. Finally we found our way into a sap, and, this ending, we had come as far as was possible. The Colonel put up his periscope to find where we were, and I jumped up on to a platform and poked my head over the parapet. You could hear the crack of a rifle now and again, but not often.

We had come to the best spot. The men and the flag were opposite. They were nearer than before, yet they had not come far over, and at this moment still looked before them in an undecided fashion. I do not doubt they cared little for the exposed position.

Almost at once Bargi climbed up beside me, and there were the three of us in a row – the Colonel looking into the periscope, Bargi standing on tiptoe, peeping over the parapet, and myself at the end of the line. The two Turks continued to delay, in fact went so far as to make a motion of retreat.

'Call them, Bargi!' the Colonel burst out. 'Tell them to come on; say it's all right!'

The little man looked anxiously about, but pulled himself together and called out something in Turkish. His words failed to carry all the way, so that he clapped hands to his mouth and cried out anew, this time at the top of his voice. At once the Turks were reassured; they scanned eagerly to find the voice, and after exchange of a sentence or two, came forward deliberately, the man with the standard bearing it high above his head.

They were entering our half of the debatable country when some fool to the right hand fired, and set a dozen others pulling triggers. The Turks turned about, and made for home at a shambling trot; but with the speed it began the fire died, and the peacemakers steadied their retreat. Then Bargi called again, in time to reassure, for they rather doubtfully came back, the standard-bearer holding his flag at top height. They drew near enough for me to see clearly their appearance, and it was plain they were men of different rank.

The standard-bearer was a cut-throat looking fellow with a black moustache and a complexion scarce lighter. I doubted he was a pure Turk. He was small and well shaped; but there was that in his expression which made me fear for any dog of an unbeliever who might pass his way. He was dressed in the green uniform, with their strange pleated cap on his head. Through all the dealings he spoke no word.

The man beside him, the empty-handed man, was quite otherwise. He was dressed as an officer, and proved to be a doctor. He was a man of manners, a man of civilisation, a gentleman. He came to the parley with French on his lips.

The two men crossed the half-line boundary, and came so close in that the Colonel put up his hand to stop them, lest they should arrive on top of our trench works.

'Tell them to stay there, Bargi!' he broke out. 'Tell them to come no farther!'

Bargi halted them. He had taken courage, the fire being dead; he spoke fluently, and seemed to enjoy his importance. His dusky face glowed with satisfaction and sweat.

'Get up, Bargi,' the Colonel said of a sudden. 'Go out and meet them. It's quite safe, man. Go on!'

Poor little Bargi almost collapsed. It was one matter to peep over a parapet top, and quite another to stand up in the open like a tree, a target for all the world. He gave the Colonel a look of agony. 'Hurry up, man!' was what he got for his trouble.

He began his climb, and I had scrambled up first and pulled him the last of the way. He made no attempt to go farther, and it did not matter, the Turks having arrived within talking distance. Yet it seemed fate would refuse us our parley, for someone let a machine-gun loose – Australian or Turk I do not know, but may Allah smite him!

The bullets sang by my head like a swarm of mad bees. There was no time for 'After you, sir'. Bargi tumbled back into the trench, and I jumped down on top of him. A brisk burst of rifle fire broke out on both sides, and then died with all suddenness. Next I was up on the parapet again.

The Turkish peacemakers had run for their own lines, but now they returned.

Bargi was sadly disinclined for a second reappearance in the open, but there was nothing for it, and presently he stood on top beside me. The Turks were near at hand again, too close for the Colonel's pleasure; and he waved Bargi forward in an abrupt fashion. Openly reluctant, Bargi went.

The meeting was a meeting of dancing masters. They put their hands to their foreheads and bowed profoundly; they advanced and bowed once more; they smiled with utmost courtesy and bowed anew. Next they fell to talking loudly, but in the accents of men who ask the other's good health, and who rejoice at the fineness of the day. And while they talked, I picked out a seat on the mound before the parapet, and sat down to watch. It was so near evening one might sit at ease out in the sunlight.

It was a sight you might seek in vain on many a summer's day. There stood up the two great armies, the Turkish Army and the troops of Australasia, filling the mouths of the trenches, and staring one another in the face. Men that had lived days on end between two narrow, sun-baked walls, men who had lifted heads above a certain level at risk of their lives, now looked over the great bare country, and widened their lungs with breezes new from the sea.

The sky was filling with clear white clouds, the ground was sown with shadows; and endless heights and depths climbed up and tumbled away. And there were swift greens and blues and greys splashed over the picture, and earthy reds, and glistening patches of sand. And for background were the big hills leaning against the sky.

And rank after rank, from foot to skyline, stood soldiers in their thousands. The reserves were countless. Look to the right hand, and look to the left, and you were met by our men, their heads lifted over the parapets, or themselves a-top swinging their legs. And between the armies lay the debatable land, pocked with dead men and broken rifles. Ye gods! It was a sight worth the looking.

Where I sat the ground fell sharply away, and a few yards down the slope rested three of our dead, lying with heads close together. And look where you would, you would come on part of a man – a pair of boots pushed from a mound; a hand; an elbow; or maybe it was the flutter of a piece of coat. The burials had been by night – graves forced from hard ground, with few minutes to give to the building. The mounds had settled and betrayed their secrets.

Of Turks fallen in the last attack there was no end: it was a day's task to count them.

There came down the line word that General Runner parleyed with the other group. I looked across. Several men stood together, but no more could I discover.

No sooner was the fire of both armies well dead than a number of Turks jumped from their trenches and fell with right good energy to filling their arms with the rifles which lay in scores about the field. Speedily men were staggering home loaded to their limit. And a sniper who sniped from an exposed position fell to digging himself in in generous style. The Colonel let out a bellow. 'Stop those men! Stop them this minute! Bargi, stop those men!'

Bargi grasped what was wanted, pointed it out to the flag-bearers, and with lusty shouting the men were recalled. But the manoeuvre gained the enemy half a hundred rifles; and methinks the sniper had a more spacious parlour from that hour.

It was our last interruption. It seemed the enemy asked for a truce for the burial of their dead. Bargi ran forwards and backwards, swollen with importance. The Colonel could do no more than receive the message; but the Brigadier was with the other group and would have more power.

In course of time word arrived empowering the Colonel to announce the enemy might send a staff officer by way of Gaba Tepe next morning, when the matter would be discussed. Bargi floundered over the explanation, and a big Lieutenant of infantry climbed up to help him. The man must have been among the largest in the army.

'You'll be a good advertisement for Australia,' the Colonel said. And seeing I was all anxiety to follow, he added, 'No, Lake, this is not your stunt.'

It was all over presently. The men of truce agreed to take back the message, and fire would open again in a few minutes. Afresh they saluted, afresh they bowed: and our men came this way, and they turned that.

The Colonel gathered up glasses and periscope; and we went off to tea. On the way we ran into a party placing in position a trench mortar. And farther on we met men hurrying up with ammunition. We had roared at the Turkish treachery; but who shall say our honour was over-nice? As I sat at tea, the firing broke out again in a great roll.

Their staff officer rode into our lines next morning. He reappeared the morning after also, and the outcome was a truce of half a day. Certain rules were framed. Parties of so many either side were allowed over so many yards, and neither party might penetrate beyond halfway. We would take their dead to them, and they would bring our dead to us.

The day and the hour came round, and peace fell over the armies. The silence was very strange. About the middle of the morning the

Colonel set off as usual for the trenches, and we started the rounds as on any other day from the B Battery observing station.

No shot was to be heard, and the trenches were emptier of men than I had seen them. Without delay we passed to C Battery on the Pimple, and there joined Colonel Irons, Major Andrews, and Major Green.

Behind C Battery and before A, the five of us climbed from the trenches on to open ground. The sun was out, but the day was cool; and it was pleasant to stand up at ease in the open. A great gathering had come about on the debatable land. It was like a day at the races, with a shabby crowd in attendance. The rule limiting the number of parties was slackly enforced, and anyone tying a white bandage to his arm to denote stretcher-bearer could go where he wanted.

In this way there were numbers exploring on their own account, exchanging mementoes with the enemy, and seeing what was to be seen. The camera fiend was at large.

The burial of the dead went forward in harmony if not in love. Our fellows were good-willed enough and eager with curiosity; but among the enemy were many glum countenances. Nor do I wonder, for it is but chilly amusement gazing into the faces of your own dead.

There were many strange sights to be found in a few hundred yards' marching; but I have not time to tell a tenth of them.

At one place was a crater in the ground where a shell had burst; and round it, like chickens come to feed at a basin, lay eight dead men. It was the prettiest bit of shooting that you might wish to see. And not so very far away was a gully, maybe twenty yards long, half that wide, and half again that deep. The Turkish stretcher-bearers had gathered dead from everywhere, and tumbled them here – the place was a-choke with bodies. Hundreds were there. They lay a dozen deep. They made me catch my breath. But it was when we turned to go over to A Battery that we passed the scene it will take me longest to forget.

Four of our own fellows lay on their backs in the grass, all within a few paces. They were of those who had fallen in the first rush on

'Eight acres of dead bodies,' The armistice 24 May 1915.

the first day, and had been overlooked. Their clothes were little stained, for no rains had touched them, and their hats were still cocked to one side in the jauntiest manner.

The first man was a skeleton, picked as clean as a century of waiting might do. His skull looked out between the tunic and the hat; and through the bones of his hands grasses had woven a road. One could only gape at the fellow.

The next man waited on his back too; but the fierce suns had done otherwise with him. The flesh had decayed under the skin, while the skin had stayed, becoming a dark parchment drawn tightly over the bones. Every hair on head and hand remained. Face and hands were tiny, the face and hands of a child they were: yet the face was full of expression, and more terrible to look on than the face of any ape.

The third man was as the second.

The fourth man had swollen up and afterwards sunk down again. I had to turn away and spit.

And those four men had been filled with great foolish hopes but a few weeks before. Amen! Amen!

Come, hang up the gun by the chimney!
Come, scabbard the sword and the dirk!
And we'll tiptoe afar,
Where the sunbeams still are,
Leaving spider and mouse to their work.
The moon yet doth ride through the night, friend,
The sun yet doth warden the day:
And we'll lie down and rest,
On the earth's ample breast,
While these rivers of blood run away.

Come, loosen the belt and the tunic,
Uncover your head from its steel!
Leave the mess-tin to rust!
Let the flask choke with dust!
There are better things needing our zeal.
The harvest is heavy with waiting.
The eyes of our women are red;
Then stay but an hour,
While the hills break in flower,
And the grasses climb over our dead!

Oh foolish, oh foolish this striving!
Oh empty this passion and hate!
I am laboured of breath:
I am weary to death:
Come, let us forgive ere too late!
Come, lend me your hand for a space, friend!
The hours and minutes race by!
But we've time to lie back
On the side of the track,
Till these channels of blood have run dry.

Frederick Loch

PEACEABLE-LOOKING MEN

Joseph L. Beeston

On 23 May anyone looking down the coast could see a man on Gaba Tepe waving a white flag. He was soon joined by another occupied in a like manner.

Some officers came into the Ambulance and asked for the loan of some towels; we gave them two, which were pinned together with safety pins. White flags don't form part of the equipment of Australia's army.

Seven mounted men had been observed coming down Gaba Tepe, and they were joined on the beach by our four. The upshot was that one was brought in blindfolded to General Birdwood. Shortly after, we heard it announced that a truce had been arranged for the following day in order to bury the dead.

The following morning Major Millard and I started from our right and walked up and across the battlefield. It was a stretch of country between our lines and those of the Turks, and was designated No Man's land. At the extreme right there was a small farm; the owner's house occupied part of it, and was just as the man had left it. Our guns had knocked it about a good deal.

In close proximity was a field of wheat, in which there were scores of dead Turks. As these had been dead anything from a fortnight to three weeks their condition may be better imagined than described.

One body I saw was lying with the leg shattered. He had crawled into a depression in the ground and lay with his greatcoat rolled up for a pillow; the stains on the ground showed that he had bled to death, and it can only be conjectured how long he lay there before death relieved him of his sufferings.

Scores of the bodies were simply riddled with bullets. Midway between the trenches a line of Turkish sentries were posted. Each was in a natty blue uniform with gold braid, and top boots, and all were done 'up to the nines'. Each stood by a white flag on a pole stuck in the ground. We buried all the dead on our side of this line and they performed a similar office for those on their side.

Stretchers were used to carry the bodies, which were all placed in large trenches. The stench was awful, and many of our men wore handkerchiefs over their mouths in their endeavour to escape it. I counted 2,000 dead Turks. One I judged to be an officer of rank, for the bearers carried him shoulder-high down a gully to the rear.

The ground was absolutely covered with rifles and equipment of all kinds, shell-cases and caps, and ammunition clips. The rifles were all collected and the bolts removed to prevent their being used

'... one was brought blindfolded to General Birdwood.' Captain Butler leads Major Kemal Ohri, blindfolded, through the Anzac Lines.

again. Some of the Turks were lying right on our trenches, almost in some of them.

The Turkish sentries were peaceable-looking men, stolid in type and of the peasant class mostly. We fraternised with them and gave them cigarettes and tobacco.

Some Germans were there, but they viewed us with malignant eyes. When I talked to Colonel Pope about it afterwards he said the Germans were a mean lot of beggars.

'Why,' said he most indignantly, 'they came and had a look into my trenches.'

I asked, 'What did you do?'

He replied, 'Well, I had a look at theirs.'

LOVE LETTER XIX

Oliver Hogue ('Trooper Bluegum')

My Dug-Out,
Braund's Hill,
Anzac.
27 May 1915

My Bonnie Jean,

So far so good. I'm still alive and kicking, though I frankly admit that is due more to good luck than good management.

We've been a week on Anzac, which is just about long enough to get one's bearings, and to know the safety spots and danger zone. Already our brigade has had some casualties. Young Murray was shot by sniper two days after we landed. Poor old Sid Parkes was shot dead in the trenches a couple of days ago. He was a good soldier. He used to call me Sergeant Quicksilver, and was always saying nice things about you.

Norman Jeffreys was killed yesterday. You remember him? He was the last man to join the brigade – came all the way from Queensland, brought his own horse and just got in at the last minute. One of the best men in the whole regiment. Colonel Cox is wounded and has been sent to Alexandria.

... We had quite a lively time landing. The Turkish battery on the Olive Grove, south of Gaba Tepe, opened a packet on us and splattered shrapnel all over the shop. Some shells landed in the sea close to our boat and others burst overhead. It was just a miracle, but not a soul was hit. We got ashore in huge barges. Then we marched up Shrapnel Valley and bivouacked on the side of a hill.

... The Turks always give newcomers a special welcome, and they spared no efforts to give us a warm reception. They plumped shells all round us for several hours. Big Jack Cheater was wounded – (you know Jack, he had a big horse called Zero, a champion jumper, but looked a cross between a camel and a kangaroo).

George Wright was wounded a couple of yards from me. Several other chaps stopped pieces of shrapnel shell. One shell passed between me and the Brigadier, missing us by inches ... It would take too long to tell you of all the lucky escapes we've had ... We spent the night digging dug-outs, but finding the place a bit too much like a target, we moved our quarters.

We are now located at the top of Shrapnel Valley on Braund's Hill, just where poor Colonel Braund was shot a short time before. The firing line is about thirty yards away. Fortunately most of the shells which miss the trenches pass harmlessly over our heads, though a certain number burst near us and make us duck ... But what strikes me most forcibly is the extraordinary cheerfulness of our Australian soldiers. They laugh and joke all day long. When wounded they generally say something like this: 'So long, chaps, see you later. I'm off for a holiday.'

One young fellow was mortally wounded, and he signalled for a pencil to write. We thought he had some message for his sweetheart or mother, but he just wrote: 'Are we downhearted?' then he shook his head in the negative and passed out.

Our brigade is temporarily reinforcing the infantry line. The three regiments are with the battalions to learn the intricacies of trench warfare. Our regiment is with the 1st Australian Infantry Brigade, which recently lost its Brigadier, Colonel MacLaurin. Colonel Smyth, V.C., is now in command.

My troop occupies a strip of trench about thirty yards long, and I am responsible for its safety. It's quite a unique experience going up and down the silent trenches at night, seeing that all the sentries are at their posts, watching and listening for the enemy who is only fifty yards in front of us. As there are hundreds of their dead lying just in front of our trenches we have to be mighty careful that others are not sneaking up. But we'd give them a lively time if they came.

We have just heard that General Bridges has been dangerously wounded and has been sent on the ship to Alexandria, but they feared he would die.

On 24 May – Queen's birthday, Empire day – we granted the Turks an armistice to bury their dead, which lay thick all along the firing line, testifying both to the vigour of the attack and the marksmanship of the Australians. Their losses were at first estimated at 6,000 but we helped to bury over 3,000 of them, and hundreds more must have been brought into their lines during the past six nights. Now we reckon that their casualties must have been at least 12,000.

I should mention that the Turks observed the terms of the armistice most chivalrously. Once, when a Turkish soldier picked up a grenade and ran with it to their lines, one of their officers ran after him, kicked him where a kick would do most good, took the grenade and returned it with a bow to Major Heane, who had charge of the arrangements. (You know Jim Heane – comes from Dubbo – used to be in the Light Horse, but came away with the 1st Brigade Infantry. Just recommended for D.S.O.)

By the bye, you will hear extraordinary stories from wounded men and others of the horrible atrocities and mutilations practised by the Turks. Well, don't believe a word of them. They are all grossly exaggerated, if not wholly false. Some started these fictions and the rest took them up.

I have, however, found two cases of mutilation, but when you remember the Armenian massacres, and know that the Turkish Army is recruited from the wilds of Asia Minor and the Caucasus, you will be surprised at the gentlemanly way the Turk has fought us.

There is little to add about the attack on the 19th. The Turks charged all round our line from north to south. They advanced as the Germans taught them, in heavy columns, with marching tapes to keep them straight. But our rifles picked them off by scores and our machine-guns mowed them down by hundreds, while our artillery played havoc with their reserves and supports. Here and there they came in thick masses right up to our parapets, but the few who did get over were promptly bayoneted.

Time and again they charged and time and again they hurled back, decimated and cowed. The German officers forced them out of the trenches with revolvers, but it was all futile. They advanced, yelling 'Allah, Allah,' 'Mahomet,' 'Allah,' and crawled back moaning and groaning.

Our supports sneaked right up to the firing line and offered bribes of tobacco and tins of milk to their pals just for the fun of swapping places for a few minutes. Others clamoured for a shot with exhortations, such as: 'Come down, Bill, and give us a shot. I'm a miles better shot than you are.' One chap, Sergeant Higginson, perched himself on the parapet and picked off the Turks one by one till he had twenty-nine. He wanted thirty, but it was getting very light, and the Turks started sniping again and then Higginson was killed. He never got the thirty.

Our losses were only a few hundred. It would have been far less only our chaps with characteristic carelessness got on the parapets and exposed themselves to the Turkish snipers. Next day, when General Birdwood asked one of the lads if he had shot many Turks, the soldier replied proudly, 'Miles of the cows.'

The mail bag closes in a few minutes.
With oceans of love,
Yours and for ever and ever,
J.B.

THE FIRST SEA LORD MEETS AN ANZAC

Roy Bridges

A young Australian, wounded in the May fighting, was taken to England to recover his strength.

During his convalescence a social event was organised at which a certain Right Honourable Gentleman came to mingle with the veterans. The Right Honourable Gentleman was in the company of his political chiefs and was interested in acquiring a few impressions from the men of Anzac.

He asked this particular Anzac what he thought of the campaign on Gallipoli.

With the hammering of the British fleet against the Dardanelles all through March in mind, the Anzac answered, 'If I'd been a burglar, and wanted to break into a place, I wouldn't have spent several nights before pelting stones on the roof.'

The Right Honourable Gentleman immediately terminated the conversation then and there and moved on with his smiling entourage.

'Didn't you know who that was?' a horrified bystander asked the Anzac.

'Usen't he to be the First Sea Lord?' replied the Anzac, unperturbed.

MY LITTLE WET HOME IN THE TRENCH

Tom Skeyhill

I've a Little Wet Home in the Trench,
Which the rain storms continually drench.
Blue sky overhead, mud and sand for a bed,
And a stone that we use for a bench.
Bully beef and hard biscuit we chew,
It seems years since we tasted a stew,
Shells crackle and scare, there's no place can compare
With My Little Wet Home in the Trench.

Our friends in the trench o'er the way
Seem to know that we've come here to stay.
They rush and they shout, but they can't get us out,
Though there's no dirty trick they won't play.
They rushed us a few nights ago,
But we don't like intruders, and so,
Some departed quite sore, others sleep evermore,
Near My Little Wet Home in the Trench.

There's a Little Wet Home in the Trench,
Which the raindrops continually drench,
There's a dead Turk close by, with his toes to the sky,
Who causes a terrible stench.
There are snipers who keep on the go,
So we all keep our heads pretty low,
But with shells dropping there, there's no place can compare,
With My Little Wet Home in the Trench.

GLIMPSES OF ANZAC

SHRAPNEL

Tom Skeyhill

I was sittin' in me dug-out and was feelin' dinkum good,
Chewin' Queensland bully beef and biscuits hard as wood.
When, 'boom!' I nearly choked meself, I spilt me bloomin' tea,
I saw about a million stars and me dug-out fell on me!

They dug me out with picks and spades, I felt an awful wreck,
By that bloomin' Turkish shrapnel I was buried to the neck,
Me mouth was full of bully beef, me eyes were full of dust,
I rose up to me bloomin' feet and shook me fist and cussed.

The Sergeant says, 'You're lucky, lad, it might have got your head,
You ought to thank your lucky stars!' I says, 'Well, strike me dead!'
It smashed me bloomin' dug-out, it buried all me kit,
Spoilt me tea and bully beef . . . I'll revenge that little bit!

I was walkin' to the water barge along the busy shore,
Listenin' to the Maxims bark and our Big Lizzie roar,
When I heard a loud explosion above me bloomin' head,
And a bloke, not ten yards distant, flopped sudden down . . .
    stone dead.

I crawled out from the debris and lay pantin' on the sand,
I cussed that Turkish shrap and every Turk upon the land.
We cussed it when it busted a yard or two outside,
We cussed it when it missed us, a hundred yards out wide.

It's always bloomin' shrapnel, wherever you may be,
Sittin' in your dug-out, or bathin' in the sea.
At Shrapnel Valley, Deadman's Gully, Courtney's Post and Quinn's,
At Pope's Hill and Johnson's Jolly . . . that deadly shrapnel spins.

I don't mind bombs and rifles, and I like a bayonet charge,
But I'm hangin' out the white flag when shrapnel is at large.
When I get back to Australia and I hear a whistlin' train,
It's the nearest pub for shelter from that shrapnel once again!

AMBULANCE WORK

Joseph L. Beeston

Once we had landed on 25 April and our tent was pitched in a gully near the beach casualties began to come in pretty freely, so that our tent was soon filled. We then commenced making dug-outs in the side of the gully and placing the men in these.

After a few days the Royal Marine Light Infantry Ambulance were ordered away, and we were directed to take up their position on the beach. A place for operating was prepared by putting sandbags at either end, the roof being formed by planks covered with sandbags and loose earth. Stanchions of four by four inch timber were driven into the ground, with crosspieces at a convenient height; the stretcher was placed on these, and thus an operating table was formed.

Shelves were made to hold our instruments, trays and bottles; these were all in charge of Staff Sergeant Henderson, a most capable and willing assistant. Close by a kitchen was made, and a cook kept constantly employed keeping a supply of hot water, bovril, milk and biscuits ready for the men when they came in wounded, for they had to be fed as well as medically attended to.

One never ceased admiring our men, and their cheeriness under these circumstances and their droll remarks caused us many a laugh. One man, just blown up by a shell, informed us that it was a **** of a place, 'no place to take a lady'. Another told of the mishap to his 'cobber' who picked up a bomb and blew on it to make it light:

'All at once it blew his bloody head off! Gorblime! You would have laughed!'

For lurid and perfervid language commend me to the Australian soldier. I have seen scores of them lying wounded and yet chatting one to another while waiting their turn to be dressed. Profanity oozes from him like music from a barrel organ. At the same time, he will give you his side of the situation, almost without exception in an optimistic strain, generally concluding his observation with the intimation that 'We gave them hell'.

The stretcher-bearers were a fine body of men. Prior to this campaign, the Army Medical Corps was always looked upon as a soft job. In peacetime we had to submit to all sorts of flippant remarks, and were called Linseed Lancers, Body Snatchers, and other cheery and jovial names; but, thanks to the Turks and the cordiality of their reception, the A.A.M.C. can hold up their head

© AWM P01815.005

'The stretcher bearers were a fine body of men.'

with any of the fighting troops. It was a common thing to hear men say, 'This beach is a hell of a place! The trenches are better than this.'

The praises of the stretcher-bearers were in all the men's mouths; enough could not be said in their favour. Owing to the impossibility of landing the transport, all the wounded had to be carried – often for a distance of a mile and a half, in a blazing sun and through shrapnel and machine-gun fire. But there was never a flinch; through it all they went, and performed their duty.

Of our Ambulance 185 men and officers landed, and when I relinquished command, forty-three remained. At one time we were losing so many bearers, that carrying during the daytime was abandoned, and orders were given that it should only be undertaken after nightfall.

On one occasion a man was being sent off to the hospital ship from our tent in the gully. He was not very bad, but he felt like being carried down. As the party went along the beach, Beachy Bill became active; one of the bearers lost his leg, the other was wounded, but the man who was being carried down got up and ran!

All the remarks I have made regarding the intrepidity and valour of the stretcher-bearers apply also to the regimental bearers. These are made up from the bandsmen. Very few people think, when they see the band leading the battalion in parade through the streets, what happens to them on active service. Here bands are not thought of; the instruments are left at the base, and the men become bearers, and carry the wounded out of the front line for the Ambulance men to care for. Many a stretcher-bearer has deserved the V.C.

One of ours told me they had reached a man severely wounded in the leg, in close proximity to his dug-out. After he had been placed on the stretcher and made comfortable, he was asked whether there was anything he would like to take with him. He pondered a bit, and then said, 'Oh! You might give me my diary – I would like to make a note of this before I forget it!'

Meantime stores of all kind were being accumulated on the beach: stacks of biscuits, cheese and preserved beef, all of the best. One particular kind of biscuit was known as the 'forty-niner' because it had forty-nine holes in it, was believed to take forty-nine years to bake, and needed forty-nine chews to a bite. But there were also beautiful hams and preserved vegetables, and with these and a tube of Oxo a very palatable soup could be prepared.

It can be readily understood that in dealing with large bodies of men, such as ours, a considerable degree of organisation is necessary, in order to keep an account, not only of the man, but of the nature of his injury (or illness, as the case may be) and of his destination. Without method chaos would soon reign.

As each casualty came in he was examined, and dressed or operated upon as the necessity arose. Sergeant Baxter then got orders from the officer as to where the case was to be sent. A ticket was made out, containing the man's name, his regimental number, the nature of his complaint, whether morphia had been administered and the quantity, and finally his destination. All this was also recorded in our books, and returns made weekly, both to headquarters and to the base.

Cases likely to recover in a fortnight's time were sent by fleet-sweeper to Mudros; the others were embarked on the hospital ship. They were placed in barges, and towed out by a pinnace to a trawler, and by that to the hospital ship, where the cases were sorted out. When once they had left the beach, our knowledge of them ceased, and of course our responsibility.

We heard many anecdotes about our recent patients. One man arriving at a hospital ship was describing, with the usual picturesque invective, how the bullet had got into his shoulder. One of the British officers, who apparently was unacquainted with the Australian vocabulary, asked, 'What was that you said, my man?'

The reply came, 'A blightah ovah theah put a bullet in heah.'

At a later period, after the Turkish offensive in May, a new gun had come into action on our left, which the men christened 'Windy Annie.' Beachy Bill occupied the olive grove, and was on our right. Annie was getting the range of our dressing station pretty accurately, and a requisition on the Engineers evoked the information that sandbags were not available. However, the Army Service came to our rescue with some old friends, the 'forty-niner' biscuits. Three tiers of these in their boxes defied the shells just as they defied our teeth.

As sickness began to be more manifest, it became necessary to enlarge the accommodation in our gully. The hill was dug out, and the soil placed in bags with which a wall was built, the intervening portion being filled up with the remainder of the hill. By this means we were able to pitch a second tent and house more of those who were slightly ill.

It was in connection with this engineering scheme that I found the value of W. O. Cosgrove. He was possessed of a good deal of the *suaviter in modo*, and it was owing to his dextrous handling of Ordnance that we got such a fine supply of bags. This necessitated a redistribution of dug-outs, and a line of them was constructed sufficient to take a section of bearers. The men christened this 'Shrapnel Avenue'. They called my dug-out 'The Nut' because it held the 'Kernel'. I offer this with every apology. It's not my joke.

The new dug-outs were not too safe. Captain Murphy was killed there one afternoon, and Claude Grime badly wounded later on.

Claude caused good deal of amusement. He had a deep-rooted objection to putting on clothes and wore only a hat, pants, boots and his smile. Consequently his body became quite mahogany-coloured. When he was wounded he was put under an anaesthetic so that I could search for the bullet. As the anaesthetic began to take effect, Claude talked the usual unintelligible gibberish.

Now, we happened to have a Turkish prisoner at the time and, in the midst of Claude's struggles and shouts, in rushed an interpreter. He looked round, and promptly came over to Claude and began uttering words which I suppose were calculated to soothe a wounded Turk. We had some difficulty in assuring him that the other man, not Claude, was the Turk he was in quest of.

Our bearers continued doing splendid work after the May offensive and right through to the August offensive. As I said, it was a long and dangerous carry from the firing line to the 'Shrapnel Avenue' ambulance station or Casualty Clearing Station on the beach and a lot of them were wounded themselves.

The miserable part of the affair was that the Casualty Clearing Station on the beach broke down and could not evacuate our wounded. This caused a blockage, and we had numbers of wounded on our hands. A blockage of a few hours can be dealt with, but when it is impossible to get cases away for forty hours the condition of the men is very miserable.

The cooks got going, and had plenty of bovril and Oxo, which we boiled up with biscuits broken small. It made a very sustaining meal, but caused thirst, which was troublesome, as it was particularly difficult to obtain water.

Shelter from the sun, too, was hard to get; the day was exceedingly hot, and there were only a few trees about. As many as could be got into the shade were put there, but we had to keep moving them round to avoid the sun. Many of the cases were desperate, but they uttered not a word of complaint. They all seemed to understand that it was not our fault that they were kept here.

As the cases were treated by us, they were taken down towards the beach and kept under cover as much as possible. At one time we had nearly 400 waiting for removal to the ship. Then came a message asking for more stretchers to be sent to the firing line, and none were to be obtained; so we just had to remove the wounded from those we had, lay them on the ground, and send the stretchers up. Thank goodness, we had plenty of morphia, and the hypodermic syringe relieved many who would otherwise have suffered great agony.

Going through the cases, I found one man who had his arm shattered and a large wound in his chest. Amputation at the shoulder-joint was the only way of saving his life. Major Clayton gave the anaesthetic, and we got him through.

Quite a number of Ghurkas and Sikhs were amongst the wounded, and they all seemed to think that it was part of the game; patience loomed large among their virtues. Turkish wounded were also on our hands, and, though they could not speak our language, still they expressed gratitude with their eyes.

One of the Turks was interrogated, first by the Turkish interpreter with no result; the Frenchman then had a go at him, and still nothing could be got out of him. After these two had finished, Captain Jefferies went over to the man and said in plain English, 'Would you like a drink of water?' 'Yes, please,' was the reply.

During one afternoon a battalion crossed the ground between us and the beach. This brought the Turkish guns into action immediately, and we got the time of our lives. The shells simply rained on us, shrapnel all the time; of course our tent was no protection as it consisted simply of canvas, and the only thing to do was to keep under the banks as much as possible.

We were jammed full of wounded in no time. Men rushing into the gully one after another, and even a company of infantry tried to take shelter there; but that, of course, could not be allowed. We had our Geneva Cross flag up, and their coming there only drew fire.

In three-quarters of an hour we put through fifty-four cases. Many bearers were hit, and several were killed. Seven of our tent division were wounded. One man reported to me that he had been sent as a reinforcement and had just arrived in Gallipoli. While he was speaking, he sank quietly down without a sound. A bullet had come over my shoulder into his heart. That was another instance of the fortune of war. Many men were hit, either before they landed or soon after, while others could go months with never a scratch.

From 2 p.m. till 7 p.m. that day we dealt with 142 cases.

This shelling lasted for an hour or more, and when it subsided a party of men arrived with a message from Divisional Headquarters. They had been instructed to remove as many of the Ambulance as were alive. Headquarters, it appears, had been watching the firing. We lost very little time in leaving, and for the night we dossed down in the scrub a mile further along the beach, where we were only exposed to the fire of spent bullets coming over the hills. Our fervent prayer was that we had said good-bye to shells.

The new position was very nice; it had been a farm – in fact the plough was still there, made of wood, no iron being used in its construction. Blackberries, olives and wild thyme grew on the place and also a kind of small melon. We did not eat any; we thought we were running enough risks already; but the cooks used the thyme to flavour the bovril, and it was a nice addition.

The 4th Field Ambulance had some ingenious craftsmen. Walkley and Betts secured two wheels left by the Signalling Corps, and on these fastened a stretcher; out of a lot of the web equipment lying about they made a set of harness; two donkeys eventuated from somewhere, and with this conveyance quite a lot of transport was done. Water rations were carried as well, and the saving to our men was great. Goodness knows, the bearers were already sufficiently worked carrying wounded.

It was while we were in this position that Warrant Officer Henderson was hit; the bullet came through the tent, through another man's arm and into Mr Henderson. He was a serious loss to the Ambulance, as since its inception he had had sole charge of everything connected with the supply of drugs and dressings, and I missed his services very much.

We were now being kept very busy and had little time for rest, numbers of cases being brought down. Our table was made of four biscuit boxes, on which were placed the stretchers. We had to be very sparing of water, as all had to be carried. The donkey conveyance was kept constantly employed. Whenever that party left we used to wonder whether they would return, for one part of the road was quite exposed to fire; but Betts and Walkley both pulled through.

As there was still a good deal of delay in getting the cases off, our tent was brought over from Canterbury Gully and pitched on the beach, the cooks keeping the bovril and biscuits going. We could not maintain it there long, however, as the Turks' rifle fire was too heavy, so the evacuation was all done from Walker's Ridge about two miles away. The Casualty Clearing Station here (the 16th) was a totally different proposition from the other one. Colonel Corkery was commanding officer and knew his job. His command was exceedingly well administered, and there was no further occasion to fear any blockage in getting our wounded off.

Our bearers did great work here also and one of them, Carberry from Western Australia, proved his worth in another manner. The 4th Brigade were some distance up the gully and greatly in want of water. Carberry seemed to have the knack of divining, for he selected a spot where water was obtained after sinking. General Monash drew my attention to this, and Carberry was recommended for the D.C.M.

Early in August, soon after Colonel Manders was killed, I was promoted to his position as Assistant Director of Medical Services, or, as it is usually written, A.D.M.S.

On this I relinquished command of the 4th Field Ambulance, and though I appreciated the honour of the promotion yet I was sorry to leave the Ambulance. We had been together so long, and through so much, and every member of it was of such sterling worth that when the order came for me to join Headquarters I must say that my joy was mingled with regret. Everyone – officers, non-commissioned officers and men – had all striven to do their level best, and had succeeded.

With one or two exceptions it was our first experience on active service, but all went through their work like veterans. General Godley, in whose Division we were, told me how pleased he was with the work of the Ambulance and how proud he was to have them in his command. The Honour list was quite sufficient to satisfy any man. We got one D.S.O, two D.C.M.s, and sixteen 'Mentioned in Despatches'. Many more deserved recognition, but then all can't get it.

PADRE

Oliver Hogue ('Trooper Bluegum')

In the training camps in Australia the chaplains conducted services, helped at the concerts, and generally made themselves useful and agreeable. On the transports they did pretty much the same thing; but somehow we never seemed to know them, and they, in turn, knew very few of us by name.

It was when we settled down in Egypt that we first began to know them, and to appreciate their work. And since Cairo has the reputation of being the wickedest city in the world, there was ample scope for the operations of the chaplains.

But one of the chaplains had adamantine ideas on theological subjects. He was a great scholar, and had other virtues, but his conscience would not let him participate in the combined services with the other ministers. So when we came away to thrash the Turk we left him behind in Egypt.

In his stead we took an Irishman – Father Bergin. He was a good sport, a good priest, brave as a lion, and with wounded soldiers gentle as a nurse. His only fault was that he always wanted to be right up in the firing line, for he dearly loved a 'scrap', being Irish.

When the 5th Light Horse Regiment had their fight near Gaba Tepe, Father 'Mike' was everywhere tending the wounded, and as a water-carrrier he rivalled Gunga Din. Those of us who were not of the 'faithful' learned to like him more and more, and if the campaign had lasted much longer I fear we would have all been 'Romans'.

Then there was Captain Robertson, young and quiet, and kind of heart. I don't think any of us ever saw him in a pulpit. Mostly he had to preach in tents or in the open air. I have heard him hold forth in an Anzac gully, with the shells bursting overhead. Again, I have sat at his feet right in the support trenches, just behind the firing line, while his sentences were punctuated by the report of snipers' rifles.

He used to dwell on 'historic associations'. He told us that our feet had trod the same streets and fields as Moses and Aaron and Pharaoh, Joseph and Mary, the Apostle Paul, Antony and Cleopatra, Helen of Troy, Mahomet Ali, Napoleon and Byron, and a host of others. His forte, however, was not preaching, but practising. He practised most of the Christian virtues. He was the soldiers' friend, and when we'd sit and smoke and yarn round the campfire at night, and if someone swore inadvertently, he was not righteous overmuch.

Our third padre, the Senior Chaplain of the Brigade, was Captain Keith Miller. As the Americans say, he was 'some preacher'. At Ma'adi we used to have the big tent packed with 2,000 soldiers. Visitors from Cairo and beyond used to go from our services as much impressed with the preacher as with the physique and bearing of the Light Horsemen.

Sermon-tasters from St. Andrew's, Cairo, nodded their heads in grave approval. Elders, with an air of finality, said, 'Yon's a fine deliverance'; and other elders answered, 'Aye'. The padre's final oration and peroration before we left for the front won the special commendation of General Birdwood, who was present. I forget now what the sermon was about – but I know I wanted to cheer at the end of it.

On one of the Turkish prisoners captured, we found a copy of a divisional order, in which the O.C. stated, 'I have many times been round the fire trenches, but have never met any Imam. I lately gave an order that Imams were to be constantly in the trenches, in order to keep up the morale of the men by preaching and exhorting; and whenever possible men should be assembled for prayer, and the call for prayer should be cried by a fine-voiced Imam.'

Now, it is pleasing to record that no such order was necessary in the ranks of the Australian division. Our chaplains since the memorable day of the landing played their part manfully in the great game. They were in the trenches day and night, talking with the men, writing letters home to their people, visiting the sick; and every man in our brigade was supplied with a neat little pocket Testament by a friend of the New South Wales Auxiliary of the British and Foreign Bible Society.

On Sundays there were services in all the brigades – in the gullies, or under the crests of the hills behind the firing line. And sometimes we couldn't hear the singing because of the cannon's roar; there was not one solitary spot in Anzac absolutely safe from enemy fire. And yet I have never heard of any soldier being wounded at any of these services!

Once Padre Miller was conducting a service in Shrapnel Valley, and had finished his firstly, secondly, and thirdly, and was just coming to the peroration, when shrapnel shells burst overhead. So the service had to be abandoned.

Yet, in spite of his many estimable qualities, I regret to state that Padre Miller had one besetting sin. It was a secret sin. Only a few of us knew of his weakness. He played chess. Yes, played chess over and over and over again. When, in Cairo, others of us would play tennis, he would slink away with some old crony and play chess. I have known him play till two o'clock in the morning at a game. (There is no doubt about the hour, because he called for me on the way back to camp.)

He was often late at mess, playing chess. He scarce had time to dress, playing chess. Admittedly he played well, and after defeating the Ma'adi champions he sought fresh victims in Cairo. The Scotch engineer on the transport was a fine player, but he couldn't checkmate the Padre.

When we landed in Gallipoli the first thing the Padre did was to dig a dug-out. The second was to seek a chess mate. There was no chess board, so he got the lid of a box. There were no chessman, so he carved Queens and Bishops and Knights and Pawns out of the flotsam and jetsam on Anzac Beach.

Then, safely ensconced in a snug little dug-out, the Padre and his mate stalemated and checkmated to their heart's content, oblivious of the shells which burst around. Immediately after his tour of the trenches, and his visit to the sick, the Padre would make for his chess mate.

Later on we found him making periodic visits to the hospital ship. I admit he religiously did the rounds of the wards, and looked after the wounded, and I frankly admit that I went on board to see the nurses, but I'm positive the driving force behind the Padre's visits was the prospect of a game of chess with the skipper.

After a few months on Gallipoli the Padre was transferred to the hospital at Lemnos. We all sympathised with him, stuck at the base, and missing all the fun of the fighting. Then we heard that the M.O. at the hospital was a great chess player, and we knew that the Padre had never deserved our sympathy.

A GLIMPSE OF ANZAC

H. W. Dinning

This spot, where Australians showed the world what manner of man is nurtured under the Southern Cross, is fair to look on.

We saw it first from the sea, in the full burst of spring. Literature, both ancient and Byronic, glows with the beauties of the Aegean spring ... and it's all true.

The prodigal flinging of colour over the shores of Gallipoli utterly surpasses in richness the colour of Australia. Here the colour ashore is glowing red, acres of poppies waving upon the green plains, and the Aegean blue waters are of a colour unknown in Australia.

Every morning we look out on the same stretch of the lovely Aegean, with the same two islands standing over in the west. Yet neither the islands nor the sea are the same on any two successive days. The Aegean changes more suddenly and frequently than ever does the Pacific. That delicious Mediterranean colour, of which we used to read so sceptically and which we half disbelieved in J. M. Turner's paintings, changes in the quality of its hue almost hourly.

Every morning the islands of the west take on fresh colour and are trailed by fresh shapes of mist. The atmosphere deludes in the matter of distance; today Imbros stands right over against you; you see the detail of the fleet in the harbour and the small ravines in the striated heights of rocky Samothrace. Yet tomorrow, in the early morning light, or more often towards evening, Imbros lies mysteriously far off like an isle of the blessed, a delicate vapour shape reposing distantly on the placid sea.

Nor is there monotony here in weather or temperature.

It is now late October and autumn and changes in temperature are as incalculable as they are in Melbourne in certain seasons. Fierce, biting, raw days alternate with the comfortableness of mild late summer. Today it may be more than your life is worth to bathe (shrapnel disregarded) and tomorrow in the gentle air you may swim and splash for an hour and still desire more as you prolong the joy by washing your garments in the ocean.

We have suffered the tail end of one or two autumn storms and have had two downright fierce gales blow up where the wind came in the night with a suddenness that found most unprepared. In half an hour many of us were homeless, crouching about with our bundled bedclothes and trespassing on the confined space of the stouter dug-outs of our friends.

Men lay on their backs and held down their roofs by the weight of their bodies until overpowered and the sea roared over the shingle beach with a violence that made even swearing and blasphemy inaudible.

For weeks men had been preparing dug-outs against the approach of winter, but they were unprepared for weather of such violence. The morning showed a sorry sight on the beach, barges torn adrift from their moorings and hurled ashore. Some were empty, some were filled with supplies; but all were battered, some disabled and some utterly broken. One was filled with rum and never before, on active service, had such a chance of unlimited spirits been offered. Many jars were spirited away before the time of unloading came.

Far more serious was the state of the landing piers. There had been three. One stood intact; the landward half of the second was clean gone and of the third there was no trace except a few splintered spars on the shore.

The mending began forthwith but so did the bursting of shrapnel over the workmen, for this stroke of vengeance from Allah upon the unfaithful was not to go unsupplemented.

By nightfall, however, the abridged pier was successfully reunited with the shore, in spite of the shrapnel and a sea that made it impossible for barges to come alongside.

For two days the after-wind of the gale kept bread and meat and mail tossing on the waters off Anzac and we were fed on bully beef and biscuit as we wistfully eyed the mail trawler pitching out there with her precious burden. For the arrival of mail eclipses all other considerations, even life and death, the fighting or even the landing of rations!

Mail has been arriving weekly for six months. Sometimes it comes twice a week, for the Army Corps Post Office never rests and instalments may be spread over three or four landings.

Most mails are landed between sunset and dawn, mostly after midnight. Post Office officials must be there to check and supervise and they get little sleep on 'mail nights'.

Incoming mails do not constitute all their work; outgoing mail from the firing line is heavy and they have other tasks to perform also.

There are the pathetic 'returns' to be dealt with, the letters to men who will never read them, written before the heavy news had reached home. A huge bulk of correspondence is marked 'Killed' and re-addressed to the place of origin of the fallen soldiers. Their comrades keep their newspapers and the parcels of comforts bring melancholy cheer to their fighting comrades-in-arms. What else is to be done with them?

Letters put a man at home for a couple of hours, and so does his local newspaper. Perusing the local paper takes him back to the old habit of picking at the news over his eggs and coffee or on the suburban business train. Intimate associations hang about the reading of the local newspaper, associations almost as powerful as are brought by letters. If relatives at home understood this they would despatch newspapers with stricter regularity.

And what can be said about parcels from home? No son away at boarding school ever pursued his voyage of discovery through tarts, cakes, sweets, pies and fruit with the intensity of gloating expectation that a man on Gallipoli displays as he discloses the contents of his 'parcel'.

'The arrival of mail eclipses all other considerations.' Mail station Shrapnel Valley.

'Strewth, Bill, look, a new pipe! And some of me favourite terbaccer. Blimey, cigars too! Have one before the crowd smells 'em. Hello, more socks! Oh well, winter's comin'. 'Ere, 'ow are you orf for socks, cobber? Take these, bonzer hand-knitted, sling them army issue things into the sea ... Gawd! 'ere's a shaving stick, that's handy ... I clean run out of carbolic soap!'

Mail deserves all the organised care the War Office can bestow; mail makes for efficiency.

There may be no morning delivery of the daily newspaper on Anzac, but we get the news. At the foot of Headquarters Gully is the notice board and wireless messages are posted daily. At any hour men are elbowing their way into the perusing circle.

There is news of operations along our own front and copious messages from the Russian and Western fronts. The Melbourne Cup finish was cabled through immediately. There were few men who did not handle their purses around the board that evening, for no war news, for months, had been so momentous as this.

The associations called to mind by the news from Flemington were strong and homely, as well as national. Men were recalled for a while from the land of blood and death to the office, the bank, the warehouse, the country pub or the shearing shed where Cup bets were often placed and sweeps made. The sporting spirit is stronger than any other Australian national trait. The Defence Department knew what they were doing when they made provision for a cabled despatch of the running of the Cup to Gallipoli.

Of course, much news is spread by rumour also. Rumours persist, for example, as to the presence of women behind the Turkish lines. Our outposts claim to have seen them and victorious attacking parties that have captured Turkish camps have been said to declare that they have found garments hanging there of the most significant lace-frilled sort.

The unbelieving diagnose that these are the highly-embellished pyjamas of Turkish officers and the whole thing is probably to be disbelieved. The Turk is too busy to be distracted by the blandishments of his women. Harems are doubtless best left well behind at home, to be revelled in when the British are finally driven into the sea.

ARCADIA

H. E. Shell

I've dwelt in many a town and shire from Cairns to Wangaratta;
I've dropped into the Brisbane Show and Bundaberg Regatta,
But now I've struck the ideal spot where pleasure never cloys,
Just list' to the advantages this choice retreat enjoys –
The scenery is glorious, the sunsets are cyclonic;
The atmosphere's so full of iron, it acts as quite a tonic!
No parsons ever preach the Word or take up a collection;
While politicians don't exist, nor any by-election.
No scandal ever hovers here to sear our simple lives;
And married men are always true to absent, loving wives.
And should you doubt if there can be a spot which so excels,
Let me whisper – it is ANZAC! Anzac by the Dardanelles.

THE HOME FRONT

E. C. Buley

The spirit of Australia can best be gauged by reading an extract from a letter written to the Australian wounded by a young lady who was a teacher at the High School in Ballarat, and which was cabled all over the world, since it echoes truly the pride of Australia in its heroes and the determination of the Commonwealth that all shall be worthy of their devotion and grand patriotism. The letter was received at the hospital at Malta, and runs as follows:

May 12

Dear Australian Boys,

Every Australian woman's heart this week is thrilling with pride, with exultation, and while her eyes fill with tears she springs up as I did when the story in Saturday's *Argus* was finished and says, 'Thank God, I am an Australian.'

Boys, you have honoured our land; you, the novices, the untrained, the untaught in war's grim school, have done deeds of veterans. Oh, how we honour you; how we glory in your matchless bravery, in your yet more wonderful fortitude, which the war correspondent says was shown so marvellously as your boatloads of wounded cheered and waved amid their pain as you were rowed back to the vessels!

What gave you the courage for that heroic dash to the ridge, boys? British grit, Australians' nerve and determination to do or die, a bit of the primeval man's love of a big fight against heavy odds. God's help too, surely.

Dear boys, I'm sure you will feel a little rewarded for your deeds of prowess if you know how the whole Commonwealth, nay the whole Empire, is stirred by them. Every Sunday now we are singing the following lines after 'God Save the King' in church and Sunday school. They appeared in the *Argus Extraordinary* with the first Honour Roll in it:

> *God save our splendid men!*
> *Send them safe home again!*
> *Keep them victorious,*
> *Patient and chivalrous,*
> *They are so dear to us:*
> *God save our men.*

What can I say further? With God the ultimate issue rests. Good-night, boys. God have you living or dying in His keeping. If any one of you would like to send me a pencilled note or card I'll answer it to him by return.

Your countrywoman,

Jeanie Dobson

That Australian purses were opened with Australian hearts is proved by the remarkable total of gifts in money and kind made by Australia to various funds on behalf of sufferers by the war. In the first ten months the Commonwealth contributed in cash the sum of £2,329,259 to the various funds arising out of the war, apart from immense gifts in kind, the value of which is not estimatable. The

State contributions are totalled as follows: New South Wales, £980,889; Victoria, £850,000; Queensland, £200,825; South Australia, £127,540; Tasmania, £36,750; and Western Australia, £133,255. Total: £2,329,259.

The Australian care for the wounded is the subject of a testimony from Sir Frederick Treves, which may be included here to show the appreciation with which this care had been met by the most eminent surgeon in the Empire:

> The generosity with which Australia has provided motor ambulances for the whole country, and Red Cross stores for everyone, British or French, who has been in want of the same, is beyond all words. I only hope that the people of Australia will come to know of the admirable manner in which their wounded have been cared for, and of the noble and generous work which that great colony has done under the banner of the Red Cross.

General Sir Ian Hamilton sent to Mr Andrew Fisher, the Prime Minister of the Australian Commonwealth, a message of which every Australasian should be proud:

> May I, out of a full heart, be permitted to say how gloriously the Australian and New Zealand Contingents have upheld the fine traditions of our race during the struggle still in progress. At first with audacity and dash, since then with sleepless valour and untiring resource, they have already created for their countries an imperishable record of military virtue.

GEORGE

Oliver Hogue ('Trooper Bluegum')

George was the cook.

He blew into the Light Horse Camp at Holsworthy when we were training. The Staff Captain gave him the job because he was a sea cook. Any man who can cook at sea ought to be able to cook on dry land. And all through the weary weeks of waiting and working, George kept on cooking.

George was small, not to say puny. His height was five feet, and his chest measurement nothing to cable home about.

Had he gone to Victoria Barracks in the ordinary way to enlist he wouldn't have passed even the sentry at the gate, let alone the doctor. But George knew the ropes. He had 'soldiered' before. That's why he took the short cut direct to camp.

We never saw much of him on the way to Egypt aboard the *Suevic*; when off duty he used to climb to some cosy corner on the uppermost deck and read dry textbooks on strategy and tactics. At odd times he would seek relaxation in *Life of Napoleon*, *Marlborough*, or *Oliver Cromwell*, but this was distinctly 'not a study, but a recreation'.

Passing through the Suez Canal we saw the Turks miles away on the rim of the desert. George got out his rifle, set the sight at 2,500 yards, and waited. But the invader kept well out of range, and George went back to his cooking.

It was mid-winter in Egypt and the nights were bitterly cold. Greatcoats were vitally necessary. How welcome were the mufflers and Balaclava caps and warm socks knitted by the girls we left behind us!

Welcome also was the hot coffee George provided to fill in the shivering gap between *reveille* and stables. And after the horses had all been fed and watered, we returned with zest to breakfast – porridge and meat and 'eggs-a-cook' and bread and marmalade. I've heard some grumblers complain of the 'tucker' in Egypt, but I've seen a bit of war by this and I'm convinced that the Australians are the best-fed army in the world. And George by the same token was not a bad cook.

*   *   *

Summer swooped down in Egypt. In its wake came heat and dust and flies and locusts. Over the scorching sands of the desert we cantered till the sweat poured from us and our horses, and the choking dust enveloped all. 'Gyppie' fruit sellers scurried hither and yon yelling 'Oringes – good beeg one'. And as we regaled ourselves with the luscious thirst-quenchers we thought of camp and the dinner that George was preparing.

We trekked along the Nile, and almost before we halted George was boiling the billy. We bivouacked at Aaron's Gorge, or the Petrified Forest, or in a desert waste, and always George was on the spot with his dixies and pans. The cook's cart was a pleasing silhouette against the pyramid-pierced skyline, when we turned our eyes westward in the long summer evenings.

When at last we started for the Dardanelles, we of the Light Horse Brigade had (as you know) to leave our horses behind, and the cook's cart stopped too. But George came along all right.

Despite the activities of the submarines we reached Gallipoli in safety, and witnessed the Allied warships pounding away at the Turkish defences. Historic Troy was on our right; before us the entrance to the Dardanelles; and on the left, firmly established on Helles, was the great Mediterranean Expeditionary Force, making its first halt on the road to Constantinople.

But we had to go further north, a mile beyond Gaba Tepe, where the Australians – particularly the 3rd Infantry Brigade – had performed such deeds of valour that Dargai, Colenso, and Magersfontein were declared by old soldiers to have been a mere picnic in contrast.

We landed amid a hail of shrapnel. Transhipping from the transports, we crowded into launches and sweepers and barges. These little boats, heavily laden with khaki freight, made straight for Anzac Cove. Fair targets for Tommy Turk, of course; so the guns of the Olive Grove Battery sent us anything but peaceful messages.

Plug-plong went the shells into the water. Zip-zip hissed the bullets all round us. But, marvellous to relate, not a man was hit. Next day some infantry reinforcements, landing in the same place and manner, sustained forty casualties. That's the luck of the game – the fortune of war. We landed everything satisfactorily.

George brought up the rear, with his pots and dixies. It is because of George that I recapitulate.

In a long, straggling khaki line ('Column o' lumps,' said the Brigade Major) we meandered past Casualty Point and Hell Spit, and up to our bivouac in Shrapnel Valley. Snipers on the hill up beyond Quinn's Post sent long-range shots at random down the track. Shells burst over our heads, and the leaden pellets spattered over the landscape. It would take too long to recount half the miraculous escapes some of our chaps had.

Our artillery worked overtime, and the row was deafening. But our gunners could not silence the elusive cannon in the Olive Grove. After a time, wherein the minutes seemed like hours, we reached the campsite, and started to dig in feverishly. We burrowed like rabbits. Picks, shovels and bayonets made the earth fly till we had scratched a precarious shelter from the blast. Like troglodytes we snuggled into the dug-outs, waiting for the bombardment to cease.

But George went on with his cooking.

Next day we changed our quarters. The German artillerymen were too attentive. We had sustained a few casualties, so we sought a more retired spot under the lee of the hill. For the first time since we had landed we were able to look about us. There was a lull in the cannonade, though the musketry fusillade proceeded merrily.

We saw the long line of Australian and New Zealand trenches whence the Turks had been driven in rout the night before, leaving 3,000 dead to mar the landscape. We heard too, definitely, for the first time of the good Australians who on this inhospitable shore had given their lives for King and Empire – General Bridges, Colonel MacLaurin, Lieutenant Colonel Braund, Lieutenant Colonel Onslow Thompson, Sergeant Larkin (who used to sit on the opposite side to Colonel Braund in the New South Wales Parliament, but found in war the leveller that makes us all one party), and hundreds of others.

Looking up to the precipitous cliffs above, we marvelled anew at the reckless daring of our infantry comrades who had scaled those heights in the face of rifle, machine-gun and shrapnel.

But we had not long to saunter and wonder. Our brigade was sent straightaway into the firing line. We were initiated into the mysteries of trench warfare, sapping and mining, bombs and grenades, observing and sniping, possies and dug-outs, patrolling and listening, periscopes and peepholes, demonstrations and reconnaissance, supports and reserves, bully beef and biscuits, mud and blood and slaughter, and all the humours and rumours, the hardships and horrors of war.

And all the time we were doing our little bit George went on with his cooking. He may have been thinking of Napoleon, or Marlborough, or Cromwell, but he did not seem to be thinking much about this war of ours – except that he had to do some cooking for it.

The Turks were shooting many of our officers down, and many of our dear old pals, but George remained – and we hoped that they would spare him. Good cooks – real, good cooks like George – are scarce.

ON WATER FATIGUE

George H. Smith

I'd like to get the Hun who sends the little bits of shell
Which buzz around as wearily I top that blooming hill.
He only does his duty, but my only shirt I'd sell
For half a chance to give the cuss a non-return to Hell!

THE DEATH OF OXBRIDGE

Frederick Loch ('Sydney de Loghe')

A group of us 'Headquarters Johnnies' had yarned outside the cookhouse since the midday meal.

My old friend Oxbridge was there, and Stone and Prince, and one or two others, I think. We sat in the open on biscuit tins or stones, or whatever was handy, for the day was sunny and quite mild. There was nothing to do, and we talked on and on.

The tireless musketry fire rolled from the valley head, and enemy shells still burst haphazardly along the beach and over the sea. But for an hour or more headquarters had been free from such attention, and that was all that concerned us.

Instead of pondering over shells, Oxbridge had grown homesick again, and was holding forth now on a theory of his own – that after six months' active service, the Government would send home all men wanting to go. His reasoning seemed a bit faulty to the rest of us; but he convinced himself.

Oxbridge was a thoughtful, gentle soul, always keen for a yarn and a theory on this and that. He was called 'Oxbridge' in mocking deference to his education and scholarly ways.

The arguments had not impressed us much, but somehow or other we stopped talking, and one looked out to sea, and one cleaned his pipe, and I went on cooking. We were all sick of this business; that was the truth.

Oxbridge was an odd fellow in many ways and easily led, but we had worked together in various staff positions since the days at Mena Camp in Egypt. In wartime you get to know men quickly and deep friendships are formed in months or even weeks. I felt I'd known Oxbridge all my life.

In spite of the lazy shelling, the beach was thick with the usual crowds. And the bay was full of vessels. Oxbridge stood up at last, tall and with a stoop, and took it all in with an unappreciative eye.

I went on stirring Welsh rabbit in a mess-tin lid, all my hopes fixed on it. The fire was nearly done, and called for new wood, and the cheese was just simmering. It was a toss-up which would win.

Men climbed up and down the hillside, moving to their dug-outs and that sort of thing; fragile clouds passed across the sun and darkened its face a few moments; the breeze rustled over the few bushes spared by the cook's axe: such things I saw while I knelt and watched the Welsh rabbit through the critical moments.

Oxbridge still stared into the distance, I noticed, and just then a gust of wind filled my eyes with smoke, and with an oath I sprang up behind him. As my eyes cleared he turned to move away, and that instant something struck him with a hard, dull sound, and he breathed out a long-drawn 'Oh!' and threw his hands forward and fell upon the ground. He got up again and fell down once more.

A shell burst along the hill somewhere behind us.

The doctor, who saw it happen, ran up, and we carried Oxbridge under shelter of the cookhouse and laid him on his back. His eyes were shut, and his breathing was loud and difficult, and already he was turning a horrid grey. The Red Cross orderlies joined us.

We, who could not help, drew back out of the way under the shelter of the cookhouse walls. The doctor leaned forward and pulled up the wounded man's shirt, baring his chest. Below the heart was a small red mark.

A second shell burst upon the hill, and a third farther along. They were ranging for us again.

None of us said a word, and only one man moved: the doctor was taking a syringe from its case. First he held it against the light, and next pushed it into the dying man's arm.

A fresh burst of fire swept the hillside, and each man looked to himself wondering if he were next. Shells began to fall about us. They began to fall fast and burst close around us.

Soon I was looking at the sea through a wall of red dust. We huddled back against the cookhouse, my heart went thump, thump, against my chest, and I lay as still as a mouse. Poor Prince had lost his head altogether, and, as the shells burst, threw his arms out to push them off. The dust rose thicker and thicker, and finally the sun shone through it in the form of a sullen red ball.

We watched the coming of Death to Oxbridge. He never moved again, except once when he turned his head slightly; but the unnatural breathing went on, went on and grew more feeble.

The doctor sat with his back to us, and his head bowed between his shoulders. He moved seldom; seldom lifted his eyes from the dying man. By him the orderlies knelt, huddled together to get what cover they could; and the shells would swoop down with a roar and a scattering of the dust.

Nobody said anything that I can remember, but time passed and left us watching the still figure, and listening to the horrible breaths.

At last the firing passed farther along the slope, and the dust settled once more. The adjutant came down from his dug-out.

'Is he badly hit?' he said, looking down and jerking his head.

'The bullet went below the heart. He is still alive, and that is about all.'

The adjutant raised his eyebrows, nodded, and went away. We became silent again.

Hawkins came back up from the valley and passed by us.

I thought he was staring at Oxbridge, but he never saw him. The doctor spoke at once. 'You had better get under cover, Hawkins. They have been dusting things up round here just now.'

'Yes, I saw that,' Hawkins said, with a laugh. And he curled up in his dug-out.

Presently the waiting was over. Death had won – the last trench was taken, the final fortress stormed. The doctor got to his feet, and spoke to the orderlies. 'Is the stretcher here?'

I looked into my dead friend's face and an old thought came back to me. Death is not often beautiful. Here was no heroic end; here was no bold gaze, which told of past duties well done. Nothing of that kind, but, instead, a silly smile where the mouth dropped, and a little blood upon the palate, and the skin turning yellow.

Not heroic, my friends, not beautiful.

I stared down at Oxbridge while they covered him with a blanket.

Thoughts I would have put aside at that place and at that hour came to me.

Friend, life owed you more years; but, knowing the type of chap you were, perhaps they would have been years without profit. Now you have died at the start of life, and others following may remember your sacrifice and take heart from it.

Perhaps you could have done no better thing. I think you will sleep soundest here, where the cliffs climb up by Sari Bair.

If you should step it out afar
To the pebbly beach of Sari Bair
Full many rude graves you'll find there are,
By the road the sappers drove there.

Crooked the cross, and brief the prayer,
Close they lie by the hillside bare,
Captain and private, pair by pair,
Looking back on the days they strove there.

There still they lie, their work all done,
Resting at ease in the soil well won
And listening hard for Gabriel's gun,
To spring up and salute, as behove there.

THE ANZAC LINE

H. W. Dinning

All Australians by now know the Anzac positions where their sons and brothers scrambled from the boats, splashed onto the fatal sand and either fell or fixed the steel and charged to conquer or fall above.

The charge was made up a steep-ridged hill opening upon an irregular tableland. Either flank of that hill is gently undulating low country and a thin belt of light sand fronts it all.

I will attempt to describe it as it appears in 1915, but there is the danger of being disbelieved because the reader, harassed by the constant war news from this smiling land, may well conceive the incongruity of the fair landscape coloured in another way, with the red dust of troop movement, the hideous discolour of bursting shells and the grey smudge of shrapnel.

A grand range of chalk hills runs south behind the pasture on the right flank. The low shore plain of the left flank is backed by a group of green pinnacles moving north towards the glittering salt lake of Suvla Bay. To the north the coast sweeps out to the horn of Saros Bay, a rough sheer-rising headland, southern sentinel of the great Saros cliffs.

Moving inshore to the foot of the plateau one gets an impression of smoothness that is a delusion. In close detail it is rough, small ravines and sandy gullies which both hindered and assisted the Anzac aggressors on landing.

Leaving behind the beach, with its feverish busyness, the climb to the trenches follows a well-engineered road levelled in the bed of the ravine. In the sides of the ravine the dug-outs are as thick as dwellings in a Cairo alleyway, which is saying a lot!

Beaten side-tracks branch off in all directions but the only real haven for mules and horses is the shelter of the banks of the ravine which have been dug out at intervals into a sort of extensive stable.

It is the height of the afternoon and there is no wind stirring under the hill. The men off duty are sleeping heavily. They have flung themselves down and lie, worn out, in the thick dust and heat of their shelters where the flies swarm.

Not everyone is sleeping. Here and there a regimental office is operating in a dug-out and the typewriters are busy. They make a strange resonance with the hum of bullets above, which does not cease.

The Post Office lies in a bend of the path. This is dug in deep with sandbag bulwarks. There is no sleeping here. The khaki-clad staff stamps and sorts in their subterranean chamber, amidst a disorder of mail bags and the fumes of sealing wax. One hopes the shrapnel will spare this sanctuary.

Half a mile up, the road peters out into a rough and dusty track under the hill crest. It is heavy climbing now and one realises for the first time what a task it was scaling up here at the first charge. It is hard work on a well-beaten road. Imagine what it was like for those infantrymen, hampered with their steel-laden rifles and equipment, with the Turks raining death from the trenches above! It took them seventeen minutes' work to reach these slopes. We have been panting and scrambling for forty minutes, and we are not up yet.

Five minutes more brings us to the sentry guarding the communication trench. He sends us stooping on our way, for you dare not walk erect beyond this point. Here the bullets are not 'spent' (though 'spent' bullets can do damage enough further down).

The labour of trench-making must have been enormous. Here is a picked trench five feet deep and half as wide again as your body, cut out of soft rock, hundreds of yards of it . . . miles of it!

Fifteen minutes looping around in this manner brings us to an exit which opens out into a battery position where two guns are speaking from deep pits. In a dug-out beside the pit lies the presiding genius with his ear to a telephone. His lingo is almost unintelligible, except to the initiated, but from the observers on our flanks he is transmitting corrections and directions to his gunners.

One man is juggling shells from the rear of the pit, one is 'laying' the gun, and the rest are understrappers.

The roar of the discharge, heard from behind, is not excessive. What comes uppermost is the prolonged 'whizz' and scream of the shell.

Artillery work is at least engaging and interesting. The infantryman aims in a direction and hopes for the best but the man

'The sleeping places, hollowed out under the lee of the wall, a foot from the floor.'

at the gun watches each shot, gauges the error, and acts accordingly for the next. His is a sort of triumphal progress towards his mark.

Re-entering the trench, we creep towards our second line. There are a few scattered marksmen at work here and there along our way.

There is a kind of comfort even in the trenches. The sleeping places, hollowed out under the lee of the wall a foot from the floor, will keep a man more or less dry in the rain. There are symbols of creature comfort scattered around, blankets, newspapers, tobacco tins, eggshells, orange peel and chocolate wrappings ... but it's harsh enough. There is little respite from the crackle of musketry, the song of the bullet and the intimate scream of the shells.

The labyrinth of trenches becomes very intricate as you approach the front line. 'Saps', communications trenches, tunnels and galleries make a maze that requires some initiation and knowledge to negotiate successfully.

In the rear lines the men off duty are resting as best they can, plagued as they are with flies, heat and dust. In general they are far too exhausted to care much, as long as they have their tobacco and a place to lie. They try to be comfortable in the squalor; some even try to cook a trifle of food at their pathetic little hole-in-the-wall fires.

The most impressive thing near the first line is the elaborateness and permanency of the trenches, dug-outs and overhead cover. Also, the impression of keenness and alertness here is in striking contrast to the easy-going aspect of the reservists in the rear lines. The men work at frequent intervals, in pairs, one observing with the periscope, the other missing no chances with the rifle.

Two things shock you and arrest your gaze.

The first is the ghastly spectacle of our dead lying beyond the parapet. They have been there since the last charge; that was three weeks ago, and they are black and swollen. They lie in so exposed a place that they dare not be approached.

The stink is revolting; putrefying human flesh emits an odour without a parallel. An hour's inhalation was almost overpowering. One asks how our men have breathed it for three and four months. The flies swarm in hosts.

The second thing you notice is the amazing proximity of the enemy trenches. The average distance is about fifteen yards.

You may be told 'Come along here, they're a bit closer' and taken to a point at which the neutral ground is no more than five yards in width, a rifle and bayonet extended from each trench would meet across it. You will need to look furtively through a loophole to verify this. Our men can hear the Turks snoring.

One result of this uncanny proximity is that the bomb is the chief weapon of offence. To shy a bomb over five yards is an easy deed to accomplish and bomb wounds are much to be dreaded as the missile does not pierce, it shatters, and there is no choosing where you will have your wound.

Working slowly back along the line you will find you are in old Turkish trenches that have been originally constructed as to fight in the direction of the sea. When our men took them they had to immediately turn around and build a parapet on the other side.

These trenches were choked with Turkish dead and to bury them out in the open was unthinkable, so they had to be buried beneath the new inland-facing parapet or thrown into pits excavated in the trench wall. The consequence is that as you make your way along the trench floor you occasionally come into contact with a protruding boot encasing the foot of a dead Turk. We had more than one such unsavoury encounter. The odour arising from our own dead is not all with which our infantry have to contend.

War isn't fun and a good deal of drivel is spoken and written about the ennobling effects of warfare in the field. The men who have had four months of this are, for the most part, pasty-faced ghosts with their nerves on a raw edge. The troops suffer from inadequate rest that is habitually broken, an entire lack of exercise, food that is scanty and ill-nourishing, a perpetual and overpowering stink of the most revolting kind and black swarms of flies that make rest impossible even if the enemy shelling and bomb-throwing did not. Then there is the nervous strain of suspense and known peril that is never lifted.

Australians have done their part with unequalled magnificence but flesh and blood and spirit cannot go at this indefinitely. God help the Australian infantryman who has less than a frame of steel wire, muscles of whipcord and a heart of fire.

In rare cases men have been driven demented in our firing line. Men who were in civilian life modest, gentle, tender-hearted and self-effacing have become bloody minded, lusting to kill. War is not fun, neither is it ennobling.

It is by way of Shrapnel Valley that we regain the beach. The Australian hospital stands on the right extremity, by no means out of danger. A sparse line of stretchers is moving down almost continuously. This is a hospital for mere hasty dressing to enable the wounded to go aboard the pinnaces and out to the hospital ship standing offshore.

Collins Street doctors who have left behind practices replete with every convenience find themselves working in hastily erected marquees where half the attendants limp or hop.

The beach is animated. There are innumerable wireless stations, ordnance stores, medical supply stores and A.S.C. depots. Here are the hard facts and hard graft; dirt, sweat and peril of righteous war. It is by these mundane means, rather than pride, pomp and circumstance, that the clash of ideals is progressing, and by which a decision will come.

Here on the beach the morning splash has become indispensable to some. Daily at six-thirty you see the bald pate of General Birdwood bobbing beyond the sunken barge just offshore, and a host of nudes lining the beach. As the weather cools the host is slowly diminishing to a few isolated fellows who are either fanatics or have come down from the trenches to clear up vermin and dust-infested skin at all costs.

Naturally men would prefer to bathe at midday, rather than at 6.30 a.m. when the sun has not got above the precipitous ridge of Sari Bair. But the early morning dip is almost the only safe one. The beach is still enfiladed by Turkish artillery from the right although this is better than previously when enemy guns from both flanks commanded the beach. The gun on the right somewhere that continues to harass us is known familiarly as 'Beachy Bill'. The one that was formerly active on the left went by a name intended for the ears of soldiers only.

'Beachy Bill' is, in fact, the collective name for a whole battery capable of throwing over five shells simultaneously. 'Beachy Bill' sometimes catches the morning bathing squad and then there is much ducking and splashing shoreward and scurrying over the beach to cover by men clad only in the garments nature provided.

Shrapnel bursting above the water raises the question: will it ever stop? Will the pellets ever cease to whip the water? The interval between the murderous lightning burst aloft and the last pellets whipping the water seems everlasting to the potential victim.

The hidden battery cannot be located. The cruisers are doing their best with searching fire, their blue-jackets are climbing the masts to observe, the balloon is aloft, the seaplanes are vigilant, our own artillery outposts never relax ... but there is no clue. It is concealed with devilish ingenuity. Every day it is costing us dearly.

All's fair in war. Turkish sniping is awfully successful. The Turkish sniper is almost unequalled, certainly unexcelled, as an unerring shot. They have picked off our officers at a deadly rate. Lance Corporals have become Lieutenants in a single night.

Transport of supplies to the flanks is done by mule-carts manned by Sikhs. The route is sniped by night as well as by day and is swept by shrapnel and machine-gun fire. Only under the most urgent necessity are supplies taken to the flanks by day and then the loss in men and mules is heavier than we can rightly bear.

Sickness also has diminished little. Colic, enteric, dysentery and jaundice are still painfully prevalent and our sick are far flung and many in Lemnos, Egypt, Malta and England. As long as the flies and the unburied persist, the wastage in sick men deported is near to alarming.

Along with disease it's the monotony that kills those away from the front lines, not hard work or hard fare. We have now been embarked here for four months and there has been little change in our way of living. Every day there is the same work on the same beach, shelled by the same guns. Presumably the same guns are manned by the same Turks, for we never seem to knock out those furtive and deadly batteries that maim and kill almost daily.

LAMENT

Lance Corporal Saxon

It ain't the work and it ain't the Turk that causes us to swear,
It's having to fight at dark midnight with the things in our
*   underwear.*
They're black and grey and brindle and white and red and big
*   and small*
And they steeplechase around our knees and we cannot sleep
*   at all.*
Today there's a score, tomorrow lots more of the rotters,
*   it ain't too nice*
To sit, skin bare in the morning air, looking for blooming lice!

THE PROCLAMATION

William Baylebridge

The men in the trench were getting ready for tea. It was about this time that the Turks' aeroplanes would be up, to see what they could do to trouble us.

There was one making over to our lines now. This machine came from beyond Suvla, like a bird sitting on the wind it floated against the blue. Those who had field-glasses lifted them here and there, and did what they could to make out what the caller would be up to. Nearer, and nearer it came, till almost above our lines.

Then our guns and rifles had their say. The light blue of the sky, where the shells burst, was patched with white smoke. Machine-guns, too, emptied their belts at the newcomer. But the fellow up there had his luck with him and we scored not one good hit.

These planes would make the trip for two reasons – to see what we might be up to, and to throw down bombs and a kind of a short arrow. Because of this we now got ready for whatever might come down. It was not long in coming. Out dropped a bomb – or what looked like it – but the thing then scattered into a great number of pieces, diving this way and that. These pieces twisted in the wind, and made slowly for the ground.

It was soon seen that they were sheets of paper, no doubt with print on them, and, by all the odds, meant for us. As luck had it, though, that airman's shooting turned out to be as poor as our own:

the wind got under this drift of paper, and carried most of it across No Man's land and into the lines held by the Turks themselves.

A number of these sheets came to earth where the Turks had meant them to: they dropped into one of our front trenches. One man picked up the cleanest of these sheets and a crowd gathered about him; and they read it through. There was many a bitter grin and many an oath at that reading.

Then someone said, 'Let Snowy do the talking.' So a man there called Snowy took hold the sheet, spat, and spoke up in these words:

PROCLAMATION TO THE ANGLO-FRENCH EXPEDITIONARY FORCES

Protected by the heavy fire of a powerful fleet, you have been able to land on the Gallipoli Peninsula on and since 25 April ...

All your endeavours to advance into the inner parts of the Peninsula have come to failure under heavy losses ...

'Aye,' said one soldier, 'but we did land.'

'For all their skite, the joke isn't through yet,' growled another.

Two fine British battleships, the Triumph *and the* Majestic, *have been sunk before your own eyes ...*

'Yes, and they'll be paid for yet,' a third man put in.

Since those severe losses to the British Navy, your men-o'-war have had to seek refuge, and have abandoned you to your own fate ...

'O, what sweet and uncorrupted liars,' said the first soldier again, hotly.

'And add to that,' said another, 'that liars want better luck. If these sons of Barabbas can believe that, who do they think does the shelling?'

Your ships cannot possibly be of any help to you in the future ...

'Well, then,' said a tall Winton man, 'all the more need for us to show some stiffness of the neck here.'

Soon all supplies will be cut off from your landed forces ...

Another man said, with a grin, 'If the grub's to be cut off, the harder will we lay on to get at theirs. It's kids' wisdom.'

Snowy turned again to his sheet.

You are exposed to certain perdition by starvation and thirst ...

'We'll chance that,' said a Queenslander, 'perhaps the politicians and the bad seasons have hit us – but we've seen worse.'

You could escape useless sacrifice of life only by surrendering ...

'And sacrifice our honour and good name too, I suppose,' said another, smacking his forehead.

We are assured you have not taken up arms against us through hatred ...

'Good guessing!' this man put in again. 'But it's all the worse for them that we kill without hating.'

Greedy England has made you fight under a contract ...

When this was read out, the men there thought it the best stroke of all. Said one: 'Yes, the world, to the last goat in it, knows how we came here. It knows how the whole joke was fixed up, with ourselves left out of it. Yet, for all that, the circus is not through yet; and, mugs that we are, we're not quitting till then.'

You may confide in us for excellent treatment ... There is enough to feed you well and make you feel quite at your comfort. Don't further hesitate. Come and surrender.

'The truth is,' said one man, with a queer sort of a chuckle, 'there's some breeding in these bastards after all. What more could they say? See, now, how they want to take us by the hand, brothers all! It pains them to think that, through all the months that they might have, they haven't killed the fatted steer to welcome us!'

'You've said it,' another put in, 'they are better beasts than we took them for. It's damned good of them. "Look," they say, "we'll welcome you and see that you go always with a full belly." And all for what? Only that we come in softly and kiss them fair upon their black arse.'

'So much for so little!' laughed another. 'It's too cheap!'

'There's a bit more of it,' said Snowy, who wanted to get it over; and he read on.

On all other fronts of this war, with your own people and your allies, the situation is as hopeless as it is on this peninsula ...

'Let it be so,' said a man standing on the edge of the group; 'it's not hope, you dungheads, but ammunition, that we need here.'

The Russian troops are surrendering. Do as they do. Further fighting is mere stupid bloodshed.

'Isn't that straight from their bursting hearts?' laughed the Queenslander. 'It's their own blood they're thinking of.'

Snowy tore the sheet up. 'If we thought anything of those who made this offer,' he said, 'it might hurt. But poor wits, and weak hearts, went into the making of it.'

'Still, something sticks and rankles,' said another, 'that they thought the idea worth trying.'

Now, there was a man there they called the Bard. He had words to waste when he wanted them; and the mob thought there was need for words now. Seeing him not a mile off, someone said, 'Pass one to the Bard; he'll fix the cows.'

When they passed the sheet to the man they spoke of he got down from a loophole, took the torn sheet and read it through slowly. After he had scratched his head enough, he turned the thing over and, taking a stump of lead pencil from his coat, he wrote this:

TO OUR GOOD FRIENDS,
THE TURKS, GREETINGS!

If we have hitherto held off from closer communion with your twice courteous selves, it was not, believe us, from any pleasure we had in that seclusion. Gladly would we give back your goodwill a hundred fold but, like yourselves, we have much upon our heart.

We would gladly ease the burden and empty our heart to you as our friend; for our joy in being here we find but a poor and perfunctory thing, except that yourselves come into it. For, as you point out, friendship between us is much to be desired.

Some men, it is true, account Friendship of so much worth that, rather than want for it, they have bought it at the price of their honour. Great errors can breed up where the counsel of a friend is false or lacking and, as we value our good name, we shall value the friend who supports it and trust his counsel.

As to your kind offer, therefore, we cannot allow you to make such a gesture without some similar offer of a condition of friendship in return.

Therefore, do these things. Firstly, take the General who commands your troops; secondly, attach to him all officers from Colonels up; thirdly, send these, bare-

headed and with rumps bare, with wire halters about
their necks, across to our lines to await our pleasure.

Such friendship shall you have then as we shall
observe always, and, being the friends you are, you will
surely find it grateful to return.

The Bard then read the joke out.

His mates – who considered that intention was everything, and
the way of doing it unimportant – thought it neat work. He then
folded the sheet small, tied a stone to it, and, swinging it on a cord,
threw it so that it fell cleanly into the nearest Turkish trench.

'Let them go to school with that,' he said.

WHY WE SHALL PREVAIL

F. J. Leigh

Not because our hearts are stouter;
Or that we are better men;
Not because we mock the doubter,
Fighting battles with his pen.
Not because our arms are stronger;
Or that we are better born;
But that we can hang on longer,
Even when we're spent and worn.

Not because our Navy's greater
Or our store of shells is more;
Not because our guns are 'later',
Guns alone don't win a war;
Not because our Empire's peerless;
Or that we have got more 'tin';
But, because, when things look cheerless,
We can set our teeth and grin.

ROBBO

Oliver Hogue ('Trooper Bluegum')

George and Bill, Tom and Dick and Harry – all a happy family, having a wonderful time. You never knew what was going to happen next. At any moment your turn might come. You could not tell. You saw old pals in the morning, and you didn't see them in the evening.

Sometimes the mate who had shared your tent and fought alongside you in the trench – the mate who was with you in Egypt, and laughed and joked with you at Anzac – was suddenly snatched away from you, and then you realised what a thin line it is that separates life from death.

Have you ever dreamed that you were standing on the edge of a precipice and that an enemy was racing along to push you over? That was how we felt during these days on Gallipoli. A moment, and then you too might be falling headlong down the precipice. But we found it best not to let our minds dwell upon it.

So we went on burrowing into the side of the hill. We banked up the sides of our dug-outs with sandbags and tins and earth. Most of the fighting was being done in the trenches. In some places they were now 1,500 yards apart, in some only twenty-one feet apart; and in the latter case life was filled with excitement. It was sap and mine and bomb and fusillade all the time.

Opposite page: 'We went on burrowing into the side of the hill.'

My brigade had now been here for some time, and despite the 'accidents' which were always occurring we all had, somehow or other, a feeling of absolute security. We laughed at the Turks, and we smiled at what Liman von Sanders said – that he would drive us into the sea. We were just waiting, content and confident, for the big move that was going to lead to Constantinople!

And as I have said, we were a fairly well-fed army. We had none of the luxuries that the British Expeditionary Force had in France and Flanders. But on the whole we did not do too badly. The brigadier ate the same 'tucker' as his batman.

We were given meat and vegetables and biscuits and cheese and jam. If only we could have had a lump of bread for a change! For the biscuits were so hard that they could be used to defend the trenches, if necessary – either as missiles or as overhead cover. Our Colonel broke one of his teeth on one. So we tried to soak them in our tea. Then we made them into porridge.

There was fighting on land and sea, in the air and under the water. Aeroplane reconnaissance was a daily spectacle. Our airmen would go aloft and have a good look at the enemy's position. The enemy's guns would boom out all the time, and shrapnel shells would burst all round the plane without ever seeming to hit it.

We thought it was great sport watching the white puffs of smoke where the shells burst. Then the aeroplanes would drop bombs on the Turks for spite, 'throw-downs' we called them. Sometimes the position was reversed, and the Germans dropped bombs on us.

Two can play at the same game in war. Take the hand grenades. You should have seen Corporal Renwick take them! Before he became a soldier Renwick was well known on the cricket field – as indeed were hundreds of others – and on Gallipoli he used to catch the bombs and throw them back before they exploded. Nor was he the only one who did this. It was like tossing live coals back and forth – playing with fire.

Some of our boys used to say it was the best 'slips practice' they ever had! Sometimes a bomb would explode prematurely and a man's fingers would be blown off, and worse than that. But the others went on with the game.

And we went swimming down at the beach, just as if it had been Manly or Coogee. Only it was more exciting. Shells took the place of sharks. Instead of the sudden cry one would sometimes hear at Manly or Coogee of ''Ware Shark,' it was ''Ware Shell!'

The Turks are not the surfers that the Australians are. They had little sympathy with such healthy exercise, and they showed their disapproval of it by opening fire on the beach; and then there was a warning whistle, and we all rushed in to shelter. Afterwards we had the pleasure of initiating some Turkish prisoners into the joys of surf bathing, but the majority of them did not take kindly to it.

And all the time the fighting went on. One night we had a great set-to. The Turks mined one of our trenches and rushed in and captured it. This was the affair at Quinn's Post. We counter-attacked and re-took the trench, killed and captured some of the Turks, and then took one their trenches.

Then the hand grenades began to come, and the cricket commenced. It was an exciting match. The Turks made a determined attempt to recapture the position. They charged in strong force, but our chaps all along the line 'hit them to leg'. We enfiladed them with rifle and machine-gun fire, and they were eventually repulsed with a loss of about 2,000.

Wiggins, of the Field Ambulance, was sitting in his dug-out, and two of his mates went out and called to him. He leaned out and said, 'Not yet; the shrapnel hasn't stopped.' Then a shrapnel shell passed between the other two and struck him on the head and killed him.

Life and death! A very thin line ... One never knows. 'In the morning the grass groweth up, in the evening it is cut down and withered.'

One day the word went round that 'Robbo' had been killed. We would not believe it at first. It seemed a silly lie, one of those baseless camp rumours that some fool starts for a joke. Some of the officers went round to see for themselves. Colonel Cox, by the dug-out, looking old and stricken. 'Robbo's killed,' he said. Then we knew it was true. Alas, alas, here was a loss! For 'Robbo' was great.

The Turks had been subjecting us to a heavy bombardment for some days, and our artillery had been responding vigorously.

Mostly their shells buried themselves in the sides of the hills, or exploded somewhat harmlessly in the air. Then one unlucky shrapnel shell burst right over the headquarters of the 6th Light Horse Regiment – and 'Robbo' was there.

Lieutenant Henry Robson lay on the floor of the dug-out, a shrapnel bullet in his breast. And we who had lived with him in camp and on the march for eight strenuous months, sorrowed keenly as will his North Coast friends. To Colonel Cox it was not only the loss of an officer; it was also the loss of an old friend who years before had shared the dangers of battles and the stress of war.

All of us liked Lieutenant Robson. His bark was far worse than his bite. He'd give a shirking soldier the full force of his tongue, but his heart – 'right there' as 'Tipperary' has it – was in the right place.

Kind of heart, genial of temper, and always willing to help others along, we mourn a man that can ill be spared. He was reckoned the best transport officer in Egypt. He knew horses as few men did.

Australians are reputed good horsemen, but poor horsemasters. But Lieutenant Robson was good all round with horses. He would get more work out of a team than anyone I know. He could get a full measure of work from his men also. But he never overdrove man or beast. That's why we liked him.

Harry Robson was forty-eight years of age when he died a soldier's death on Gallipoli Heights. He was one of the original Northern Rivers Lancers, and went to England with the New South Wales Lancers in 1893. Later on he went home with the Lancers under Colonel Cox in 1899.

Standing six feet two in his socks, he was as straight as the lance he carried. He was an expert swordsman, and won several prizes at the tournaments in Scotland and at Islington. At tent-pegging he was an acknowledged champion. On the transport and in Egypt we had many bouts with the sword and singlesticks, but none of the younger officers could worst Robson, although he was old enough to be their father.

When the South African war broke out, he was a Sergeant Major in the New South Wales Lancers under Colonel Cox, they being the first Colonial troops to land at the Cape. He went right through the war, and participated in the battles of Modder River, Magersfontein, Grasspan, Paardeberg, Driefontein and the Relief of Kimberley. He was with French's column during the main advance.

When the 3rd Imperial Mounted Rifles were formed, Lieutenant Robson became transport officer under Colonel Coz, and saw a lot of service in Natal, the Orange Free State and Eastern Transvaal. He participated in Kitchener's big drive, wherein his resourcefulness was of great help to the column.

On one occasion Remington's column was held up by an impassable, boggy morass. The Inniskillens and Canadians were bogged. The Australians halted. Lieutenant Robson improvised a crossing with bales of hay and reeds, and got his transport over while the others were wondering how far round they would have to go. On another occasion in the Transvaal, by a simple device, he crossed the Wilge River with all his mules and wagons at a place reckoned absolutely hopeless for wheeled transport.

After the South African war he settled down on the Northern Rivers, and prospered. But when this great cataclysm convulsed the world, he heard the call of Empire, and responded like a patriot. He wired to Colonel Cox, offering his services, and left the comforts of home for the discomforts of war.

On board the transport he was most painstaking and zealous in the performance of his duties. At Ma'adi he had his transport running as smoothly as a machine. When we found we were going to Gallipoli without our horses, we thought that Lieutenant Robson would be left behind. But at the last moment the regimental quartermaster fell ill, and Robson filled the breach. And so for nine weary weeks of fighting he looked after the needs of the regiment, and not one trooper ever went to bed hungry. (I say 'bed', but none of us has seen a bed for many months.)

As quartermaster, there was no need for him to be poking about the trenches and up in the firing line as he did. But it was not in the firing line he was killed. That is the fortune of war.

He was standing just near headquarters watching the warships gliding over the Aegean Sea. Then came the fatal shell, and 'Robbo' passed out to the Beyond.

SIDELIGHTS OF BATTLE

The Sun, Sydney

'I'll never forget,' says Corporal Carnegie, 'my first feeling after killing a man. I took aim and that, all right, I fired and he fell dead. I shook all over, and felt as if I had murdered him, and then I heard myself saying to my neighbour, "There now, I've killed him, the poor beggar!" You soon get over that, though, and after a short time become as deliberate and callous as possible.

'It is marvellous how short a time war takes to change the make of you. When I arrived in Gallipoli I fancied the men I saw must be a different kind to myself. They paced up and down the trenches looking like wild beasts. You never saw anything like the look in their eyes – wild and staring. And when, after the evacuation, I got back to Cairo, the chaps who had not yet been into action remarked the same expression in my own eyes! So there you are!'

Corporal Carnegie's expression now is the mildest and cheeriest in the world. You cannot imagine that it was ever wildly staring. He, like others, found waiting for the order to charge the most nerve-racking of all war's trials.

'Five minutes to go!

'Three minutes to go!

'Over!

'And then men who have been trembling and fearful leap over the parapet with shouting and laughter.

'I saw a bit of a kid cowering in a corner when the order was given to fire. I took not a bit of notice of him, and my mate said, "All right, leave him alone; he'll be at it presently." And sure enough, in a little while the youngster got up and took his rifle. His face was white as death, but I saw him lean right over the parapet and take aim. His gun was hot before he stopped firing, and the enemies' bullets were kicking the dust up all around him.

'There was another youngster I shan't forget in a hurry. It was his first experience of bombs. One burst in the trench, and he ran just as hard as he could to the end of the sap. Yes, he came back again very ashamed of himself, until I told him, "It's all right, laddie, I've felt that way myself."

'During a bombardment you don't feel in the least excited or nervy. It's the next day, or when you try to sleep, that it gets to you. Dream? I should smile. But they generally give you rum after heavy action, so that you fall into a sound sleep without any trouble.

'I used to duck like anything when first I saw action, but it was not long before I laughed with the rest when a sniper took off the branch of a tree above my head. Funny, when you're going into the firing line you never feel it's yourself won't come back again. You are quite sure you'll get through all right, and you feel sorry for the others when you look round during the service beforehand, and consider that never again will this complete set of men stand round while the chaplain reads.

'Once at Gallipoli we saw a young Turk lying dead in the most beautiful position for firing. He was prone with his rifle sighted. Our fellows waited till night to drag him in and go through his papers. He was only nineteen, and there was a half-written letter in his pocket to his mother. It was in Arabic. In his kit bag we found a nice clean suit of pyjamas, a tin of roast beef, and clothes nicer than our own. His mother must have been fond of that kid.

'We ate the roast beef, and my word it was a treat after Gallipoli bully beef!'

NOT DEAD YET

Joseph L. Beeston

Anzac will be a wonderful place for tourists after the war is over.

For Australians particularly it will have an unbounded interest. The trenches where the men fought will be visible for a long time, and there will be trophies to be picked up for years to come. All along the flat land by the beach there are sufficient bullets to start a lead factory.

The beaches are pleasant and the water is perfect for swimming and fishing.

Our men had a novel way of fishing; they threw a bomb into the water, and the dead fish would either float and be caught or go to the bottom – in which case the water was so clear that they were easily seen. There was one fish that was common, they were something like a mackerel, and were delicious.

One thing that was really good in Anzac was the swimming. At first we used to dive off the barges; then the Engineers built Watson's Pier, at the end of which the water was fifteen feet deep and as clear as crystal, so that one could see every pebble at the bottom. At times the water was very cold, but always invigorating.

General Birdwood was an enthusiastic swimmer, but he always caused me a lot of anxiety. That pier was well covered by Beachy Bill, and one never knew when he might choose to give it his attention. This did not deter the General. He came down most regularly, sauntered out to the end, went through a lot of Sandow exercises and

'Swimming was popular with all hands.' General Birdwood swimming at Anzac Cove.

finally jumped in. He then swam out to a buoy moored about a quarter of a mile away. On his return he was most leisurely in drying himself. Had anything happened to him I don't know what the men would have done, for he was adored by everyone.

Swimming was popular with all hands. Early in the campaign we had a Turkish attack one morning; it was over by midday, and an hour later most of the men were in swimming.

I think it not unlikely that some of the 'missing' men were due to this habit. They would come to the beach and leave their clothes and identity discs ashore, and sometimes they were killed in the water. In this case there was no possibility of ascertaining their names. It often struck me that this might account for some whose whereabouts were unknown.

While swimming, the opportunity was taken by a good many to soak their pants and shirt, inside which there was, very often, more than the owner himself. I saw one man fish his pants out; after examining the seams, he said to his pal, 'They're not dead yet.'

His pal replied, 'Never mind, you gave them a hell of a fright.'

These insects were a great pest, and I would counsel friends sending parcels to the soldiers to include a tin of insecticide; it was invaluable when it could be obtained.

I got a fright myself one night. A lot of things were doing the Melbourne Cup inside my blanket. The horrible thought suggested itself that I had got 'them' too, but a light revealed the presence of fleas. These were very large able-bodied animals and became our constant companions at night-time; in fact one could only get to sleep after dosing the blanket with insecticide.

Another thing that was good all the time on the Peninsula during the campaign was the tea. The brand never wavered, and the flavour was always full. Maynard could always make a good cup of it. It has been already mentioned that water was not at first available on shore. This was soon overcome, thanks to the Navy. They convoyed water barges from somewhere, which they placed along shore; the water was then pumped into our water carts, and the men filled their water-bottles from them. The water, however, never appeared to quench our thirst. It was always better made up into tea, or taken with lime juice when we could get it.

A well-known firm in England puts up a tin which they term an Army Ration, consisting of meat and vegetables, nicely seasoned and very palatable. For a time this ration was eagerly looked for and appreciated, but later on, when the men began to get stale it did not agree with them so well; it appeared to be too rich for many of us. We had plenty of jam, of a kind – one kind. Oh! How we used to revile the maker of 'Damson and Apple'! The damsons coloured it, and whatever they used for apple gave it body.

Tobacco, cigarettes and matches were on issue, but the tobacco was of too light a brand for me, so I used to trade off my share of the pernicious weed for matches. The latter became a precious commodity. I have seen three men light their pipes from one match. Captain Welch was very independent; he had a burning glass, and obtained his light from the sun.

Perhaps the most common stores on the beach were the stacks of 'forty-niner' biscuits which, as I mentioned previously, we used for protection when sandbags were not available.

My little dog Paddy enjoyed the swim almost as much as I did. He was a great favourite with everybody but the Provost Marshal. This official was a terror for red tape, and an order came out that dogs were to be destroyed. That meant that the Military Police were after Paddy. However, I went to General Birdwood, who was very handsome about it, and gave me permission to keep the little chap. Almost immediately after he was reprieved he ran down to the Provost Marshal's dug-out and barked at him. Paddy was very nearly human.

One day we were down as usual when Beachy Bill got busy, and I had to leave the pier with only boots and a smile on. I took refuge behind my old friends the biscuits, and Paddy ran out to each shell, barking until it exploded. Finally one burst over him and a bullet perforated his abdomen. His squeals were piteous. He lived until the next day, but he got a soldier's burial.

No account of the war would be complete without some mention of the good work of the chaplains. They did their work nobly, and gave the greatest assistance to the bearers in getting the wounded down. I came into contact chiefly with those belonging to our own Brigade – Colonel Green, Colonel Wray, and Captain Gillitson, who was killed while trying to get to one of our men who had been wounded.

Services were held whenever possible, and sometimes under very peculiar circumstances.

Once service was being conducted in the gully when a platoon was observed coming down the opposite hill in a position exposed to rifle fire. The thoughts of the audience were at once distracted from what the Padre was expounding by the risk the platoon was running; and members of the congregation pointed out the folly of such conduct, emphasising their remarks by all the adjectives in the Australian vocabulary.

Suddenly a shell burst over the platoon and killed a few men. After the wounded had been cared for, the Padre regained the attention of his congregation and gave out the last verse of 'Praise God from Whom all blessings flow'.

There was one man for whom I had a great admiration – a clergyman in civil life but a stretcher-bearer on the Peninsula – Private Greig McGregor. He belonged to the 1st Field Ambulance, and I frequently saw him. He always had a stretcher, either carrying a man or going for one, and in his odd moments he cared for the graves of those who were buried on Hell Spit. The neatness of many of them was due to his kindly thought. He gained the D.C.M., and richly deserved it.

All the graves were looked after by the departed one's chum. Each was adorned with the Corps' emblems: thus the Artillery used shell caps, the Army Medical Corps a Red Cross in stone, etc.

On 21 August an attack was made on what were known as the W Hills – so named from their resemblance to that letter of the alphabet. Seated on a hill we had a splendid view of the battle.

First the Australians went forward over some open ground at a slow double with bayonets fixed, not firing a shot; the Turks gave them shrapnel and rifle fire, but very few fell. They got right up to the first Turkish trench and all the occupants turned out and retired with more speed than elegance. Still our men went on, taking a few prisoners and getting close to the hills, over which they disappeared from my view.

Next, a battalion from Suvla came across as supports. The Turks meanwhile had got the range to a nicety; the shrapnel was bursting neatly and low and spreading beautifully – it was the best Turkish shooting I had seen. The battalion was rather badly cut up, but a second body came across in more open order than the others, and well under the control of their officers; they took advantage of cover, and so did not lose any men.

The fight was more like those one sees in the illustrated papers than any hitherto – shells bursting, men falling, and bearers going out for the wounded. The position was gained and held, but there was plenty of work for the Ambulance.

We also watched the *Bacchante* do some splendid firing, right into the trenches every time. With one shot, amongst the dust and earth, a Turk went up about thirty feet; arms and leg extended, his body revolving like a Catherine wheel. One saw plenty of limbs go up at different times but this was the only time when I saw a man go aloft *in extenso.*

There were very few horses on the Peninsula, and those few belonged to the Artillery. But at the time I speak of we had one attached to the New Zealand and Australian Headquarters, to be used by the despatch rider.

Anzac, the Headquarters of General Birdwood, was about two and a half miles away; and, being a true Australian, the despatch-carrier declined to walk when he could ride, so he rode every day with despatches. Part of the journey had to be made across a position open to fire from Walker's Ridge.

We used to watch for the man every day, and make bets whether he would be hit. Directly he entered the fire zone, he started as if he were riding in the Melbourne Cup, sitting low in the saddle, while the bullets kicked up dust all round him.

One day the horse returned alone, and everyone thought the man had been hit at last; but in about an hour's time he walked in. The saddle had slipped, and he came off and rolled into a sap, whence he made his way to us on foot.

When going through the trenches it is not a disadvantage to be small of stature. It is not good form to put one's head over the sandbags; the Turks invariably objected, and even entered their protest against periscopes, which are very small in size. Numbers of observers were cut about the face and a few lost their eyes through the mirror at the top being smashed by a bullet.

On one occasion I was in a trench which the men were making deeper. A rise in the bottom of the trench just enabled me, by standing on it, to peer through the loophole.

On commending the man for leaving this lump in the floor of the trench, he replied, 'That's a dead Turk, sir!'

WHEN 'BEACHY' PUTS ONE OVER

Lance Corporal King

Oh, Anzac Beach is a busy place with scores of men at work,
And, though we never man a trench, we help to fight the Turk,
Carrying stores and carting shell, they 'do their bit' and they do it
well.
But it's duck and scatter that the load don't matter,
Drop it, hop it, you don't want to cop it ...
You bet it isn't clover ...
When 'Beachy' Puts One Over.

Indian fellows with their mules, Ghurkas and Maltese,
English and Australian lads, a mixed up crowd are these.
But we've all one thought the same when 'Beachy' starts his game.
It's duck and scatter, where don't matter,
Don't be slow, keep down low, let things go,
Make a dive for cover.
When 'Beachy' Puts One Over.

We mustn't stay down long, there's whips of work to do,
Those chaps up in the firing line need food and water too.
Don't think of looking glum, matters not where you come from,
After the scatter it's a laughing matter,
It's grin, buck in and load that tin,
But again we'll play the rover
When 'Beachy' Puts One Over.

THE BREAKOUT

ANZAC ALPHABET

'IFSH'

A is for Anzac, renowned evermore,
B is for Beachy who bursts on the shore.
C is for Colic which follows directly,
D is for Dose taken paregorectly.
E is for Exercise climbing the hills,
F for Fatigues which come faster than bills.
G is the German who makes the Turk fight,
H is for Hell which we hope is his plight.
I is for Indian, excellent fellow,
J is for Jaundice which makes us turn yellow.
K is for Kobber, Australian for friend,
L the Last Post which comes right at the end.
M is for Mule who's as game as a sparrow,
N is the Nuisance of saps much too narrow.
O is for Oaths, some of which are ripsnorters,
P is the Pain they produce at headquarters.
Q is the Quiver that runs down your back,
R the big Rooster which shells from Chanak
S the Soft Jobs you get back at base,
T is for Turk who's a pretty tough case.
U is for Underground where we all rest,
V is for Vickers, the man-killing pest.
W the Whisky we sigh for in vain,
X for Xcitement, 'The mail's in again!'
Y is for 'Yes' if we're asked to go home,
Z is for Zero, we're chilled to the bone!

LONE PINE

William Baylebridge

Of all those battles fought by our troops at Anzac, none was more fierce, and few were more bloody, than that waged at Lone Pine.

Shut too long in their trenches, with little room to pass beyond them and taking death, night and day, from the shells the Turks hurled into their lines, our troops' only desire was to be out and upon the move. Not only did Australian bayonets bring it through to a right end, but such things as were done there put Australian courage forever past doubt.

Lone Pine stood against the centre of our line. It was high land and so strong was the Turks' position there, both in defence-works and men, that any soldier, skilled in his trade, would have thought it impossible to be taken at all. The Turkish front trenches were roofed in with heavy logs which were covered up with earth. Shelling, from our guns and ships, had little effect there.

Machine-guns were set into the Turkish front line and room had been made there for snipers and for those who threw bombs out. In front of all these traps lay an ugly tangle of barbed wire. The open land further out was swept clean by rifle fire from both ends of the ridge, for the Turks controlled a dozen positions further north, and also many to the south. Turkish artillery had the accurate range of this country to a hair.

On the afternoon of the sixth day of August, a great bombardment of shellfire, from our ships behind us and our batteries on land, was

'The open land further out was swept clean by rifle fire.'

poured into the wire and the Turkish back trenches at Lone Pine. These back trenches were not covered up and great numbers of Turks had been gathered there to defend that position. Those back trenches were soon choked up with dead and wounded.

While this was going on the Turkish gunners, shooting as often as they might, gave back something of what they got. With the roaring of guns, and the screech of that flying shell, there was little peace that afternoon. But then, all at once, our guns ceased firing and the charge was blown. Like hounds loosed from a leash, off raced our men: with bayonets fixed, up and over the parapet they leapt, and charged.

That charge might well have stirred the blood in any man! Those men raced toward the enemy trenches, spat upon by rifle fire from every loophole, cut down by machine-guns, torn through by a rain of shrapnel, and not one hesitated. Thick they fell but they cared not. Believe me, it was not hard, later, to see the way they had gone, so heavy-sown it was with men dead.

Thinned out, but with Australian hearts yet, those who could swept on, pushed through the twisted wire, and swarmed at last up the parapet of the Turks. Once up and on that parapet, did these Australians wait? No, they tore up the roof from those front trenches and leapt down into a darkness ripe with death.

Then was there bloody work! In and home went their steel; it had a thirst in it for the blood of those Turks. Then did they fight like the men they were, now thrusting, now holding off, now twisting, now turning, now wrenching out their bayonets from this crush of flesh, now dropping down with their limbs shattered, with their bowels slit and torn out by the foe.

Along through those trenches, dark and stinking, men fought hand to hand. Many, with clubbed rifle, spilt out the brains of others, trodden soon to mud on the floor there. Bombs, knives, whatever came next to hand, both foe and friend brought into use. The bombs, bursting in little room, did great hurt: many a press of tough men they tore up, limb away from limb, making a right sickening mess.

Here and there the Turks got together in knots so that they might better hold out; but the steel of Australia ploughed a passage through those trenches. Little then did it help those Turks to know every corner, each turn and short cut, of that place; little then did their valour help them. As the two sides fought on in the heat and choking stench of that darkness, the dead lay thick under foot, here two-deep, three-deep there, and there four-deep.

Now, you have heard how these men of Australia, that tore the roof up and off those trenches, got *their* part done. While all this was doing, there were others who took those Turks in the rear. These men had charged on over the roofed trenches and struck out for the trenches behind. Coming up to these trenches – filled now with the death our guns had dealt – they pushed in, and sealed up behind them the passages that linked the back trenches with the front lines, so that the Turks could by no means get out.

Thus, taking the foe both in front and upon the rear, our steel drove them in and back upon themselves, and slew them like sheep in some accursed shambles. Too many of our own men as well were slain there! Neither friend nor foe escaped and the trenches were choked up with dead men and dying.

So thick lay the dead that we later piled them to the height of a tall man, and had to prop them up behind logs, and hold them up out of the trench with ropes, so that one side of the passage might be kept clear. Never, surely, was there a battle fought more fiercely hand to hand!

Our men, at last, got the better of those Turks. Those still alive and stirring, we drove up out of the ground and fell upon. Some we slew fighting; some, making off as they best might through the open, we caught with our machine-guns; some we pushed up into saps where they were glad to give over.

As for their counter-attacks, the Turks made many, and in fine style; but, though these attacks cost us many good men, they cost the foe more, and were but lost labour.

Three days and three nights this battle lasted. The loss upon our side was a hard loss – we buried above 2,000 slain.

As for the men who fought in this battle, all were infantry. There were men of the 1st Brigade in the first attack and, in the relief and making good the victory, men of the 2nd Brigade.

THE 3RD BATTALION'S RUM

H. W. Cavill

There is one humorous incident connected with the famous Lone Pine charge that deserves to be recorded; that is the story of the 3rd Battalion's rum.

The officers of the 3rd Battalion were addressed by their Colonel the evening before the fight, and one of the matters that came up to be decided was that of rum. Two issues of rum were due on the day of the fight, and the question was when should they be given.

The Colonel was an old Australian soldier of the Instructional Staff – one of the finest fighters at Gallipoli. He was wounded three times in the next twenty-four hours and was carried dying from the trenches he had won.

At this conference, the night before the fight, he laid down his view: 'I believe the issue will be a good tonic to the men in their present condition,' he said, 'but I do not like the idea of giving it to men just before they go into action. We will have one issue in the morning, and the other after the fight is over.'

It was next day, about two hours after the charge, when a man with a demijohn on his shoulder came along, up Shrapnel Valley and into the firing line trenches. The Brigadier himself was at the mouth of that sap receiving messages. He was trying to clear the sap to let some of the most urgent traffic through. All traffic to the front had to pass through thirty yards of narrow, pitch dark tunnel, and then out over the heath, facing the gauntlet up to the parapet of the Turkish trench.

Endless lines of men with ammunition, men with bombs, men with water, men with picks, shovels, sandbags, signallers, messengers, engineers, stretcher-bearers, were filing at funeral pace into it, and the whole tunnel was constantly blocked, while they carried one or two poor badly wounded fellows back.

I remember one pitiful procession that emerged from it, after at least ten minutes' struggle through the dark interior – first a seriously wounded man in a folding cane stretcher, next an army medical man, and after him, crawling on hands and knees out of the tunnel and down the trench towards the rear, another wounded man.

Only those men whose presence was urgent were allowed to go through afterwards.

'What are you carrying?'

'Bombs, sir.'

'Well, put them down here a moment, and stand by until that tunnel is clearer.'

'And what are you carrying, my man?'

'The 3rd Battalion's rum, sir.'

'What?'

'The 3rd Battalion's rum, sir. Colonel put me in charge of it, and told me to see the ...'

'Well, put it down here, and stand by.'

'The Colonel told me to take it through, sir.'

'Well, put it down here for the present.'

'The Colonel told me ...'

'Look here! Never mind what you were told; put it down there at once!'

The rum carrier put his heavy load down on the first step, and retired, obviously unsatisfied, for the moment. The Colonel had told him the men would want their rum, and it was his duty to see it through. For a couple of minutes he watched the Brigade staff dealing with infinitely more important messages.

Then, the first time the Brigadier looked up, he stepped forward again.

'How 'bout the 3rd Battalion's rum, sir?'

'Oh, well, get along with you,' answered the Brigadier, amusedly.

And so he shouldered it and trudged out contently towards the heath and towards the bullets, and, I suppose, the 3rd Battalion got its rum.

LOVE LETTER XXXI

Oliver Hogue ('Trooper Bluegum')

Ryrie's Post,
Anzac.
7 August 1915

My Bonnie Jean,

There are big things doing on Gallipoli now. It may be – nay, it should be – the beginning of the end. The whole plan has been admirably conceived by Sir Ian Hamilton, and the Staff work has been excellent down to the minutest detail. It now only remains to be seen if our tactics are equal to our strategy.

Yesterday was a day of glorious achievement: of victory in one place and defeat in another; of terrific fighting, heavy bombardment, wild charges over storm-swept fields, night charges up and down precipitous hills and gullies. It was a day of slaughter for Turkey and of losses that will fill many Australian homes with grief unutterable.

Oh, the pity of it all, Sweetheart! Hundreds of fine young fellows in the prime of life – now lying huddled inert khaki lumps on the bloody field.

It was a fourfold plan of attack. First there was an artillery duel with all the guns on Gallipoli waxing wrathful. Our guns blazed away at the Turkish trenches and in defences, but I reckon the bombardment was not nearly long enough nor strong enough. The terrific fire which opened on our boys the moment they charged was proof of that.

Second: There was the work of the gallant Australian Division; a demonstration on the right, attack on Lone Pine in the centre, and on the left an attempt at German Officers' trenches and Walker's Ridge.

Third: The New Zealand and Australian Division on the left of the Anzac semi-circle made a magnificent drive, pushing the Turks before them over hill and dale, capturing several lines of trenches, stores and ammunition, and almost doubling the area held by the Army Corps.

Fourth: Those three, big efforts though they were, constituted the minor phase of the big battle of Sari Bair. The fourth and main phase of the operation was the landing of a new force of two Divisions of British troops at Suvla Bay, with a view to stretching a cordon across the Peninsula and crumpling up the right wing of the Turkish Army, which was already shattered by the victorious

© AWM G01126

'The Turkish front trenches were roofed in with heavy logs which were covered up with earth.' Anzac troops in the captured trenches at Lone Pine.

pursuit of the New Zealand and Australian Division. The sequel will show if this eventuated.

Such, my dear, as clearly as I can make it out, was the big battle of Sari Bair, which began yesterday, is now raging furiously on the left, and may last for days and days. You will see by the casualty lists – which doubtless have reached home by this – that our brigade has but few casualties, and got but little honour and glory out of the affair. For we held the extreme right of our line with our outpost resting on the sea just north of Gaba Tepe.

All the 2nd Light Horse Brigade and the 3rd Infantry Brigade had to do was to hold their line, make a demonstration, and bring enfilading fire to bear on the Turks on Pine Ridge, when they attacked the right of the 1st Brigade. Most of our casualties were caused by shellfire, for according to his invariable custom, the enemy plastered the whole of our lines with shrapnel and high explosives.

The other two Light Horse Brigades, 1st and 3rd, got right into the thick of it. The 3rds had an almost impossible task to perform, and though they charged with magnificent gallantry against the Turkish position, they withered away under a scathing fire from a swarm of machine-guns and a well-directed hail of musketry.

The 1sts, in spite of the splendid charge and the capture of three lines of trenches, were gradually driven back by successive Turkish counter-attacks, and finally bombed back to their original position with seventy-five per cent of casualties and only one officer unscathed out of all who sallied forth.

The historians will tell of the dogged but unsuccessful attempt of the 2nd Infantry Brigade to capture the German Officers' trench, and of the stirring capture of the almost impregnable Lone Pine position. I did not see the former. I did see the latter and can still see the scores of khaki figures so still and silent in front of the Turkish trenches. All dead Australians, fine young fellows, who a day ago were full of lusty life.

The 1st Australian Infantry Brigade – our own lads from sunny New South Wales – have covered themselves with glory in this exploit. It was magnificent the way those lads charged, even though they knew that hundreds must perish in the charge.

Talk about the Charge of the Light Brigade!! Well, all I've got to say is that this war will make us readjust the estimates of old-time battles and exploits. The capture of Lone Pine was a feat of arms that the Pretorian Guard or Cromwell's Ironsides or Napoleon's Old Guard would have gloried in having to their credit. We who watched were spellbound.

The irregular khaki line charged with reckless indifference to the hail of shrapnel and rifle fire and machine-guns. A well-trained regiment of Gay Gordons or Grenadiers or Fusiliers would have charged in a beautiful line – and probably would have been mown down like wheat before the scythe. But our chaps don't fight that way. They raced forward as individuals, not as a battalion. Each man's initiative spurred him on to do deeds of valour with his own hand. But for this their casualties would have been far greater.

We saw them falter just for a second – but it was only to hack the barbed wire out of their path. Then they jumped into the trenches and slaughtered the Turks with the bayonet. Oh, Honey, it was magnificent! It was War. Once again we Light Horsemen stand and salute and do honour to our comrades of the Infantry.

When the heroic band reached the Turkish trenches they found them protected with overhead cover, pine logs and brushwood and earth, with only an opening here and there. But with magnificent daring our boys bayoneted the defenders, jumped down among the swarming Turks and plied the bayonet like demons.

Then our supporting columns, dashing across the intervening hell, overran the first line of trenches, captured the second defence, captured or bayoneted the inmates, linked up with the storming party, and Lone Pine was ours ... A hundred years hence the people of Australia will talk with bated breath of the glorious charge. Our 2nd Light Horse Brigade and the 2nd Infantry Brigade held the ridge against all the furious counter-attacks of the Turks, but it was the gallant 1sts who deserve the most of the glory.

Yours till the end of all things,

J.B.

EDDY ANZAC'S HOMING SONG

Anon

Way out in Australyer we heard the fightin' call,
So we quit the footie ground and dingy picture hall.
Said goodbye to mother, shook everybody's hand
And then we humped our packs and guns to Abdul's blighted
    land.

CHORUS
But, Oh, Gawd, 'ow we miss old Australyer!
The land that we all call our own.
We miss the beaches, the wide open spaces,
And the bush where we used to roam!
Though tough has been the job, still we didn't quail.
We couldn't let Old England stand alone.
Yet we'll cheer like 'ell on the day we sail,
To our sunny southern home.

We found it weren't no picnic, life not all deluxe,
(Even blooming officers lived minus frills and tucks)
Our French and Tommy cobbers were showin' wear and tear,
An' us Aussie blokes are 'ere to do our bleeding share!

CHORUS

But one day you will see us on the transports out at sea –
As we say goodbye to Johnny Turk and cursed Gallipoli!
When Suez is behind us an' Colombo fades away,
We'll know that we are almost home and this is what we'll say!

CHORUS

THE WOUNDED CORPORAL'S STORY

E. C. Buley

We lay under cover in the dark waiting for the word to go. Every man had his bayonet fixed and his magazine empty. The work before us had to be done with cold steel. The Turks had three lines of trenches on the hill slope opposite.

Suddenly I became aware of a stir among the Maoris on my left; I was right up against them. Next to me was a full-blooded Maori chief, a young fellow of sixteen stone, as big and powerful as a bullock, a lineal descendant of fighting Rewi, the Maori chief from whom all the legends descend.

Once Rewi and his tribe were surrounded by a force of white men who outnumbered them three to one. The whites had got between them and the stream of water on the top of the hill, which is unfair fighting according to Maori rules. Then they sent a message to Rewi bidding him surrender. He replied, 'Ka Whawhai Tonu, Ak'y Ak'y Ak'y.' (We fight on and on; for ever and for ever and for ever.) 'Then send away the women and children,' was the next suggestion. 'The women fight too,' says brave old Rewi. An hour later the Maoris rushed out of the trap with Rewi at the head of them and before the astonished whites knew what was doing they had cut a way through and escaped.

This descendant of Rewi's is a different sort of chap. He has two good university degrees and is a lay preacher. I once saw him in a frock coat and silk hat, talking on the virtues of cleanliness and the nobility of hard work.

But now he had dressed for the occasion in a pair of running shoes and shorts which covered about eight inches of the middle of him. I could see his brown skin glistening with perspiration in the dim light as we waited for the whistle to blow and send us over the top. His head was moving from side to side and his lips were twitching. From time to time he beat the earth softly with his clenched fist.

Then I got the rhythm of it and realised what was happening. I suppose those 500 Maoris picked me up into their silent war song.

I know the words of the Haka well, and though they could not dance it they were beating out the measure of it with their fists on the ground. After each soft thump I could feel that their bodies strained forward like dogs on a leash. They caught me up in their madness and I longed to be at it. I thumped the ground with them, and prayed to be up and dancing, or out and fighting.

Their eyes were rolling and their breath was coming in long, rhythmical sobs. The groaning sound of it was quite audible; in another minute they would have been up on their feet, dancing their wild war dance. But then came the signal; and Hell was let loose.

'Ake, Ake,' they shouted, 'we fight for ever and for ever.'

Up to the first trench they swept. I could hear some of them yelling, 'Kiki ta Turk' ('Kick the Turk'). Those were the fellows who had kept on their heaviest boots, and meant to use their feet. God help the Turk who got a kick from a war-mad Maori.

Our blood was up; I know mine was. We were not far behind them to the first trench, and you never saw such a sight in your life.

The Turks had been bashed to death; there is no other word for it. We got up to them at the second trench, where there was a deadly hand-to-hand going on. Some of them had broken their rifles and were fighting with their hands. I saw one Maori smash a Turk with half-a-hundredweight of rock he had torn up.

I don't remember much more, because I was in the thick of it myself by then, that's why I am here in the hospital.

I don't know anything more at first-hand but I hear a good many of them came back, though I shouldn't have thought it possible. The Turks who escaped will not wait next time when they hear the Maoris coming ... and you can hear them coming all right.

THE MIGHTY NEW ZEALANDERS

E. C. Buley

The men of New Zealand had to defend the extreme left of the Australasian lines along Walker's Ridge, facing almost due north. During the month of July, too, the New Zealanders took over the defence of Quinn's Post, and by very skilful sapping operations made that once dangerous post one of the safest places in the whole camp.

Farther north than Walker's Ridge itself, the New Zealanders also held two isolated posts known as Outpost No. 1 and Outpost No. 2. Communication with the main lines from these outposts was maintained through deep saps, which had been dug by the New Zealanders themselves.

Outpost No. 2 was held by the 500 Maori and was sometimes known as Maori Outpost. This place was used as a base for stores; and here in the first days of August an immense amount of munitions and food was accumulated. At this outpost, during the night of 5 August, the men of New Zealand and the 4th Brigade of Australian infantry were massed for the attack which began on 6 August.

Between this point and the great hill of Sari Bair (Hill 971) were a number of high points, among which were two flat-topped hills known as Greater and Lesser Tabletop and also Bauchop's Hill. The sides of these hills were almost perpendicular, and a network of trenches made them impregnable if held by any considerable force

'Outpost No. 2 was held by the 500 Maori.' Maori art at Anzac.

of men. In the early days of August it became known that very few men occupied these defensive trenches, and one of the objects of the attack of 6 August was to take these positions by surprise.

After dark on 6 August, the New Zealanders and the 4th Brigade of Australians marched out from Maori Outpost, stepping silently through the scrub in a northerly direction. From the beach a series of gullies, running at right angles to the shore, give an entry to the hill slopes that lead up to the main ridges of Sari Bair and Chunuk Bair, the highest points of the mountain mass separated by a deep ravine.

Up these gullies the New Zealanders made their way, clearing the enemy out of the trenches dug to bar the approaches to Sari Bair. Charging up one gully, the men of Wellington surprised and captured the Tabletop hills. Up a parallel gully the Auckland Mounted Rifles went and took possession of Rhododendron Ridge.

The Maoris charged up yet a third gully, to take Bauchop's Hill and the trenches beyond it. The fierceness of that charge, when they swept every Turk out of their path, has become legendary among the men of Anzac. The impetuosity of the charge carried them right through their own gully and into that which the men of Auckland had taken.

They came over a spur of the hills, yelling with excitement, and seeing in the dim light that a trench before them was occupied by armed men, rushed upon it, shouting their war cry. The men before them were the men of Auckland, who at once recognised the war cries of the Maoris. Fortunately the average New Zealander has a fair smattering of the Maori tongue, and the Auckland men shouted at them what phrases of Maori they could summon up in such an emergency, and the charge was stopped right on the parapet of the trench.

By such wild fighting the men of New Zealand steadily won their way upwards, through the tangle of gullies and steep hillsides toward the crest of the big hill. By day they hung on doggedly to the positions they had won, resisting attacks by bayonet and bomb. By night they moved stealthily on, through dense scrub and broken country, converging by parallel paths toward the desired crest of the hill.

No words can paint the gallantry of the fighting on those four days and 9 August saw a gallant little band of New Zealanders planting their artillery flags on the trench that spans the summit of Chunuk Bair. From that vantage point the bold pioneers could see all they had striven for through many weary weeks of constant fighting.

Away to the south-east were the forts of the Narrows. At their very feet ran the road from Gallipoli town to the main Turkish position at Achi Baba. They could see the trains of mules and the transport vehicles passing along this road. The goal of all their efforts was there, The Dardanelles, in their full sight. To their right and left, on higher crests, the Turks were massed in force, determined to drive them from Chunuk Bair.

Desperately the New Zealanders hung on to what they had gained, until support should come. Their attempt to hold that hilltop is one of the most glorious deeds in all the annals of war. Eventually the best of the Turkish commanders, Mustafa Kemal, led a huge force against them.

Finally, after sixteen New Zealanders kept a long section of trench against a whole host of enemies for three hours, the position was abandoned and the New Zealanders had to retire. Many would rather have died where they were ... and a good many of them did so.

The losses of those four days can best be judged by reference to the casualty lists. The Auckland Mounted Rifles, 800 strong on the day of 6 August, had thirty-seven uninjured men at roll-call on 11 August.

Over 400 New Zealand wounded spent those four days in a place they christened the Valley of Torment. It was a deep depression in the hillside on the rugged side of Sari Bair. On one side of it rose a perpendicular cliff that would have defied a mountain goat to climb it. On the other rose the steep declivity of Rhododendron Ridge.

The only way in and out was from above, where the New Zealanders were fighting like possessed beings for the foothold they had won on the crest of Sari Bair. Below, the valley opened out upon a flat plateau, so swept by the guns of both sides that no living thing could exist for one moment upon its flat, open surface.

To this valley the stretcher-bearers carried the men who had fallen in the fight, a sad little group of wounded men whose numbers increased hourly. Those less severely injured crawled there and unwounded soldiers carried their stricken mates there for shelter from the hail of bullets.

A devoted band of Red Cross men lent them what aid they could, stayed their wounds with bandages, tied tourniquets round limbs to check the flow of arterial blood, and made tortured men as easy as circumstances would permit. There was no doctor nearer then the dressing station on the beach.

The approach to this valley was so dangerous to attempt by daylight and there was no water there, until one man dug into a moist spot far down the valley, and chanced on a spring that yielded a trickle of brackish water.

By midday on 8 August, 300 men, suffering from all the terrible manglings that exploding bombs and high explosive shells can inflict, were in this place of refuge, and more were continually arriving. Some sought to cheer the rest by predicting a great victory as the result of the attack. Here and there a man could be heard reciting verses to those who would listen.

No one moaned, and no one uttered a complaint. When a man died of his wounds they expressed their thanks that he had been spared further pain. As the little spring filled, each man would have his lips moistened with the brackish water.

When night at last came, the weary stretcher-bearers tried to move some of them over the ridge to a safer valley on the other side. But these men had been working for days and nights without rest and the task was beyond their strength, for the steepness and roughness of that hillside is beyond description.

The next day came with a hot sun, and clouds of flies. Also there came many more wounded to the Valley of Torment, until the number exceeded 400.

That day many died and among those who lived, the torture from tourniquets that had been left too long on wounded limbs became unendurable. Many of them will never recover the free use of their limbs.

At last that day ended too, and evening brought a cool breeze. Then they heard, from the safe gully that lay beyond the ridge, the stealthy approach of many men in the dark. One of them, out of thankfulness, began to sing the hymn –

At even, 'ere the sun was set,
The sick, O Lord, around Thee lay.

Nearly all of them took up the singing and, while they were still singing, over the ridge came large number of soldiers who put them all on stretchers. The newcomers, some thousands in number, ranged themselves in two rows that stretched up the crest of the ridge and down the other side into the safe gully.

Each stretcher was passed from hand to hand, to the safety on the other side where a long procession was formed, bearing the wounded down to the sea. Two miles it stretched from start to finish and so the wounded men of New Zealand were carried out of the Valley of Torment.

I have met many of the men who suffered there; and I know that in their eyes the real tragedy is not the torture they experienced. It is that their comrades eventually had to withdraw from the hilltops that had been won by so much loss of life.

THE ANZAC V.C.

Oliver Hogue ('Trooper Bluegum')

As there passes before my mind's eye a kaleidoscopic picture of the wild fighting of the early days of Anzac, and the rough and tumble jumble of Lone Pine, I can't help thinking of the luck of the game.

Were honour to bestow her crowns on those who had a right to
    them,
The skull upon the battlefield would often wear a diadem.

So many unknown heroes lie buried on Anzac. So many passed the crucial test of supreme trial and with strong arm and true heart performed prodigies of valour – but no one saw them.

As a rule there was hardly time to take stock of everything. Time and again did individual Australians do great deeds, but the historians will never know of it. They are mostly too modest to talk of it and the officers who might have reported and recommended are dead.

Take that wonderful landing on the fateful day, 25 April, when Australia made such a gloriously picturesque début. How many men of MacLagan's gallant 3rd Brigade in that never-to-be-forgotten charge up the heights deserved the greatest military honour that the King can bestow? Many of those men really deserved the V.C. but so many officers were picked off, who was to know? The only solution seemed to be the conferring of the coveted medal on the whole Brigade. But there was no precedent for this. So none of them got it.

Our first Australian V.C. was Jacka of the 4th Brigade. He was young and didn't have the splendid tall physique of most of the Australians, but he was greased lightning with the bayonet. It all happened on Courtney's Post. The Turks had been sapping in towards the front trench, and after a shower of bombs they swarmed in and captured the trench. Lance Corporal Jacka, posted behind the traverse in the fire trench, blocked their advance. An officer and a few men hurried up and volunteers were immediately ready to eject the intruders.

Then, while the officer and three men engaged in a bombing exchange with the enemy, Albert Jacka jumped from the front trench into the communication trench behind, ran round and took the Turks in the rear. He shot five of them and bayoneted two. The officer's party then charged and shot the four remaining Turks who tried to escape. They found Jacka leaning up against the side of the trench with flushed face, a bloody bayonet in the end of his rifle and an unlighted cigarette in his mouth.

The boys who took Lone Pine in that fine charge, amid a shower of lead and shrapnel such as the war had not previously seen, got no V.C. for their valour. But the lads who held the hard-won post against all the subsequent counter-attacks did manage to secure a few. One of these was Captain Shout. But he never lived to wear the cross. For three long days and longer nights he participated in the furious hand-to-hand fighting in Lone Pine.

Captain Shout with his bombing gang was ubiquitous. Laughing and cheering them on he time and again drove the Turks back, and then when he reached a point where the final sandbag barrier was to be erected, he tried to light three bombs at once and throw them amongst the crowding Turks. To throw a single bomb is a risky job. To throw three bombs simultaneously was a desperate expedient. One exploded prematurely, shattered both his hands, laid open his cheek and destroyed an eye, besides minor injuries. Conscious and still cheerful he was carried away. But he died shortly afterwards.

The heroic 7th Battalion – victorious Victorians – participated in the great charge of the 2nd Australian Infantry Brigade down at Helles, the charge that made the French and English marvel at the dash of the young colonials. Four men of the 7th Battalion – Captain Fred Tubb, Lieutenant Symons, Corporal Dunstan and Corporal Burton – won the V.C. at Lone Pine.

On the night of 8 August, while the British troops in the Suvla area were struggling to wrest the hills from the Turks, the Turks round Lone Pine were vainly endeavouring to recapture this stronghold from the Australians. On the right of the 7th Battalion, things were particularly sultry, and early on the morning of the ninth some determined attacks resulted in six of our officers and several men being killed and wounded. A bit of the front sap was lost, but Lieutenant Symons headed a charge, retook the sap, shot two of the Turks with his revolver and finally erected a barricade which defied all the attacks of the enemy who set fire to the overhead cover in the hope of driving back the 7th. But the fire was extinguished and the position held for good.

It was give and take, attack and counter-attack all through 9 August, that showed the qualities of pluck and determination which won the V.C. for Captain F. H. Tubb, Corporal Dunstan and Corporal Burton. Three times the enemy attacked with bombs, blew up our barricades, and swarmed into the trench, but each time Tubb and his companions returned to the assault, repulsed the invaders, rebuilt the barricades, and in spite of a shower of bombs held the post. Captain Tubb was wounded in the head and arm, but stuck to his job throughout.

Lance Corporal Keyzor was one of a band of heroes who did wonders in the hell-zone at the south-eastern corner of Lone Pine. It was a murder hole and after much slaughter we found that we could not hold the outer trench, while the enemy found that he also was unable to hold it. Finally it was abandoned as No Man's land.

As a bomb-thrower, Keyzor was pre-eminent. He was one of those who repeatedly caught the enemy's bombs and hurled them back before they could explode. It was here that Colonel Scobie was killed shortly afterwards, and here it was that for days and nights

Keyzor moved amongst the showers of bombs with dead and dying all around, and threw bombs till every muscle ached and he could not lift his arm.

John Hamilton was very young, just nineteen. But lots of these young Australians had old heads on their young shoulders. It was at Lone Pine, where the 3rd Battalion was defending a section of the line against the repeated attacks of the Turks, that young Hamilton won the coveted honour. He climbed on to the top of the parapet and with a few sandbags as a precarious shield against bombs and bullets he stayed there for five solid hours sniping merrily, potting off any stray Turks that showed up, and giving warning to the officer below each time the enemy started out to attack. There was plenty of shrapnel flying and the zip of bullets into the sandbags grew monotonous. But young Hamilton hung on.

It was away on the left of our line at Hill 60 that Lieutenant Throssell of the 10th Light Horse performed his great act of valour. There was one section of the enemy's line that obstinately defied the Australasian attack. At last the 3rd Light Horse Brigade received orders that the redoubt had to be taken. The Brigadier sent the 10th Light Horse Regiment out to do the job.

*   *   *

Just after midnight – 28–29 August – the Westralians suddenly leaped on to the parapet and charged ahead. They were met with a hail of machine-gun and rifle fire and a shower of bombs, but nothing could stop those horseless horsemen. A brief melee on and in the Turkish trenches and the position was won. But holding it was a far more difficult matter. Lieutenant Throssell, in charge of the digging party, worked overtime putting the new line in a state of defence.

Soon the Turks massed for the inevitable counter-attack, and Throssell, with Captain Fry and a troop of the Light Horse, repulsed the first charge. But just as dawn was breaking the Turks came again with a shower of bombs as a prelude. The grenades were smothered as they fell or were thrown back again, but Captain Fry

'These attacks cost us many good men, they cost the foe more'.

paid the final penalty. One bomb rolled over the parapet into the trench, and spluttered. The men yelled, 'Let it rip.' But the only safe thing to do was to smother the bomb or heave it out. The gallant Captain chose the latter alternative, but the bomb exploded and killed him.

The holding of this threatened elbow of the line devolved upon Throssell, who rose manfully to the occasion. With his rifle he shot half a dozen Turks and with his cheery example he heartened his command, and the enemy attacked in vain. Twice indeed they swarmed in and the Light Horsemen had to give ground. But only a few yards and a fresh barricade was immediately erected. Early in the afternoon Throssell was wounded in the shoulder. But he kept on. At four o'clock he got another bullet in the neck, but still he kept on. Just after nightfall relief came and his superior officer sent him back to the field hospital.

There were other Australians who gained the V.C., Captain William Cosgrove of the Royal Munster Fusiliers, who did such a fine performance down at Helles, and others. But other historians will tell of their deeds. Corporal Bassett of the New Zealand Signallers won his V.C. for a daring exploit – laying a telephone wire right on to Chunuk Bair in broad daylight under a heavy fire.

Scores of the boys did big things that in lesser wars would have won distinction. Here they just were numbered with the unknown heroes. Every man on Lone Pine deserved special honour.

If they had been Germans they would have been covered with Iron Crosses. As it is they are just satisfied that they were able to do their job. Anyhow, Australia won't forget Lone Pine.

THE NAKED ARMY

Tom Skeyhill

Not since the prehistoric stone ages has such an army been seen in warfare as the Australian Army Corps now fighting on the Gallipoli peninsula. These suntanned, athletic colonials display an utter abhorrence for superfluous clothing. In marked contrast to the British regulars, who never discard clothing no matter under what circumstances they are fighting, the Australians are becoming famous throughout Europe for their hard-fighting, hard-swearing and nakedness, even up to a point of indecency.

Egyptian English Press, 1915

[The following poem was written in response to this article]

We've forgotten all our manners and our talk is full of slang,
For there ain't no time for grammar when you hear the rifles
*   bang.*
We never wear our tunics, unless it's cold at night,
And shirts and socks and puttees? Well, we chucked them outa
*   sight.*
The heat here, and the vermin, had drove us nearly barmy,
So we peeled off all our clobber and we're called 'The Naked Army'.

We only wear a pair of shorts that don't reach to our knees
And we're burnt as brown as berries, but we'd sooner sun than
*   fleas!*
The rookie, when first landed, hangs on to all his clothes,
But, when the greybacks bite him, it's to the beach he goes.
Then off come shirt and tunic, boots, socks and puttees too,
And he dives into the briny and does what the others do.

For the air and sun won't hurt you, in this land of fleas and strife,
So we chucked away our clobber, we prefer the simple life.
If our girls could only see us, the way we're fighting here,
I wonder if they'd hug us, and smile and call us 'dear'.
Perhaps they will still love us, although we're burnt and lean,
But we'll all need a girl who has a sewing machine.

THE FINAL PHASE

ON POST

'Tambour 8'

Peepin' through a loophole during weary hours of night
Listenin' till yer eardrums nearly crack.
Waitin' for the Corporal to bring the new relief,
Bendin' till the pains run down your back;
Starin' till your eyeballs are just about to roll,
What a lovely life for men to lead;
Who would be on sentry post along the Anzac line,
With bully beef and biscuits for yer feed?

Standin' up with leaden feet and toes that can't be felt;
Boots wet through and stickin' to the bank –
Nose tip like the apex of a blanky icicle,
Hair all wet and clingin' thick and dank:
Teeth that chatter freely in the bitter bitin' cold,
Jove! I used ter think that home was bad,
Now I'm doing sentry post along the Anzac line
Strewth! A bloomin' bloke like me is mad.

When the flamin' snow came down the other blanky night
I was draped in white from head to feet;
I musta been a picture to the officer of the watch,
When he came along to do his beat.
When I think of all me pals and cobbers stayin' home
And all the things us blokes have given up;
How I'm freezing doing sentry post along the Anzac line
When I mighta been in Melbourne for The Cup.

But, what's the good of grumblin' at blokes that stayed at home?
When I think of mates like Jim and Ted,
Down in Shrapnel Gully with a little wooden cross,

It sorta makes me cooler in the head.
I'm still doing sentry post along the Anzac line,
But, maybe, when I've seen me last big 'show',
I'll be down there in the gully somewhere near me two old pals,
And that's the last 'rest post' to which I'll go.

ABSOLUTELY!

Roy Bridges

'What nationality are you?' asked a smiling nurse, as she stood by his bedside in Alexandria. His hand went up stiffly in salute. 'Australian, miss!' he answered proudly.

'That name'll carry you through anywhere,' he adds today, chatting to me about his experiences in the last few months of 1915.

I ask him why he enlisted, and how he came to get through, for his grizzled hair, and burnt, weather-beaten face suggest that he is well past the prescribed age of forty-five years.

'It was this way,' he says. 'I was walking down the street one morning – it was 21 January – when a little boy came running up to me. And he says, "Wouldn't you like to be thirty years younger, Bill?" he says. "So's you could go to the war?"

'I says to him, "Sonny," I says, "a year or two won't make a bit of difference to me. I'm going."

'And I made up my mind on the spot to go. We'd been talking a lot about the war, and men being wanted. And I'd been thinking they could do with me. I was as fit as most men a good many years younger. I was fit then.

'So I went along to the Town Hall right away that morning; and I said I'd come to enlist. "But aren't you over age, Bill?" the shire secretary says to me. "You mustn't be over forty-five," he says. "And how old are you, Bill?"

'"Well," I says, "you can put me down as forty-two."

'He looks at me and laughs – I don't mind telling you I'm fifty-six today, and that was only last year. But I wanted to go; and they wanted me and others. I was strong enough. I could do a good day's work with the best of them.

'My chest wasn't stiff, before I got hit by one of the boats, when the *Southland* was torpedoed, that morning off Lemnos. And my foot wasn't this way then. It got frostbitten in the cold, the time we left Gallipoli. I'm not the man I was then. I'm fifty-six today, but I was forty-two when I wanted to enlist.'

Not a man of the men of Anzac has a word of regret, or of complaint against his sufferings. This man tells me his tale simply, without repining that his adventures have robbed him of the sturdy strength that brought him good wages as a labourer about the Victorian township. Yet he has suffered cruelly in the cause of the Empire. He has done his best bravely.

Today he limps about, yarning cheerfully of the wonders that he has seen; and the perils he has faced. He stood stark naked on a raft after the torpedoing of the transport *Southland* in the Aegean Sea and rescued many of his comrades struggling in the water, after a boat had been overturned. He toiled as a pioneer through the last months of the Anzacs at Gallipoli. He marched down the gullies with them on the silent grey twilight of the evacuation.

'One chap says to me,' he tells, 'what a rotten thing it was to have to leave the place after all we'd done. I says to him, "I think we're lucky to get out of it so easy".'

Military experts endorse his view.

For years past he had been known in his district as a solid worker, rouseabout, shearer, labourer, gardener – whatever rough, hard toil he cared to turn his strong hands to. He was known, too, as a staunch supporter of the Labor Party and an active canvasser in the Labor cause at election times.

He carried the same vigour and enthusiasm into his work as a member of the reinforcements for the men of Gallipoli. He played his part heroically for the last weary months of Anzac.

Frostbitten, crushed, he has come back an aged and broken man. Still able to do a day's work, though, with the same cheerful humour as before. And this is how he tells his tale of the wonders of Egypt; the heroism of the men of the *Southland*; and the last dreary weeks upon Gallipoli.

'When I got down to town,' he says, 'I went into camp at Broadmeadows, and was there a good while but finally, on 8 May, my mates and me went aboard the transport *Ulysses*, with Colonel Linton in command; and off we sailed for the front. They treated us well aboard, nothing to complain of all the time – absolutely.

'The first place overseas we stopped at was Colombo, it's got a wonderful harbour, and it's a very nice place, but we came there in the hot weather. It was 135 in the shade, absolutely! We didn't stop there very long, though, we went on to Alexandria, got there at one o'clock in the afternoon. It's a very nice place, too, but there again it was very hot – 135 in the shade, not less.

'From there we went down to Heliopolis. I saw some of the finest buildings round there as ever I saw in my life, and some of the oldest in the world. Out of the Bible, some of them!

'Some of the buildings in Egypt are some of the most remarkable I ever saw. The walls are covered with designs of animals, and all manner of curious things. There's no building in Australia like them, absolutely none.

'And on Sunday, 28 August, we marched away in file from Heliopolis to go to the front; and we went to Alexandria.

'We all wanted to get to the front, to give our comrades a hand. We knew they wanted us. They wanted every man. And if there'd been a few more like 'em, they'd have got right through to Constantinople and we'd have finished up in Berlin long ago.

'At six o'clock on Monday morning we set out for Lemnos. We went on the *Southland*, a big liner, which, I think, had been taken from the Germans. I heard so at the time.

'There were close on 2,000 men on board, and Colonel Linton, he was the Brigadier. We were sailing for Lemnos, but the ship was torpedoed in the Aegean Sea before we got there.

'At about five to ten on the morning of 2 November some men on deck saw the line of a torpedo through the water coming toward the ship. I chanced to be working below at the time, cleaning things up a bit, when all of a sudden a big explosion occurred. We'd been hit by the torpedo.

'A mate of mine was standing near to me yarning and smoking, and the shock threw us both down. He sang out, "My God, we've been hit by a torpedo!" And we had been – sure enough. And I saw that he was cut right across the face, and the blood was starting to run down.

'And then I heard four whistles blown, which meant "Every man to his post!" and my post was to stand on guard with fixed bayonet at the magazine. So I hurried off and took my stand there.

'They thought the ship was sinking, and they started to lower the boats. Some of them got away safely; some of them didn't. I stood on guard over the magazine for a time; but they didn't keep me there. They wanted a bit of help lowering the boats; for the ship was listing a bit on the side where the torpedo had blown a big hole in her; and the boats were not getting straight down into the water.

'Forty feet by ten, that hole was; and the officers had only given a bit of time before the ship sank. The water had started to rush in.

'It was an Austrian submarine torpedoed our ship. Some of us it got – seven or eight poor fellows were writing letters home, down below they was; and when the torpedo tore a hole in the side of the ship it killed them. And others were drowned; and others died afterwards.

'But the men on deck weren't scared at all. They were standing ready; and some of them were smoking and laughing; and some of them were taking off their puttees and coats, getting read to swim for it.

'One of the boats had been upset in lowering it; and the men who'd been in it were cast into the sea. So they called out for volunteers to right the boat, and bale her out, and pick up the men who were in the water. So, some jumped overboard to help the men who were in the water, and they righted her again.

'While we were lowering the boats, these words were said, "Are we downhearted?" and the answer was, "No!" "Are we prepared to die?" And the answer was, "Yes!" Then we all sang the song "Australia will be there!"

'We were only five or six hours' sail from Lemnos when we were struck. It was a fine clear morning; and the sun was shining on the islands. We sang "Australia will be there!" all the same; and we wasn't afraid to die, though we thought we was going down. We'd have gone down singing that song.

'But we didn't go down, and we didn't all have to die. The ship was seen by other boats to have been hit; and the first boat to come up full steam was a big hospital ship; and then another big ship and three destroyers; and then more; and they all stood by to assist us.

'All this while I hadn't had much time to think about being drowned or being afraid to die. The officers had only given us a bit of time, before we sank, but the boats were getting away properly now.

'There were still many of us left in the ship, though, and if it had sunk as fast as those officers said, we'd have had to sink too.

'At last I got over into one of the boats. I carried a machine-gun with me, thinking we might want it in the boat to fire at that darn' submarine, but we didn't see her; and we didn't get her.

'I got down into the boat and dropped the gun. I turned round then; and I says to my comrades who was in the boat with me, just casting off, I says, "I'll just chuck these two casks overboard," thinking to make a bit more room in the boat. We'd had to climb down into her by ladders from the ship's side.

'I turned round, and was putting my weight against the casks, when all of a sudden, because of the weight of the gun it was, the boat rolls over; and all hands get turned into the sea – forty-five of us. I went right under – but I come up again just like a cork.

'Swimming round I strikes against a raft; and I climbs on top of it; and starts helping my comrades out of the water and on to it till it could carry no more. We were right alongside the ship and all I remember is seeing men struggling in the sea; and me trying to help them out.

'I think all seemed to be recovered; I couldn't say whether any were lost in the sea or not. I didn't have any time to think. I'd got out of my clothes; and I stood up naked as the day I was born. Nothing else. Absolutely!

'And just then one of them still in the water grabs me by the leg, and splash I goes again into the sea; and under once more; and up once more. But you couldn't drown me, I wasn't born to be drowned. I gets back to the raft again; but not before a boat hits me in the chest; and that's why I've got this weakness here today. I'm not the man I was before the war.

'Colonel Linton, you know, he died. He got away in a boat at the last, I heard after, and he was capsized. He was a big, strong man; and when they saw him swimming in the sea, someone calls to him from a boat, "How are you getting on?" And he says, "I'm doing all right. Save the others," – just as an Australian officer would do. But when they picked him up, he was too far gone. Whether he'd got hurt, or what it was, I can't say, but he died.

'So, I was on the raft, pulling other soldiers out of the water, though my chest was bad then, when at last a boat comes and picks us up and takes us aboard the hospital ship, where they treated us very well. And we sets sail for Lemnos and gets there this time.

'But the *Southland* didn't sink after all. The captain, he called for volunteers to stop up the hole, and some of our officers and men offer; and they went below stripped to their breeches and boots, and somehow they got up steam and got the pumps to work. And they brought the old *Southland* safe into Mudros Harbour at Lemnos to be docked and have the big hole that the torpedo knocked in her patched up.

'When we were sailing off for the firing line the *Southland* gave four blasts with her whistle, so as to wish us all "God speed". And I tell you we whistled back again from our boats. It was 7 September, I think, when we saw her brought in.

'Lemnos is not a bad place – not bad; and it has a fine harbour, better than Sydney Harbour even. I've seen Sydney Harbour, and it's not so good to my thinking.

'A few days after we'd been brought in, we was off for the firing line. We'd been hearing all the time about what our men had been doing; and we were anxious to be with them. They wanted us, and they wanted more. If they'd had more they'd have got through and wouldn't have had to leave the place those nights in December.

'So we landed at Anzac Beach; and we went up into the trenches right away – about opposite to Lone Pine. All the time I was there I was working at the head of the pioneers. And I heard the great guns and I saw the fighting; and I just came off with my life once or twice. But I'm back here now; and only wish that I'd not had to come back but was away with my comrades in France.

'The Turks are good fighters. And they're not bad chaps after they're taken prisoner. I saw a lot of them while I was there. We were fighting all the time. On 27 November the Turks bombarded our lines at Lone Pine. Hundreds of bombs must have gone against Lone Pine. But we held them; we held them; and they didn't drive us into the sea, as they wanted to.

'The Australians are great fighters; and they'd have fought their way through if there'd been enough of them.

'Still we had a fine time at Anzac, though it was dangerous at times. The big gun of the Turks – Beachy Bill we called him – would start banging away, and go on and on. And I'd say to my mates, "There's the last bit of shell from Constantinople." But it wasn't, not by a long way.

'Many's the time I've been digging the graves of my poor comrades – I've had to jump down into the hole I'd dug to get out of the reach of Beachy Bill.

'On the last night before the evacuation, I was sitting near a mate of mine; and a shell seemed to come right between the two of us. Over we went; but that shell lobbed seven feet back or more and never exploded. If it had gone off that would have been the end of him and me – absolutely!

'After that big bombardment on 27 November, we had some days silent and then Lord Kitchener came to see how we were getting on. And, when he saw how things was, he gave the word of command that, on 16 December, or thereabouts, they should start the evacuation of Gallipoli.

'I didn't know about it at the time, they didn't tell me, but at last I got the idea what was going to be done. We were going to leave the place.

'The hot weather was over then, and the cold had come. I couldn't stand the cold at the end. It was snowing once for eight days, and after that came the blizzards. Some poor fellows lost their fingers and toes. I got my foot frostbitten, and that's what makes me lame.

'The cold was sorer than the guns firing. I got used to the firing, but I couldn't get used to the cold, being an Australian.

'Some say the Turks were in the know about the evacuation, else we'd never have got away. But, if they had been in the know, we'd never have got away as we did, without missing a man. Them Turks never missed us until the next morning after the last of us had gone.

'About nine o'clock on the night of the evacuation,' the old Australian told me, 'I marched down Dead Man's Gully. And all my mates were cut up about having to leave after all they'd done. But I says to this mate of mine, I says, "We're darned lucky to get out of it so easily." And we was! Absolutely!'

THE FINAL PHASE

Oliver Hogue ('Trooper Bluegum')

Days dragged drearily on. Pessimism peeped into the trenches. Later, in the solitude of the dug-out, pessimism stayed an unwelcome guest, and would not be banished. All the glorious optimism of April, the confidence of May, June and July had gone, and the dogged determination of August, September and October was fast petering out. The Turks had fringed the dominating hills with barbed wire and bayonets, and in very surety Australia was 'up against it.'

Not that anyone dared talk pessimism. The croakers would have been squelched instantly. But deep down there was a feeling that unless heavy reinforcements arrived we could never break through to Constantinople. But at Helles, Anzac and Suvla the British hung on, desperately, heroically.

September's cold snap was forgotten in the unexpected warmth of October – just like an afterglow of summer. Then came the wintry winds of November – and the blizzard ... Of course we have snow in Australia. Kosciusko is all the year round covered with a soft white mantle. Down on Monaro it can be bleak and wintry. And the old Blue Mountains now and then enjoy a spell of sleet and snow ... But taking us by and large we are a warm-blooded race, we Australians. That is why we viewed the approach of winter with some concern.

We knew the Turks could never, never, never break through our lines, and drive us – as Liman von Sanders had boasted – into the sea. But we were beginning to fear that we were a long, long way from Constantinople.

The blizzard swooped down on Anzac. Just like a shroud the white visitation settled on Gallipoli. It was cold as a Monaro gale. Soldiers crowded round the fires, and at night in the trenches it was terribly hard to keep awake.

The cold was something to remember. We could keep our hands a bit warm by giving 'five rounds rapid' and hugging the rifle barrel. Talk about cold feet; we had heard of 'cold feet' when we were in Egypt, but this was the real thing.

How we invoked rich blessings on the heads of the Australian girls who had knitted us those warm socks! How we cursed the thieves along the lines of communication who pillaged and pilfered, while the men in the firing line went begging! But through it all the indomitable cheerfulness of the Australian soldier would not be crushed. They laughed and joked when their teeth chattered, so that clear articulation was impossible.

To preserve some circulation they stamped their feet till exhaustion bade them cease. But the blizzard was inexorable. The

'The blizzard swooped down on Anzac.'

cold permeated everywhere. We got just a glimpse of what the British Army suffered in the Crimea.

Frostbite was something to fear and dread. It was agonising. Hundreds of men were carried down to the field hospitals and sent across to Lemnos. There were scores of amputations daily ... We had cursed the heat of July and the plague of flies, but now we prayed for summer again.

Now and then the English home papers blew in and we eagerly scanned the pages of the dailies for news of the war. We were astounded at the tone of the criticism hurled at the Government. So much of it was Party criticism, captious criticism. So little of it was helpful constructive criticism.

In Parliament and in the Press the critics were "agin the Gov'ment' rather than against the Hun. We felt wonderfully proud of the commendable restraint of our politicians. Not one word of captious criticism had there come from responsible Australian papers and people.

We knew that mistakes had been made. We knew that it was a big gamble sending the fleet to hammer their way through without the aid of an army. But we did not slang-wang the Government. In the dark hour when everybody was blaming everybody there was only one message from Australia. Press and politicians struck the same note. It was merely a reiteration of the Prime Minister's message that the last man and the last shilling in Australia were now and always at the disposal of the Empire.

Then came talk of evacuation. It staggered us. In the House of Commons and in the Press columns were devoted to discussing the Dardanelles question and evacuation was freely recommended. The Australians rose in wrath and exclaimed, 'We're d****d if we'll evacuate. We are going to see this game through.' It was unthinkable that, having put our hands to the plough, we could turn back.

The Turks and their German masters were kept well informed of the discussions at home and it made them tremendously cocky. England had practically admitted failure. The great Dardanelles expedition – the greatest crusade in the world – was an admitted fiasco. Then the Turks reasoned together. And they agreed that even 'the fool English' would never talk so much about evacuation if it were even remotely likely. But it was worth an army corps to Abdul, and it did not make General Birdwood's task any easier.

Then Kitchener came. Many of us had seen him in Australia and South Africa. We had confidence that he would see the thing through. He landed on the beach and soon the word buzzed through the dug-outs, up the gully, and along the firing line. 'K of K' was on Anzac and the boys off duty congregated to give him a rousing welcome. He went round the Anzac defences with General Birdwood, saw everything and then started in to weigh the pros and cons of a knotty problem.

Ever since the day of landing, we had discussed in an offhand way the possibility of 'getting out'. Not that we had ever considered it remotely possible that we should ever turn back. But just as a strategical and tactical exercise, we had figured out how it might be done. And it seemed that the job of getting out was fraught with more potentialities of disaster than the job of getting in.

The landing on 25 April was responsible for some slaughter. The evacuation, we reckoned, would be carnage. At a most moderate computation twenty-five per cent of the Australian and New Zealand Army Corps would have to be sacrificed to ensure the safe withdrawal of the remainder. But of course this was only a theoretical exercise. It was really outside the sphere of practical politics.

Then like a bomb came word that in very surety we were going to evacuate. In the House of Commons members had asked in an airy way why the troops were not withdrawn from Suvla and Anzac.

To them, in their ignorance, it was merely a matter of embarking again and returning to Egypt or Salonica or France. So simple it seemed to those armchair strategists. They did not know that the beach at Anzac, our main depots, and our headquarters were within a thousand yards of the main Turkish line; that the beach had been constantly shelled by 'Beachy Bill' and other batteries for eight solid months on end.

However, the powers that be had so ordained it and that was sufficient. The Australians had talked about 'never retreating', but that was only a manifestation of the unconquerable spirit that animated them. They might talk, but they never yet disobeyed an order. It nearly broke their hearts to leave the spot where so many thousand gallant young Australians had found heroes' graves; but they knew how to obey orders. The only kick was for the honour of being the last to leave. So many wanted to be amongst the 'diehards'.

It was to be a silent 'get-away.' Absolute secrecy was essential for its success. It sounds just like a wild bit of fiction. Just imagine the possibility of withdrawing an army of 90,000 men with artillery, stores, field hospitals, mules and horses, and all the vast impedimenta of war, right from under the nose of an active enemy, and all on a clear moonlit night. One single traitor could have queered the whole pitch. But British, Indians, New Zealanders and Australians were loyal to the core.

The final attack of the Turks on the right of our line had been repulsed by the 2nd Light Horse Brigade, though the enemy in determined fashion had pushed forward with sandbags right to within a few yards of our trenches.

There were half a dozen spots in the Anzac firing line where we and the Turks could hear each other talking: Quinn's Post, Lone Pine, the Neck, Apex, Turkish Despair, Chatham's Post. It would be fine fun sticking it out here while the army made its get-away. Men clamoured for the honour of being the last to leave ...

It is the night of 19 December; the fatal night which will see the evacuation of Anzac. Men talked cheerily, but thought hard. Had the Turks any idea of our projected departure? Two nights ago, a little after midnight, there was an unrehearsed incident. A fire broke out in a depot near North Beach. Soon the whole sky was reddened with the glare and the rugged outline of Anzac was brightly illuminated. Bully beef and biscuits blazed merrily. Oil drums burst with terrific force.

Then we wondered if the Turks would deduce anything from this. Would they guess it was a preliminary to the 'get-away'? It was hardly likely. The 'fool English' would never burn the stores till the last minute. So the accidental fire did no harm. Maybe it did good. For during the past month the Anzacs had tried by all manner of tricks and subterfuges to induce Abdul to attack. But Abdul knew how costly a business it was attacking the Australians, and after a few abortive attempts he remained on the defensive ...

Now all was normal. Down at Helles the British had, during the afternoon, made a big demonstration. The warships had joined in the fray and the bombardment of the Turkish lines was terrific. But on this last night there was nothing untoward happening.

General Birdwood during the day had gone the rounds of the trenches and the boys yarned with him as of old. It was a good thing for us to have had a General like that – one who understood the devil-may-care Australian character. That's why the boys called him the 'idol of Anzac'.

* * *

Away to the northward at Suvla on the shoulder of Chocolate Hills the British divisions are getting ready to retire. On Hill 60, which saw so much sanguinary fighting, the stolid Indians are awaiting orders. This way a bit the New Zealand and Australian Division has started its first parties towards North Beach. On the right above Anzac and opposite Gaba Tepe the Australians were streaming away; all but the rearguard and the final 'diehards'.

Before the morning Anzac will have seen a great tragedy, or else the greatest bluff in history ... There is the usual desultory interchange of musketry at odd places along the line, now and then punctuated with the rattle of a maxim ... nothing abnormal. Down at Helles there is a fierce fusillade. This will help us ...

Since dusk the first contingents had been steadily streaming down towards North Beach and Anzac Cove. Quickly and silently they embarked in the waiting flotilla of small craft and streaked out to the transports. Like guardian angels the warships hovered around seeing to the security of the army.

Up at Suvla we knew similar scenes were being enacted. Along the line the musketry played its usual accompaniment to the intermittent bombing. But the whole plan was working beautifully. The tension was gradually relaxing. There would be no twenty per cent casualties as the pessimists foretold. Already from Suvla and Anzac over 60,000 soldiers had re-embarked without a single casualty.

Now and then there was a round of shrapnel sent by Beachy Bill on to the southern depot at Brighton Beach. This clearly showed that the enemy suspected nothing. Yet it is bright moonlight ... It is midnight, and nearly all the men have embarked save the thin khaki line of 'diehards' in the trenches.

An odd bomb or two is thrown by the Turks. Then from the Apex, after a final volley, streaked the first batch of the skeleton rearguard. There is a breach in the brave Anzac line at last. But Abdul does not know it yet. Soon the daredevils at Quinn's Post heave a few bombs, then silently slink back, down the precipitous hillside, and along the gully to the beach.

From Courtney's and the Neck and the Pimple and Ryrie's Post and Chatham's all along the line came the 'diehards', full lick to the beach. But to their unutterable surprise there is no attack. They are not followed. The trenches that for eight long months defied the Turkish attacks are now open, not a solitary soldier left. But Abdul does not know it. There is still an intermittent fire from the Turkish trenches. They think our silence is some trick ...

At half past three on the morning of 20 December there was a burst of red flame and a roar like distant thunder. This was repeated shortly afterwards, and our two big mines on the Neck blew up. It was our last slap at the Turk. We cannot say what harm it did, but thinking the explosions were a prelude to attack the Turkish line all round Anzac burst into spiteful protest. There was a wild fusillade at our empty trenches, and on the transports the Australians smiled grimly.

Shortly afterwards the Light Horsemen on the extreme right – Ryrie's lucky 2nd Brigade rearguard – entered the waiting cutters on Brighton Beach. Then the stores – such as we could not take away – burst into flame. Only two men were wounded.

Before dawn word came that the whole force had been safely taken off, together with many of the mules and horses and guns which it was thought would have to be abandoned. At dawn the Turkish batteries opened a wild bombardment of our trenches, all along the line. Marvellous to relate, the enemy had not yet ascertained what had happened. But the silence soon told them the truth. Then they charged in irregular lines over the skyline at our empty trenches.

The warships fired a few salvoes at the enemy swarming over the hills, and they hurriedly took cover in our old trenches. These were the last shots fired over Anzac at the Turks. Then the flotilla turned its back on Gallipoli and swung slowly and sadly westward.

So ended the great 'get-away', a feat quite unparalleled in the annals of war. Historians will pay tribute to Sir Charles Munro and the Fleet.

We only take our hats off to General Birdwood and his staff and the staffs of the Australian divisions. But deep down we know the wonderful work our navy did during the eight months of the Gallipoli campaign. The army may make mistakes, but the navy is all right.

As we swing off, our last thought is not concerned with the bitterness of defeat. We think of our comrades quietly sleeping on Anzac. They gave their lives gladly, proudly, for Australia and the Empire. They showed the world that Australians could live and fight and die like Britishers.

There are many sad hearts on the transports tonight. And there are very many breaking hearts back in dear Australia. But old England has showered so many good gifts on her Colonies. The Colonies will not grudge this sacrifice for Empire.

WHEN WE RETURN

E. P. McCarthy

What hand could write the gladness that waits us on the day
We say farewell to Anzac and steam across her bay.
When all the fighting's over in this long cruel war
And we are rocking southward, beyond the Grecian shore.

When Imbros lies behind us and Lemnos fades from view,
When Suvla Bay's forgotten, and Achi Baba too.
When Lone Pine is a mem'ry that's fading from us fast,
And Khalid Bahr's becoming a nightmare of the past.

When we have left the trenches and dugouts on the hill,
Each heart will leap as never we thought men's heart could thrill.
Away from horrid mem'ries of death moans and of pain.
God speed the twenty-knotter that takes us home again.

And to the coast of Egypt, with sun haze on the sand,
While racing down the Suez, we'll wave a farewell hand:
We'll cast no backward glances across the Indian Sea,
Our thoughts will fly before us and light of heart we'll be.

And when the big boat's nearing her berth by Sydney quay,
And two black eyes are watching the side rails there for me,
Oh, let them drop the anchor and get the gangway down!
And let us see the land again in our old Sydney town.

We'll kiss the girls who waited through those long years so true.
Our patient loving sisters and grey haired mothers too.
We'll find familiar faces and friends on every hand
When we return ... if we return ... to that sweet southern land.

A 'CLASSY' EVACUATION

H. W. Dinning

The evacuation effected at Anzac was particularly 'classy'.

When the notion of evacuation was first mooted there was misgiving. We had our backs to the sea, so to speak, and we were hemmed in along a narrow sector of coast, with no ground whatever to fall back upon.

There was no one who did not expect disaster in evacuating a position such as that. The only debate was as to the degree of disaster. What would it cost in lives and money? There was a greater fear unspoken, the hideous reflection that an evacuation would make the heavy losses of eight months' fighting seem in vain.

Everyone hoped against a giving up. But soon there was no mistaking the signs of the times, the easing of the landing of supplies, the preliminary and experimental three days' restraint from fire all along the line and the added restriction upon correspondence (especially the order to refrain from any reference to the movement of troops, either present or prophetic, known or surmised).

Notice to quit was quite short. On Sunday afternoon, 12 December, the O.C. came panting up the gully.

'Fall in the unit at once!'

They were given an hour and a half's notice to have all ready for transport to the pier. Notice was, in many cases, far shorter, resolving itself into minutes, but an hour and a half is brief enough. Then there was a bustle and feverish stuffing of kit bags.

The dug-out which had been a home for four months was dismantled and left in dishevelment in half an hour.

It's hard to leave a dug-out, your shelter from shrapnel and the snowy blast and the bitter Turkish frost. It's where you smoked the consolatory pipe for so many months, consumed the baksheesh steak and marmalade, read the home letters and the local news of home from Australia. It's where you played nocturnal poker, yarned with a fellow townsman and spread out a frugal late supper.

Your dug-out has been home in a sense other than that you ate and slept there. It was home indirectly, by virtue of home mails, home talk, home memories and visualisations nurtured under its shelter in the night watches. It was also home because it was in Turkey, where your duty lay.

Now, in a few minutes, it was rudely stripped. Bunks were overturned, the larder ratted and the favourite prints brushed down from the hessian in the bustle.

The vultures from neighbouring dug-outs flocked around for the spoils. The men who had as yet no notice to evacuate came for baksheesh. With a swelling heart you disgorged your little stock of luxuries that you would have taken but had no room for.

It breaks your heart to give over to the hands of strangers your meagre library, your little table, your butter and strawberry jam, potatoes and oatmeal, surplus luxuries in clothing and the vital parts of your bunk. It also breaks your heart to pass on the odds and ends of private cooking utensils that have endeared themselves by long and frequent service at the rising of the sun and at the going down of the same, and late at night.

Though the life of a soldier is chequered, with hurried moves by flood and field, we had had so many months at Anzac, in the one spot, that we had broken with tradition and made a sort of home in a sort of settled community. And this was the rude end of it all.

We took a hurried snack as the mule carts were loaded. The cooks made merry. Cooks always contrive to have a convivial spirit at hand and they called on all and sundry to have a farewell drink with them while they scraped and packed their half-cold dixies. It was a melancholy toast.

We followed the transport to Walker's Pier. This thought was uppermost: 'What if Beachy Bill should get us now?' To a man we took all the cover there was. No one, so close to deliverance forever from that shell-swept beach, neglected precautions.

Round at Walker's the beach was thickly peopled with units awaiting embarkation. The bustling and shouting were almost stupefying.

Impromptu piers had been run out and were lighted by smoking flares. Pinnaces and barges moved noisily between them. Military landing officers and naval transport officers and middies and skippers of trawlers bawled orders and queries and responses.

On the beach men lay about on their baggage and non-commissioned officers marshalled them and moved them off. Mule transports threaded a way amongst men and kit bags. Officers who knew their time was not yet stood in groups chatting and joking.

The men, always free from responsibility, played cards and formed schools for two-up. Some dipped into their haversacks and munched, or raised to their lips drinking vessels which were not always mess tins, and did not only contain cold tea, or even cold tea at all.

We waited. The hour of embarkation was postponed from six to nine. At nine most of the excitement had subsided and the men lay quiet. As the hour drew on (embarkation was now postponed till ten), there was melancholy abroad as the significance of leaving was realised.

The rifles cracked on the ridges, the howitzers spoke, the din of bombs came down the ravines. There were those fellows being left in the trenches to see the last of it, and to get off as they could.

Not even the most resolute optimist could have looked towards the bloodless evacuation which the event has shown to an astonished world. Every flash of the guns in the half moonlight, every rifle fusillade, called up the vision of a last party attempting to leave and perhaps failing fatally to the last of its number.

'If I could get drunk,' said a man wearing most of his equipment, 'I would be blue-blind paralytic. I never felt so like it in my life!'

We waited for about another hour and a half. Then the order came suddenly to go on board, so suddenly that half of the equipment had to be left. The first load was got down and a return was being made for the other. 'Can't wait,' roared the N.T.O., 'leave your stuff or be left. The barge is leaving now, Cast off for'ard! Go ahead cox!'

This was not bluff and there was a scramble for the barge. Behind us lay the cook's gear and half of our private kit, to be despoiled, so we said at the time, by some barbarous Turk.

'Put that match out! No talking!'

Liberty to talk or to smoke would have been a boon. There was some talking in whispers, better than nothing but cigarettes were quenched, along with the spirits of that unhappy, close-packed load of silent men.

We puffed out, in silence, into the Aegean darkness and the spent bullets sang overhead in a kind of derision, getting lower and more intimate as we moved on. Soon they were spitting about us and tapping the barge and coming unreasonably near to tapping skulls and chests. After long wandering and hailing of many ships in the darkness we got to the side of the darkened transport untouched.

There was complete exhaustion at the end. The men dropped down against their kits and slept fitfully till the dawn. It was bitter cold.

When we woke it was to our last look at Gallipoli. For a time we could see only the great grey mass flecked with an occasional spurt of flame where the guns were still belching. Then the glorious sun uprose and revealed the detail.

There were the old and well-remembered and well-trodden heights of Anzac, and lower down we saw all the positions we had known, and we now saw them more clearly than ever before.

We looked along the deadly Olive Grove where lay the Beachy Bill Battery, which every day had rained screaming hell over the Anzac beach, and was even now speaking sullenly in the early morning glow.

Achi Baba rose up to the south in a sort of soft splendour; how different from the reality! That rosy-tipped mountain in the distance, could we have seen its detail, would show looming bastions, high forbidding ridges with galleries of guns and rugged ravines that had flowed with the blood of our storming parties. Now it stood there, sloping gently down towards Helles behind the high, quiet headlands and bays of the coast.

Soon we were abreast of Helles, part of the multitude of shipping in the strait's mouth. So on down behind Imbros and under Tenedos we went, then away over the freshening sea to Lemnos, which appeared as a pale cloud on the starboard bow.

By midday we lay in the quiet waters of Mudros Bay, safely looking over the canvas-clad slopes of the island.

PULLTHROUGH

Tom Skeyhill

He came straight in from the woods, where he used to earn his
    goods
Splitting timber for some railway line out West.
He slung no fancy grammars, and knew no parlour manners,
But somehow, I liked him better than the rest.

He stood over six feet high, and I don't suppose that I
Ever knew a man as skinny, or as true.
You could pull him through a gun, and we used to say in fun,
That he should have been our regiment's Pullthrough.

With a smile upon his mug, he would sit in our old dug,
And yarn about his travels everywhere,
And if anything went wrong, he could cut loose hot and strong,
And 'fair dinkum', he could teach the world to swear.

When lead was flying about, and the boys were dropping out,
And everybody around was looking blue,
When the odds were ten to one, and the line was nearly done,
It was always old Pullthrough, who pulled us through.

He was never known to rest, and he used to say in jest,
That he was too thin to stop a bursting shell.
His old honest smiling face, was well known throughout the place
And our section would have followed him through hell.

I still recall the night, when we hopped out on the right,
And charged clean through that storm of splintering lead,
As we smashed against their steel, I saw old Pullthrough reel,
Then I dropped out with a bullet in me head.

When I pulled around again, I was fairly shook with pain,
And as I looked around for someone that I knew,
I saw near me on my right, with a face so awful white,
And bleeding badly from the chest, my chum, Pullthrough.

He was fighting hard for breath, and the misty grey of death,
Was settling on his dear old features fast.
With a sob I gripped his hand and he seemed to understand,
'Cos he smiled a bit before he breathed his last.

I found out through the day, that he'd carried me away
To a dugout where he meant to get me dressed,
He had got me back all right and was binding me up tight
When a bullet came and plugged him through the breast.

There's a soldier up in Heaven. His number's two one seven,
And the colours on his wings are white and blue.
When they call the heroes' roll, there's a cheer from every soul,
And the angels kiss the hands of old Pullthrough.

You can have your fancy girls, with their pretty golden curls,
And the smiling lips and eyes that men adore.
Give me back my mate again, and I'll never more complain,
And upon this earth I'll ask for nothing more.

They say heroes never die, so I'll meet him bye and bye
In that land where men always staunch and true
As I slip in through the gate, once again I'll meet my mate,
Then I'll dig in up above, with old Pullthrough.

RIGHT AWAY

Roy Bridges

Following on the visit of Lord Kitchener, it was resolved by the Allied War Council that the peninsula must be evacuated.

The perils of the withdrawal were not underestimated. It was realised that, if the Turks had any inkling of the proposal, it would lend courage to their assault. If that occurred the evacuation must necessarily entail the loss of many thousands of lives, in addition to those sacrificed during the eight months of the campaign, and millions of pounds' worth of stores and munitions.

The only hope was to mislead the Turks as to the nature of the preparation for withdrawal, and under the cover of the winter darkness take off the men gradually.

The plan formulated in secret council was to put up the bluff that a winter rest camp was being formed at Imbros owing to the severity of the weather conditions; and that the troops were being taken there by turns. Thus, it was hoped, it might be practicable to remove in two or three stages about two-thirds of the army on the Peninsula, while the remaining third lightly manned the defences, until, the time being opportune, a dash might be made in the dead of night for the beach, where the boats would be waiting.

It was not hoped to get off without cruel losses and dread filled the minds of the commanding officers at the manner in which the troops would receive the news.

It was anticipated that the disappointment in Australia would be bitter, and the protest of the people indignant, left in the dark as they had been from month to month by the reports that had been allowed to go through regarding the state of affairs on Gallipoli.

The policy of imperfectly informing the public had convinced Australians that the grip upon the peninsula was comparatively secure, that sooner or later the Turks would be dislodged, and the portals to the East forced open.

This belief in a certain sense compensated for the loss of over 6,000 young Australians who had died, and for the 20,000 other casualties. Actually the people took the news courageously when it came, and without expression of bitter resentment. The very wonder of the withdrawal, and the relief, tended to reduce any popular feelings of resentment.

The evacuation of Gallipoli was as potentially hazardous as the landing at Anzac. It commenced on the night of 13 December when the whole of the 14th Battalion and about one hundred other Australians were taken off in barges. It meant that three battalions were left in the front line, and no brigade reserves at all. At two

© AWM P01436.004

'Guns and stores had been withdrawn without loss.'

hours' notice the 15th Brigade packed up their belongings and withdrew from the peninsula. About 600 of the 4th Brigade with all their impedimenta got away that night.

On the following day the men were engaged in making away with stores, grenades, bombs, picks, shovels, food supplies and ordnance gear. A hard problem was to get away the heavy guns; and these had to be left to the last moment, so that they might be used in action against the Turks.

Plans were prepared to fight a rearguard action, which was never fought, and the pick of the 13th and 16th Battalions were selected for the purpose.

Supplies of fresh meat and bread had stopped by now; and the forces were living on hard biscuit and bully beef.

The men made no sign, all pretended that they suspected nothing, although officers understood that the men realised that the move to Imbros meant the actual abandonment of Gallipoli.

On 15 December a boisterous north wind was blowing, and the sea was rough, rendering it extremely difficult to load luggage. At one front a casualty clearing station was set up to accommodate 300 patients with a full staff of doctors and dressers, in anticipation of heavy fighting during the final stage of embarkation.

On 16 December the wind had dropped. During the past couple of days the total strength at Anzac had been reduced from 45,000 to 20,000 men to continue to hold the lines against 170,000 Turks.

It had been decided to carry out the final stages of the withdrawal on 18 and 19 December, conditional on the weather holding up.

The weather remained steady and on 17 December, General Birdwood himself came over from Imbros and visited the Australian lines. He shook hands with the officers, and expressed the hope that many of them would come through alive.

A withdrawal without bitter loss was not to be hoped for. About 170 diehards had been selected to hold the lines till the last moments, and a few of the most daring had been instructed to remain in the front trenches and keep up a fire for another ten minutes.

Each man of the diehards had received instructions as to the minute when he must leave the trenches and what he must do: carry a machine-gun, its tripod or belts or throw a bomb or light a fuse to blow up a gun-cotton mine; or complete a barbed-wire entanglement on a track down which the Turks might race in pursuit. Each man knew, too, the exact way in which he must reach the beach.

The last day on Gallipoli – 19 December – came calm and clear. The sea was smooth, the air cloudy and foggy; a light misty drizzle of rain fell. During the morning the Turks bombarded the beaches, as they had done many and many a day in all the weary months.

By 8 p.m. there were not more than 500 troops in the whole of Anzac to hold the front line against 170,000 of the enemy. During the afternoon the fleet had carried out a heavy bombardment of Helles, as if to suggest that another attack was to be launched.

By nine o'clock the last patrol came in and reported at headquarters that they had heard the enemy digging, and setting out wires on Green Knoll and Hackney Wick, two points at which the Australian lines had been close to theirs. They had suspected nothing those last days, it seemed, and they suspected nothing now.

By 1.35 a.m. came the withdrawal of the last of the Anzacs from Gallipoli. Silently they left. Down the black gullies in the darkness, having fixed their devices to fire the rifles, they stole in little groups of six to twelve men, an officer coming last and pausing to bar the gully with a frame of barbed wire, or to light a fuse to fire a mine to wreck a sap or tunnel, by which the enemy could come if he pursued. Then four continuous files – one from the south, two from the east, and one from the north – marched silently and steadily down to the beach.

The night was grey; blackness over the land and blackness over the sea. So timed was the withdrawal, that at the same moment the heads of the columns reached Brighton, Anzac, Howitzer, and North Beach. Each line passed on to the allotted jetty, their footsteps muffled by the floors of sandbags laid in readiness. Man by man they stepped down into the motor barges.

Silence then but for the throbbing of the motor engines; and on the distant hills the splutter of rifle fire against the empty trenches.

'Right away!' and slowly the barges moved from the piers. As the last barge at Anzac Pier cast off, an engineer joined the terminals of an electric battery, to fire the big gun-cotton mines, which with a roar of sound blew up Russell's Top – the hill at the head of the western branch of Monash Gully. The sound came thunderous; and columns of fire and dust cut the greyness over the hill.

Instantly a very storm of rifle and machine-gun fire burst from Sari Bair – the Turks believing that the explosion meant the signal for a new charge. Bullets, aimed at the empty trenches high on the range, whistled over the boats and fell into the sea.

The pale moon looked out from a break in the clouds; and the sea-mist screened the barges, as in Homeric days when the gods came down to spread a mantle of protective cloud over heroic Greeks or Trojans.

Forty-five thousand men, millions of pounds' worth of guns and stores, had been withdrawn without loss; and the Turks had suspected nothing!

LETTER HOME*

Walter Gamble

On the eve of evacuating Anzac sixty men were selected to man the firing line and cover the retreat of the battalion. Ivor and I were included and held one post together. We mounted duty at 4 p.m. on the nineteenth and kept observing and sniping continually for almost a full round of the clock.

About 12 p.m. it was reported that all was going well on the beach and the next three hours seemed like an age. I thought the time would never come but, about 3 a.m., the word was passed quietly along and we sneaked through the tunnels (with about six layers of blankets wrapped around our feet), out into the open, down the winding saps to the beach, onto the lighter and away, without halting for one moment.

It was a wonderful piece of work, wonderfully carried out to the smallest detail, even to marking our tracks by a trail of flour and salt, so that we would not lose our way in the dark.

* an extract

FIRST FOOT*

P. J. Anderson

In Scotland and many parts of England it is customary on New Year's Eve for the household to 'see in' the new year by sitting up after midnight.

'First foot' is the first person to cross the threshold after midnight. 'First foot' lets in the new year and many superstitious folk insist that the best and most desirable 'first foot' is a dark man who, it is said, brings good luck to the house. He must bring something with him of which all can partake. Usually the 'something' is in a bottle.

We were having our regular evening grouse, myself, Old Melancholy, Sandy and The Doc.

Whenever possible during the long months of fighting at Cape Helles we would gather in the Doctor's dug-out about the hour of twilight to cheer each other up by reviewing our troubles.

'No mail in today', 'no fresh meat tomorrow', etc, etc. We'd recount the latest rumours of submarine disasters and diplomatic and military blunders. In fact we'd marshal all our latest grievances and then part, more or less happy, having got them off our chests before we grabbed a few hours' sleep.

On this particular evening we were in tip-top form. Each of us had had a real good grouse. The campaign commanders, the weather, the food, our Turkish and German enemies; all our pet grievances were well and truly aired, expounded upon and roundly condemned.

It hardly seemed right when, after we'd all had a good grouse, Sandy suddenly brightened up and told us to do the same.

'Well,' he remarked, 'it's all good an' well ta grouse, but can ye no brighten up a little and count ye blessin's just for this once?'

This was hardly playing the game. We thought immediately it was possibly brain trouble and myself and Old Melancholy decided it was a case for The Doc to investigate.

The Doc was quite concerned himself and, taking his cue from our comments, he questioned Sandy as to the symptoms.

'When did you begin to experience these untoward and uncharacteristic symptoms?' asked The Doc. 'Was it during the heavy shelling yesterday?'

'Symptoms be hanged!' Sandy exclaimed. 'Ye're a lot o' miser'rable bounders. Is there no a mon o' ye bethought himsel' o' the occasion? D' ye no ken it's the last day o' the year and that t'nicht is the nicht o' nichts?'

'New Year's Eve!' we exclaimed in chorus.

'Ay 'tis that,' said Sandy, 'and well I may tell ye,' he added emphatically, 'it's got to be kept up, so I expect ye'll all come roun' to ma dug-out and see aboot it at the appropriate time.'

So, despite our usual fatigue and lack of sleep, we dutifully gathered again in the Scotsman's dug-out about eleven o'clock and set to yarning, while the dug-out filled with tobacco smoke.

We all did our best to try and let the new year in with a smile but, as New Year's Eve is really the Scotchman's feast of feasts and we were all there at Sandy's behest, we felt it was up to him to make the thing work properly. So, we put Sandy in the chair and he made a few appropriate but unprintable remarks as the witching hour drew nearer.

We were all called upon to tell a yarn and make our summary of the year 1915 from our own point of view. Very little of what followed was printable.

Around 11.50 p.m. Sandy commenced to search the recesses of his valise and after some rummaging hence he produced and displayed proudly ... ye gods ... a bottle of whisky!

We stared in blank amazement. Such a thing we had not seen for ages and here Sandy had sat on it, slept on it and hoarded it up all through the long campaign. Hoarded it up when there was no guarantee of a tomorrow in which to enjoy it. Hoarded it up when it would have brought a fabulous price, and possibly, who can tell, even promotion had it been used tactfully.

'It would be a sad New Year wi'out a bottle o' whisky to see it in,' said Sandy quite matter-of-factly as he operated the corkscrew in a manner born of experience. 'Help yersel' and pass it around.'

There were no bells to ring out the old year and ring in the new, but never did men honour the occasion more truly or wish themselves more heartily a 'Happy New Year'.

'Now, I wonder who'll be "first foot"?' said Sandy. 'Custom says its got to be a dark man, ye ken, if we're all to have good luck this year, and he must na' come empty-handed.'

At that very moment we heard the noise of feet outside the dug-out and a soldier's low voice made an enquiry for the Captain. It was Old Melancholy who was being sought and, on acknowledging that he was indeed inside, the voice responded, 'Patrol just brought in a Turk, sir.'

'Bring him in here,' ordered Old Melancholy and a moment later the prisoner was pushed in ahead of the escort. He was about the darkest white man one could wish to meet.

'Well, he ought to bring us all a lucky New Year,' said Sandy gleefully. 'Let's see what he's brought along wi' him.'

The big Turk was quite happy to be searched but all that he had brought along was a little money.

'Well, it's a bit of a conundrum,' said Sandy, rubbing his chin, 'but we must all take something for luck, so I'll take the money, it'll help to pay for the whisky.'

This left us rather in a difficulty, but British soldiers rarely stop at difficulties.

So Old Melancholy fetched his notebook and took the prisoner's depositions and The Doc took his temperature.

As for me, well, I took the unfinished bottle of whisky and slid off to let the New Year in elsewhere and, if the coming year doesn't bring better luck and success to us all ... don't ever talk to me about those silly New Year superstitions.

*Anzac and Suvla were evacuated by 20 December 1915. The British forces at Cape Helles, however, remained in place until 7 January and were evacuated on 8 and 9 January 1916. British troops were, therefore, still in place on the Gallipoli Peninsula for New Year's Eve 1916, making this story at least plausible.

ANZAC

'Argent'

Ah, well! We're gone! We're out of it now. We've something else
    to do.
But we all look back from the transport deck to the land-line far
    and blue:
Shore and valley are faded; fading are cliff and hill;
The land-line we called 'Anzac' ... and we'll call it 'Anzac' still!

This last six months, I reckon, it'll be most of my life to me:
Trenches, and shells, and snipers, and the morning light on the
    sea,
Thirst in the broiling midday, shouts and gasping cries,
Big guns' talk from the water, and ... flies, flies, flies, flies, flies!

And all of our trouble wasted! All of it gone for nix!
Still ... we kept our end up – and some of the story sticks.
Fifty years on in Sydney they'll talk of our first big fight,
And even in little old, blind old England possibly someone might.

But seeing we had to clear, for we couldn't get on no more,
I wish that, instead of last night, it had been the night before.
Yesterday poor Jim stopped one. Three of us buried Jim.
I know a woman in Sydney that thought the world of him.

She was his mother. I'll tell her – broken with grief and pride –
'Mother' was Jim's last whisper. That was all. And he died.
Brightest and bravest and best of all – none could help but to love
    him –
And now ... he lies there under the hill, with a wooden cross
    above him.

That's where it gets me twisted. The rest of it I don't mind,
But it don't seem right for me to be off, and to leave old Jim
* behind.*
Jim, just quietly sleeping; and hundreds and thousands more;
For graves and crosses are mighty thick from Quinn's Post down
* to the shore!*

Better there than in France, though, with the Germans' dirty
* work:*
I reckon the Turk respects us, as we respect the Turk;
Abdul's a good, clean fighter, we've fought him, and we know,
And we've left him a letter behind us to tell him we found him so.

Not just to say, precisely, 'Goodbye' but 'Au revoir'!
Somewhere or other we'll meet again, before the end of the war!
But I hope it'll be a wider place, with a lot more room on the
* map,*
And the airmen over the fight that day'll see a bit of a scrap!

Meanwhile, here's health to the Navy, that took us there, and
* away;*
Lord! They're miracle-workers – and fresh ones every day!
My word! Those Mids in the cutters! Aren't they properly keen!
Don't ever say England's rotten – or not to us, who've seen!

Well! We're gone. We're out of it all! We've somewhere else to
* fight.*
And we strain our eyes from the transport deck, but 'Anzac' is out
* of sight!*
Valley and shore are vanished; vanished are cliff and hill;
And we may never go back to 'Anzac' ... But I think that some of
* us will!*

THE AFTERMATH

TRAVELLER, HALT

Necmettín Halíl Onan

Traveller, halt on this quiet mound.
This soil you thus tread, unaware,
Is where a generation ended ... Listen!
The heart of a nation is beating there.

RAIN

Roy Bridges

And the rain did not come through the spring, when the sun was a white fire in the sky of blue glass and the springing wheat grew yellow and withered away.

Through the summer, when the sun burnt like a scarlet ball in the smoke of the bush fires and the north winds bore blackened gum leaves and scraps of fern down into the paddocks and whirled up the sand, the stock died.

Through the autumn, when the plains were a brick-field; and the sand storms whirled up over them and the sun burnt yellow from its rising to blood-red at its going, paddocks burnt up, dams dried and water was carted from the railway station to supply the house.

All this while, the boy was in Egypt, writing home cheery letters, filled, as his mind was filled, with the wonders of the country.

And then the last letter came from him, written before they sailed from Egypt for the Dardanelles.

After that no more letters.

Perhaps he wasn't allowed to write.

No promise of rain.

'It's to be hoped it rains, before he gets back,' his father said. 'Otherwise he won't know the place. Scarcely a thing left on it.'

He'd laugh mirthlessly to the mother, trying to cheer her up and realising all the while that the boy's absence was more to him than the drought – the loss of all things.

He wanted him back badly, he admitted to himself, wandering out to the stable to fling a few handfuls to chaff to the horse. All the time hoping to himself that the rain would come before the boy came back. Not wanting him to come home to find everything burnt up by the drought.

He had read in the local papers that when bad news came through it was always broken to the family by their minister. He should be afraid, if he saw the minister even coming to call. He hoped that he would not chance to come any time while he was away from the house, because the mother knew; she read the papers too.

*　　*　　*

The year drifted into May and still the rain had not come. Days were warm and still now, evenings too, in a muggy, clammy sort of way, as if baked plains sent out the heat of the dead summer day.

It was looking very black to the north in the mornings and the wind was getting up now and then. It might rain.

For almost a week the cloud built up and broke up in the evenings and mornings.

Then the day came when the blackness kept growing over the day and the wind sighed drearily.

The leaves from the blackened gum trees fell on the stable like drops of rain.

He fed the horse and, going out to the stock-yard, stood peering out at the growing blackness. The sand was whirling across the wastes and a sudden shining fork of light flashed from the profundity to the north – like the tongue of the snake.

Thunder afar.

'It must rain,' he said aloud to himself.

He noticed a shovel that he'd left out against the fence. He walked over, picked it up, walked with it into the stable and hung it up in its place.

He felt the wind buffet the tin shed and something pattered on the roof. 'Just leaves perhaps,' he thought.

As he walked to the house cool wind gusts caught at his clothes.

He walked through the house to the kitchen as the first drops hit the roof.

She was there.

'It's here,' he said.

And then it was raining!

At first it pattered in big drops upon the roof, a broken pattern, then it picked up quickly into a roar of noise.

Conversation was not possible. They sat and listened until it settled into a steady drumming.

Though it was only midday, it was dark almost as night, until the lightning burnt in blue flames out of the blackness.

They were sitting together in silence, the mother and he – listening to the steady din on the tin roof. And the regular thunder – the guns at the Dardanelles must sound like this thunder.

They sat, understanding that the drought was broken and what it meant to them. Understanding what it meant to the boy when he came back ... listening to the drumming and the thunder ... or was it all the drumming and the thunder?

Then they realised at once that someone was rapping hard at the front door, shut against the pelting rain.

KILLED IN ACTION

Harry McCann

Where the ranges throw their shadows long before the day's
  surrender,
Down a valley where a river used to tumble to the sea,
On a rising patch of level rest the men who dared to tender
Life and all its sweetness for their love o' liberty.

In a thousand miles of ugly scrubby waste and desolation,
Just that little space of level showing open to the sea;
Nothing here to lend it grandeur (sure, it needs no decoration)
Save those rows of wooden crosses keeping silent custody.

There's a band of quiet workers, artless lads who joked and
  chatted
Just this morning; now they're sullen and they keep their eyes
  away
From the blanket-hidden body, coat and shirt all blood-
  bespattered,
Lying motionless and waiting by the new-turned heap of clay.

There are records in the office – date of death and facts pertaining,
Showing name and rank and number and disposal of the kit –
More or less a business matter, and we have no time for feigning
More than momentary pity for the men who have been hit.

There's a patient mother gazing on her hopes so surely shattered
(Hopes and prayers she cherished bravely, seeking strength to hide
  her fear),
Boyhood's dreams and idle memories – things that never really
  mattered –
Lying buried where he's buried 'neath the stars all shining clear.

There's a young wife sorrow-stricken in her bitter first conception
Of that brief conclusive message, harsh fulfilment of her dread;
There are tiny lips repeating, with their childish imperception,
Simple words that bring her mem'ries from the boundaries of the
dead.

Could the Turk have seen this picture when his trigger-finger
rounded,
Would his sights have blurred a little had he heard that mother's
prayer?
Could he know some things that she knew, might his hate have
been confounded?
But he only saw his duty, and he did it, fighting fair.

Just a barren little surface where the grave mounds rise ungainly,
Monuments and tributes to the men who've done their share.
Pain and death, the fruits of battle, and the crosses tell it plainly,
Short and quick and silent suffering; would to God it ended there.

AT RANDWICK HOSPITAL

The Sun, Sydney

It is at Randwick Hospital, Sydney.

'Allow me to introduce Pte. Donnelly, 1st Battalion, commonly known as "Glutton", on account of having tried to eat a machine-gun,' says the man in pyjamas and overcoat.

'Couldn't swallow it,' laughs Pte. Donnelly, bringing his wheelchair to a standstill.

You are a trifle bewildered, and want to know more. 'Let us hear about it,' you ask.

'I'm afraid I've forgotten everything since I had shell-shock,' comes from the wheelchair.

'He's stringing you!' the other convalescent protests. 'Go on, Donnelly; be a sport!'

'Did you really suffer from shell-shock?' demands the visitor.

'Yes, from eating peanuts!' says the incorrigible one; but a few more protests set him on the narrow pathway of truth, and you learn that after four months on Gallipoli he got so badly peppered by a machine-gun that his mates suspected him of having tried to eat it.

He was taken off to Malta with a complement of thirty-two bullets. He marks off the joint of his first finger to show the length of them. His right arm is of use only when lifted in a certain way, and it will be a week or two yet before he is able to discard the wheelchair. His legs show several crevices where bullets entered.

'I'll have to wear stockings in surf-bathing now,' he says whimsically, and with eyes too rueful to be anything but comic. 'This was a bull's-eye,' he continues, opening his tunic so that you can see a cup-shaped wound in his chest. The bullet came out through the shoulder.

During the Gallipoli campaign Pte. Donnelly went from a Friday afternoon until the following Tuesday with five hours' sleep. 'In action,' he says, 'you never feel tired, even when you've been at it for as long as three or four days; but as soon as you come off duty you go flop.

'I remember being sent into the trenches. There were regular rooms where you could lie down. They were shell-proof, and, as you may imagine, very dim. I went along the trench looking for a place to rest, and I met one of my pals. "Oh," he said, "the big room along here is all right. I'll wake you when your time's up."

'I stumbled along, and when I got there the place was full except for one bit of floor just big enough for me. I tiptoed over the others to it, and lay down, with my water-bottle for a pillow. There were two big chaps either side of me, and as they'd been there before me I took it they'd had a pretty fair innings, so made myself more comfortable by shoving one of them against the wall. My pal woke me at 9 p.m. I asked him for a cigarette, and when I struck the match I said to him, "My word, those fellows are doing well, sleeping so long."

'He laughed, and I took another look at them. I had been sleeping between two dead Turks! But you didn't take any notice of things like that out there!

'On the day of the armistice I and two others were at a part of the lines known as the Chamber of Horrors. It was the unfinished section of what we hoped would eventually join up with Quinn's Post. There was only room for three in it, and it was quite close to the German officers' quarters in the enemy trenches. The enemy did not know that, though, and we had strict orders not to betray the unfinished state of the lines, as had they charged us there we should have had no place of retreat but the tunnel which was being gradually made with the idea of joining up.

'One of the three suggested taking a peep over on this day. I did so very cautiously, and, to my surprise, saw a big German officer in his shirt sleeves advancing with a white flag. I told the others. But this time more were advancing. One of the boys in the Chamber of Horrors thought that at least this section of the enemy was surrendering. He leapt up on the parapet, shouting, "Good for you, matey! Are you going to quit? Come and shake hands with us." He was dragged down, and the news of the armistice soon passed along to us.

'The quietness of those few hours was almost more than we could bear after continual firing. If a man spoke to you, you jumped at the sound of his voice. It was uncanny the way all the little singing birds came back as soon as it was quiet. The whole thing got on our nerves, and we were glad when the time came for the armistice to end.

'The Turks had the right to start off again, and I never heard anything so puny as the first shot that was fired. Then the old naval guns got to it, and we were happy again.

'During the armistice I made friends with a Turk. He spoke perfect English. He had been coming out to Sydney to join his uncle and nephew in business, but five days before his departure he was called up. We exchanged cigarettes – I gave him a box of those awful Scotch things we used to get out there, and he gave me the real Turkish article, which, I can tell you, I enjoyed.

'While we smoked he said, "Strange, you know! Today we smoke, chat, and are happy together; tomorrow we shall probably pour lead into each other!" He was taken prisoner afterwards, and I saw him again. He was a really good fellow, like many of the other rural Turks against whom we fought.

'Life in the trenches? Well, there wasn't any dinner bell! We took bully beef and biscuits with us, and opened the beef whenever we were hungry and had the chance of eating.

'There was one fellow who had been a shearer's cook. He made a sort of grater by piercing a piece of tin with holes. He used to grate the biscuits and beef, and make rissoles and cutlets and things. My word, we wouldn't have lost him for a fortune. We were the envy of the lines.

'One day someone shot a hare (the first and last I saw on the peninsula). It was a lord mayor's banquet! We grilled it, and as soon as a bit was cooked it would be hacked off, and it was "Goodbye, hare".'

* * *

Pte. Donnelly was in London for Anzac Day. He says that most of the Australians had fresh tunics made for the occasion, more smartly cut than usual. He and several others were in a theatre during the day. In the seat in front was a broad-shouldered Australian in khaki. They recognised him as a pal.

'How bout it, Nugget?' said one of the soldiers, laying his hand on the shoulder of the Anzac in front. 'Nugget' turned round, and, to their dismay, they saw the crown of a General on his shoulder. 'Beg pardon, sir,' said they; 'thought you were one of ourselves.'

'Well, damn it all, aren't I?' said the General. 'Come out and have a drink.'

He refused to tell them his name, and they have never discovered it.

COBBERS

Roy Bridges

The motorcar waited by the kerb as he came limping out of the hospital. His mates, lounging at the gate in the yellow spring sun, observed the chauffeur giving Bill his arm to help him into the car. They conjectured that Bill had picked up some pretty swagger cobbers. He grinned back at them as the car whirled him away. His grin was sickly and he pulled a rug over his knees and leaned back on the cushions.

Bill didn't like the job he was taking on. Didn't feel up to it. Meeting his dead pal's mother and family. They lived in a big place; had money; they were a different class to him, but he knew he really had no choice, he just had to go.

His pal's mother had written a letter asking him to come; saying that her son had often spoken of him in his letters; and that she wanted to meet him. She would have come to him at the Base Hospital; only she did not go out now. She would send the car for him, if he would come and see her; she hoped that he would.

He had spent the better part of the evening writing his answer. He had promised to come, and so she had sent the big car.

The spring sunlight was all yellow and the sky was very blue, flecked with clouds. It would have been fine, whirring along the road at that pace in the big car in the sunshine – if it wouldn't be pulling up soon at his pal's house.

And then the thought of him, that he had lived there not so long ago, his pal ... the best of pals. And then the thought of him lying dead on Anzac Beach the morning of the landing, shot through the heart as they waded ashore, before he even had his boots on dry land.

Poor Harry Vane, poor chap! And so hard on his mother and family, when they had heard. And now he was headed to see them.

Out of the city into the suburbs. Lines of shops whirling past; tramcars going by with clanging bells. Lines of red-tiled suburban cottages; larger houses, finer gardens – wattle in yellow masses growing there.

He lay back wearily on the cushions, feeling clammy and cold, in spite of the rug and the warmth of the sun. He didn't feel inclined to yarn to the chauffeur, a big chap, too old to go, though, by the look of him.

The car pulled into a drive and passed through great iron gates. They went slowly up a gravelled drive, between lines of pine trees, green lawns and flowerbeds. He could see the tennis court with wire netting around it where his pal must have played often – not so long ago. The house stood up before them, red brick, Virginia creeper painting it with tender green spring leaves. A flight of steps up to the veranda where a girl was waiting in a pale grey gown with a garden hat on her head.

She was tall and fair, like his pal had been; and his eyes were misty as the car pulled up. The chauffeur jumped out to help him; but she came forward, her hand stretched out to welcome him. 'It's kind of you to come and see us, Mr Lawson,' she said, giving him her hand. 'We're so glad to see you. Harry thought so much of you.'

She was so like his pal. She spoke just like him.

He managed, 'Pleased to meet you,' his eyes not meeting hers. He remembered her brother, smiling, in the boat just before they set foot on the beach, and then going down, as soon he set foot upon Gallipoli. And later his white face, seeming to smile still, when he had gone back to find him laid out dead on the beach with the others that afternoon.

'Mother has been looking forward so much to meeting you. The steps are rather steep; let me help you,' offering her arm.

'Oh, I'm not that bad, thank you, miss. I can walk all right.'

'You're getting better?'

'Fine, thank you.'

He went slowly up the steps by her side. They crossed a wide veranda, tiled red and white, and passed into a hallway with big soft couches, covered with some bright stuff with flowers on it.

'You can leave your cap and coat here,' she said, then, noting his difficulty, 'Let me help you with your coat.'

He thanked her and she ushered him into a room off the hallway. 'Mr Lawson, Mother.'

She rose, as he came in, smiling in welcome, her hand outstretched. Tall, very pale, white-haired, but still very like him.

'I am so glad to meet you, Mr Lawson. Thank you for coming.'

He made an awkward bow as he took her hand, 'I'm only too glad to come, Mrs Vane.'

'I hope you didn't mind my not coming to the hospital,' she said. 'I don't go out at all these days, you see. Please take a seat.'

'Shall I go, Mother?' the girl asked quietly.

'No, dear, sit with us. We've both been so anxious to see you, Mr Lawson. Harry wrote of you so often. He thought a great deal of you.'

'He was a fine chap,' he answered awkwardly. 'I never had a cobber like him.'

'And he really liked you,' the mother said, watching him, 'although you only met in camp, didn't you? He felt you were a very close friend.'

His impression of the room was mostly one of comfort, the sun pale yellow through the windows, soft rugs on the polished floor. There were silver-framed portraits on the mantel and he knew some would be of his pal, Harry Vane. There was a sense of Harry in the room.

'Curious thing,' he said awkwardly, 'us meeting like that when we enlisted and cottoning to each other from the jump.'

'Yes, he said that, too,' she replied, smiling encouragingly.

He had dreaded the visit. He had thought that, if he spoke of Harry, he would upset the mother. Now he wondered that she could speak so easily of the dead. And yet he welcomed it. He wanted to speak of him. The other chaps – he couldn't talk to them about Harry Vane. They had seen so many die.

'Well, I believe we did, right from the start, too. Though we wasn't – well, not quite from the same backgrounds.'

He looked down at the toe of his boot.

'You were comrades in arms,' she said, still smiling, 'both in the ranks.'

'Oh, he could have got a commission, if he'd wanted one,' he said. 'I couldn't. Not got the head for it. Couldn't even get a stripe!'

'Harry didn't try for a commission,' she said. 'It would have meant waiting. And he was so anxious to be away. I often think now, if only he'd waited!'

Her voice shook a little, but her face made no sign. The girl was sitting quietly listening and he wondered at the strength of the two. His own throat was husky when he spoke.

'We was cobbers, too, all the time on the ship. He knew so much, I learnt a lot from him. And then, in Egypt, he knew all about the Sphinx and the Pyramids, and what we'd see. And knockin' about with him was ...' he broke off the reminiscence and a silence followed.

'Yes,' she said quietly, 'that was our Harry, such good company and always laughing ... and so knowledgeable about so much.'

'Yes, he certainly was that, Mrs Vane,' he replied, 'he certainly was.'

Another small silence enveloped them and then she said, 'One thing I can't quite bear is that he was so anxious to do things in the world. And all that he had learnt, and all he might have done, counted for nothing. Landing there that morning, and being shot – before he even had his chance.'

For the first time her face was turned from him; and watching her, he saw how white her fingers stood out against the chair, as if she grasped its arms to steady herself. He noted this as his heart jumped within his chest for she had just expressed what he'd been wondering all this time! How such a chap as Harry Vane could be blown out – in the first minutes of the landing, while he was left. Harry Vane, who'd have done so much.

Before he had gathered himself to reply she went on.

'Not that I think,' she said, 'that he could have done anything finer in the world ... anything bigger I mean ... than he ... than you and all the other Australians ... have done. Even if he'd lived to be quite old, and done the things he had wanted to do ... the things I'd wanted him to do ... written books, made a career ... that sort of thing,' she hesitated, 'I only mean ... if he could have lived just for a while ... an hour ... a day ... done something brave and fine. Saved someone's life. Anything that would have been remembered.'

Her voice quivered as she sought to control it. Then she turned her face resolutely to him, and smiled at him.

'But I didn't ask you to come here, Mr Lawson, to listen to me talking about our sorrow. I just wanted to meet you as Harry's friend, to talk with you about yourself, if you won't mind, and about your plans for the future.'

'I'd sooner talk of 'im,' he said, swallowing hard.

He understood her feelings exactly, the bitter thought of waste, the wonder of it, the hopelessness of understanding it. He, too, had wondered, ever since the morning of the landing, why Harry Vane should have died, without doing anything; have passed out at once, when he wanted to do so much.

She smiled and seemed to relax a little.

'If you wish to I'd appreciate it,' she said softly.

Feeling more alive than he had for months he spoke as thoughts and purpose were forming in his mind.

'I want to know,' he said, 'who told you that yarn of him. I mean, getting killed at once.'

'The Colonel wrote,' she said, looking at him with a sudden flush of colour in her pale cheeks. 'Why?'

'He couldn't have got the facts,' he said, meeting her eyes with his. 'Things were confused that day.'

She stared at him, her lip trembling. The girl had also turned her gaze to him.

'It wasn't on the beach. It happened up in the first or second gully. A bullet knocked him clean over. I stopped and wanted to help him down to the boat, but he told me to get on with the other chaps. He made me go!'

He dropped his gaze to his boots again, drew a long breath and said, 'I saw him there, alive for the last time, as I went on. I went on because he told me I had to go. I heard him cheering the other chaps on, too. Cheering them on, bad as he was hit. He wouldn't let any man stop to fix him – not one. He knew that it'd take us time to get him down. And what our orders was.

'You see,' he went on, 'if we'd stopped, we wouldn't have done what we did. Chaps have told me – many of 'em – that he wouldn't let 'em stop to give him a hand down. Chaps who knew him and me was cobbers. And they went on.'

He paused and lowered his voice, 'And him gettin' weaker; and still not lettin' 'em stop ... wasn't that a big thing, the sort of big thing he'd have wanted to do?'

She nodded but no words came.

'And why didn't I stop, and help him down, Mrs Vane,' he continued, 'when it might have saved him? Because I'd always done what he'd wanted me to do. I knew how he'd have felt if he'd kept me back, instead of sendin' me on, where I was wanted.

'Could he have done anything bigger?' he asked as his voice finally broke with a sob and the huskiness returned. 'I ask you, Mrs Vane, could he?'

He looked up then to meet her gaze, but could not see her face for her clasped hands.

THE MAN WHO WASN'T LET FIGHT

E. C. Buley

Perhaps he was let, eventually. But when I met him he was emphatically 'the man who wasn't let fight'.

I met him in London, a tall, well-built Australian, wearing the all-wool khaki of the Commonwealth and the neat leather cap of the Australian Divisional Supply Column, the 'Leatherheads'. He was a thirteen-stone man, but without a spare ounce of flesh on him, and over his right eye he wore a pink celluloid patch.

This decoration moved my curiosity, for I knew the Leatherheads were on the very eve of embarking; therefore I opened a conversation by asking if he was off 'to the front'.

'No, worse luck,' he said, with some bitterness, 'I'm the only man staying behind. They won't let me fight.'

A little sympathy, judiciously expressed, started him talking; and in the monotonous drawl of the Australian bush, he unfolded the strange story of his wanderings in search of a fight.

He told me who he was, and what he was; they are not essential to the point of his story. It is enough to say that he sacrificed a very good income and excellent prospects to join the Australian Expeditionary Force.

'You see,' he said, 'I've got only one eye, my left; but it's a good one. I lost the other eight years ago – mining. I had a glass eye fixed up in Sydney, just like the other one, and you couldn't tell the difference.

'I was always fond of soldiering, and joined the militia. I got my musketry certificate, which shows you a man with one eye can shoot as well as any man with two, and a sight better than most of them. I've done some 'roo shooting, too, and a fellow that can knock over an old man 'roo running at 300 yards with a worn Martini, don't need any spare eyes.

'When I was in Sydney I learned to drive a motor-car, and never had any trouble. A man who can take a fast car through the Sydney traffic don't want to worry about being shy one eye.

'Nobody ever noticed; I used to get on well with girls, and all that; and they're the first to grumble if a man's got anything wrong with him.

'I've seen a lot of bush life and was never sick or sorry in my life. So, naturally I volunteered when the war came, having no one dependent on me. I passed the medical examination all right. Of course, the doctor never tumbled to my glass eye, and there was nothing else the matter with me.

'When they found I could drive a motor, they put me among the Leatherheads. I had to pass a driving test first, and that was no child's play. But still nobody tumbled to my glass eye, and I wasn't saying anything. I went into camp in the Domain, and everything was all right till they innoculated me against typhoid.

'It took pretty bad with me; they tell me that's a good sign. But I was feverish and felt rotten, and had to go into hospital. When the doctor came round the second day, I had a dirty tongue and a temperature, and he whistled a bit.

'"Let's look at your eye," he said; and before I knew what he was after, he had pulled back my bottom lid to see if there was any inflammation there. Of course, my old glass eye rolled out on the pillow.

'You oughter seen that doctor jump. He went quite white in the face, too. Well, there was nobody about, and presently he burst out laughing, which I took to be a good sign. So I said, "Are you going to be a sport, Doctor? No one knows but you, and there's no need for you to know."

'"Are you sure nobody knows?" he asked, still laughing fit to burst.

'"Not a soul," I told him.

'"Wonderful," he says; "I don't know either."

'So I got away with the Contingent.

'When our boys got off at Egypt we came on here, because our motor outfit was no use in the sand there. We've been five long months in camp at Romsey, when I really only want to be at The Dardanelles.

'All that time I've been doing the same work as the rest; transporting gravel in the motor wagon, and all the rest of it. And not a soul ever tumbled to my glass eye.

'Then it was settled that we should be sent – somewhere. But before we could go, the whole lot of us had to go through a fresh medical examination; British Army doctors this time.

'I was going to chance it; and I don't think they would ever have found me out. But you never know what you're doing with these English doctors; they're not reasonable chaps like in Australia, as you shall see. And I didn't want to get the C.O. into trouble; he's a grand chap, Tunbridge.

'So when the doctor came to me, I made a clean breast of it; you ought to have seen the C.O.'s face. He was dead surprised; so would anyone be. But the doctor turned nasty.

'"I can't pass you," he said. "A one-eyed man driving a car! Disgraceful!" And so on.

'Nothing I could say or do was any use; I was rejected. I'm as strong as a Monaro steer, and my eye is as good as three ordinary ones. But it's not good.

'So I got a week's leave, and went off to see a bit of England. Down at Southampton I fell in with some Canadians; real good chaps, they were. We had a drink or two, and I found they were off to the front that very night. Here was a chance!

'I fixed things up with them, and borrowed a hat; then I made my cap into a neat parcel, and left it at the railway parcels office. There was I, as good a Canuck as any of them. Except that I had "Australia" on my shoulders instead of "Canada", but that didn't matter.

'It was dark when we lined up on the pier and they called the roll. I got into the back row, and they called everybody's name but mine; and everybody said "Here" except me. Bit neglectful, I call it; but I was there all right. Australia *will* be there.'

'We got over to Havre, and everybody was fussing about his kit, so I fussed about mine. Of course I didn't have any, but I gave such a good description of it that to get rid of me the orderly said, "It's over there." So I got on to the train, and up to the front we went.

'We were all billeted in a big barn with stacks of grub; and next evening my pals were detailed to go out into the trenches. I got hold of a rifle and some ammunition; there was no difficulty. And I went off with them.

'It was dusk, and about 400 yards from the communication trench we all went down on our hands and knees and crawled. I crawled, too, and kept low, as they told me, when we got to the communication trench; and presently we were all snug in the first line of trenches.

'Then my luck turned. Along came a Canadian officer, to inspect. "Are you all right here, sergeant?" he says. "How many men have you got?"

'"Twenty-one, sir," says the sergeant in quite a little voice.

'"Twenty, you mean."

'"No, sir, twenty-one. There's a long Australian galoot here, that wants to have a shot at the Germans, so we brought him with us."

'Now if that'd been an English officer there'd have been a row, and I should have been shot, or something. But this captain says, "Here, that won't do. Let's have a look at you." So he ran the rule over me, and examined my papers, he even felt my khaki! He knew a bit, that Canuck captain.

'Then he said, "I believe you are telling the truth, but I can't have you here. You'll be getting wounded or something; you're just the sort of fool that would."

'He spoke very nice. "You wouldn't have the sense to get killed," he said. "You'd be wounded, and I couldn't account for you. So, get," he says.

'"How am I to get out?" I asked.

'"The same way you got in," he says, very short.

'"And where am I to go?"

'And I wouldn't like to tell you where he told me to go.

'Well, I stooped and went back along the communication trench. I wasn't going to draw the fire on the boys who were in the firing line. But when I got to the end of it, I stood up, and put my fingers in my mouth and I whistled as loud as I could. I couldn't shoot at the Germans, but I did want a bit of fighting.

'I put my hands in my pockets and strolled back over that ground where we'd been crawling; and I whistled "The Wild Colonial Boy". Nobody took a bit of notice.

'I slept in the billet that night, and had a real good breakfast; then the wounded began to come in. There was a pretty lively scrap through the night; of course I slept through it all – just my luck.

'I made myself useful – stretcher-bearing and whatnot. But I could see that if I stayed there, I'd only get myself into trouble, and somebody else, too, very likely.

'I went to the little base hospital, and I said, "Can you give me an eyeshade. My eye is paining me." And they gave me this. They were just making up a hospital train for the coast, so I chucked away my glass eye – I was disgusted with it anyhow – and put on the shade. Then I got on the train as one of the poor wounded.

'Presently another doctor comes round – this place seems stiff with doctors – and examined me. "That's getting on nicely," he says, looking very hard at me.

'"Yes, Doctor," says I, as if I was in pain. Of course he must have seen there was something wrong, but he was too busy to worry about a little thing like that.

'We had a pleasant journey down: nurses fussing around, and so on. And what do you think I struck on the ship? Another blooming doctor!

'He was so pleased with my quick recovery that he brought an assistant to look at me. They seemed quite dazed about it, but they were busy men: plenty to keep them occupied without troubling about me, which is just as it should be.

'I got my cap at Southampton, and joined up with my old corps. No fighting for me.

'Now I've got to send in my papers. But I've not come 12,000 miles for a fight with the Germans to go home without firing a shot. I'm getting a new eye made here in London; I've seen it in the rough and it's a beauty, the real thing. They know how to make them here.

'And I'm going to have it riveted in, and soldered down and fastened in its place with concrete; then I'm going to enlist with Kitchener's boys. If they find me out, they can only jug me. Do you think they would?'

I couldn't tell him, but it's more than likely. A strong man with a glass eye, who insists on fighting the enemy at a time like this, is apt to be considered a danger in this country. Especially when he has an *undetectable* glass eye.

A DREAM OF ANZAC

William Baylebridge

By 8 August the gallant 29th Division had pushed well into the containing battle at Krithia. At Lone Pine the 1st Brigade of Australian Infantry had taken the Turkish positions, and the New Zealanders, the right covering column of the main attack, had charged and secured the almost impregnable old No. 3 Post.

The gullies, won at a bitter price in blood, were open to the two attacking columns which, even now, were advancing to the assault.

The Turks, threatened as they had never expected to be, put forth their entire strength to cut us off from the crests that meant final victory. Their reserves were brought up in great numbers to meet this threat which, had the odds not been insuperable, would have meant an end to their hopes.

The men of our right attacking column, paying with their lives for every foot of territory won, toiled up the gullies and formed a rough line up past the Table Top. Then they threw themselves into the confused struggle which led on towards the stubborn heights of Chunuk Bair.

Our remaining column, the Australians and their comrades on the left, laboured up the crags and across the chasms of the Aghyl Dere. They had set their hearts on attaining the high ultimate goal – Koja Chemen Tepe. This peak, dominating the whole peninsula, was the key to make victory ours.

In this last column there was a Queenslander named McCullough.

Because he was much given to dreaming queer dreams, men called him the Prophet. But, though his strange dreams and premonitions had run to many new and strange things, none were as strange as this delirious dream he was living now. To any sane man this advance seemed to be the nightmare of a madman.

With their blood up, and with a will that was more than human urging them on, these men struggled forward, cursing, killing, almost drowning in the billowing smoke and dust spread by exploding shells. Great masses of earth were torn away and entombed them. Men were spattered with the bowels and brains of comrades. The hungry wire raked at their flesh, and was left dripping with their blood. Bombs and bayonets dispersed them on the shaking earth.

Night turned to the agony of dawn, and day to night again, and those who were not dead still moved on. Many would think that those who had been left in the scrub below, now just shapes without human meaning, were the lucky ones, for they had done with all this agony.

And in the shambles down there – one of those countless uncommemorated souls – lay Pat McCullough. He had struggled on with that marvellous company of men till he was exhausted from his wounds, his sight had become confused and his senses had lost their reckoning. Then he had dropped in a limp heap beside that track, a track watered with the blood and sweat that shall give it significance, and sanctify it, to Australians forever.

* * *

When McCullough woke, he found himself among boulders in a small depression, shut in with scrub. He stretched himself, rubbed his eyes, yawned, and sat up. The air was clear, and almost without sound. There was some touch of freshness that told him it was still early in the day. Nothing looked amiss – a pair of doves sat preening each other on a fir bush. Up aloft an intent hawk cut lessening circles against a background of pale blue as if he had sighted some business in the neighbourhood.

'Strange!' thought McCullough. 'How did I get here?'

He scrambled to his feet, took a few steps into the undergrowth, and discovered that the ground about him was the summit of an insignificant hill.

In a flash all that he had been through came back to him – all that had happened before this awakening – that mad scramble to death or victory up the blood-sodden gullies.

But what was this?

Pressing his hand to his forehead, as if to help his memory, he gazed about in an effort to understand. The place looked, he thought, like the discarded pit some artillery battery had used.

'Strange!' he repeated.

What struck him was the weird stillness of the place. The roar of our guns, the heavy rumbling of far-off howitzers, the bursting of shells, the vicious snap of rifles, the shouting of men on the beach, the human noise of men cursing, or singing at their work, or crunching along hard roads were all gone. The thousand sounds of war that once echoed through these hills might never have been.

It was so quiet. What did this mean?

And then, in a flash of perception, a reason came.

Deaf! Of course, he was deaf. Had he not been partially deaf many times before from the artillery and shrapnel? His hearing had gone now for good.

Yet, even as he asserted this, he knew that he was not deaf. A fitful morning was blowing in from the sea, flapping the leaves of a shrub nearby. That, beyond question, he heard. Yes, and he also heard, up in the silent air, a lark singing; and there were pigeons, in the scrub below, making an audible job of their wooing.

'Surely,' he thought, 'I am still Pat McCullough, and this is Anzac; but, if that's so, my wits are totally out somewhere.'

There was plainly need for some tough thinking; and selecting a spot for this, he sat down to do it. He felt his limbs, gingerly, with trepidation. They were as solid as a rail – the scarred but substantial flesh and bone of a soldier – and none, thank God, missing!

Then it struck him that he had no clothes on: he was bare. In the same breath he felt a queer tickling on his belly and found that a great bunch of hair had set up the titillation.

'What's this?' he began and then, breaking off, stroked his chin and burst suddenly into a laugh.

'A beard!' he exclaimed. 'Verily,' he laughed, 'the Prophet hath his beard!'

So grotesque did this transformation seem to McCullough that he questioned his very identity. Had he died down there in the gully? Was this mystery to be explained by the transmigration of souls? Had he left his former flesh and gone, by some dark process, into a different body?

It flashed on him, at this point, that he could clear up this question easily.

He felt under his left breast. The old scar was still there! Another piece of shrapnel, he remembered, had knocked two teeth away on the right half of his jaw. He put his hand up, and found the gap.

He brought to mind other marks, marks that had cost the foe something – and these he went through carefully till he was convinced he was McCullough. This was his skin, and the same bone, and the hair – at least some of it – that had gone shearing with him from Carpentaria to down below Bourke.

Having settled this point, he breathed easier.

The next question to clear up was the identity of the place. Though the soil and the scrub were certainly just as at Anzac, this silence was uncanny. It was entirely out of keeping with the stir and ear-shaking noises that never stopped on the battlefield.

McCullough got up, and made for a little spur which, as he expected, commanded a good view of the country round about. He pushed carefully through the gorse, taking great care to protect his bare flesh, and came out onto a crumbling pinnacle, running almost sheer to the ravine below.

The land beyond this ravine was fairly flat; it was patched with crops, and carried groves of grey-leafed olive trees. This part he did not know well; but that hill in the distance, that stubborn-looking lump on the skyline, was surely Achi Baba, a hill of many memories.

To McCullough, the weightiest thing in life now was to make sure.

Picking his way to another spur, he looked hard and long. Before him, now, lay a confused mass of broken hills. McCullough rubbed his eyes. Surely he knew that landscape, and that peak! Hell and death, he ought to! But what was that great, imposing mass, stuck there on the top of it?

The peak should be Koja Chemen; but the building, or whatever it was, that caught the rays of the ascending sun on its bright surface, what was that? And what were these other marks – that looked so odd here – these structures (if they were indeed that) which had cropped up where, until now, only snipers had crawled?

Was it Anzac, and yet not Anzac? Or was he mad? Or was this dreaming?

Noting the position of the sun he pushed over to that side of the hill which, if the place was still what it had been, must look out to the Aegean Sea.

What he should see there would fix it. There would lie the swarm of multi-shaped barges, laden with munitions for both guns and men, and longboats, lined with the wounded, would be putting out in tow to the hospital ships. The fidgety destroyers and the battle-ships would be there, and the bones of wrecked shipping, too.

A few steps now, and one glance would decide it. He would soon know how his case stood, for the scene was as well known to him as his own home. Hurried forward by these thoughts, he shoved his way through the brush, and stood breathless on the hill's edge.

If McCullough had found marvels before, now there was really something to gape at!

What could this mean?

There was the beach he had fought up in that ghostly dawn of the twenty-fifth. He knew every foot of that. There, before him, was the first ridge – heaped, when he had seen it last, with almost its own weight of stores, and honeycombed with dug-outs. But, there was no trace whatever now of those stores, and there, in the near distance, lay the scarps under which they had so recently fought that bitter fight, on the seventh, eighth and ninth of August ... this August? ... last August? ... or what August?

His eye, still in quest of a solution to this riddle of the familiar and the unfamiliar, travelled back to the beach, curving around, in the shape of a boomerang, to Suvla.

It was the beach, positively, beyond doubt, where men had laughed, and cursed, and swum, and died. Ah, what soldier who had taken his baptism there could mistake it? The waves of the blue Aegean Sea broke gently upon it as they did often of old.

Yes, Anzac, it was Anzac in truth, it was; but yet not the Anzac it had been – not *his* Anzac.

For there he saw a pretentious pier, and a smug modern hotel was perched where the field hospital had once perched on the hill! A hotel it must be, surely. But for what? For whom?

There were also different trees which looked well established. Many of them, in a blaze of gold, threw the perfect colour across the drab landscape before him. What trees were these?

As if to answer his question, the breeze carried up a perfume which he sensed with a sudden wonderment of delight. Wattle!

Well, that was something. The men there would at least sleep among their own trees, the trees they had slept among so often in their own land. But all these things that belonged to a world so remote, how did *they* get there?

To McCullough there was something about the whole business that was more than uncanny. It was as if he was living in two worlds, and was a lost soul in each.

God! If only he could but shake off the obsession of either world and struggle back somehow, as a complete and satisfied entity, to one of them – no matter which!

He saw what he saw; all the life of the place as he had known it, from the beach to the top trenches, had disappeared. But why should it? That strip of shore, where men had loafed, or hauled guns and lumber to land, or shouldered ammunition, and beef, and biscuit or waited their turn for water, had become his whole existence.

These things were no longer on the shore. They had given place to this – the antithesis of all that had been there formerly. But why? How?

McCullough could make nothing of it.

So absorbed was he in all of this, trying to save his wits from a collapse, that he did not hear the footsteps of a stranger who just now arrived, after a stiff climb, at the summit of the hill. The newcomer, mopping his forehead, and peering in all directions as he did so, saw McCullough half-hidden in the scrub.

'Seen a platoon of turkeys about here, mate?' he called out.

McCullough turned sharply and there, looking human enough, was the shape which had addressed this question to him. He came out of the scrub and confronted a stoutfellow, very red in the face, attired in shorts, and carrying a shot-gun.

Both men stared in surprise. McCullough, clothed as Adam had been, gave the newcomer a queer sensation about the spine. The gentleman held his gun ready for emergencies.

'Seen some turkeys about here, mate?' he repeated, edging off a little.

McCullough found no words to reply with. His ideas got confused again. If this fellow was looking for the enemy with a weapon no better than that in his fist, he was mad.

'They're the best table birds the boss has,' the man went on, evidently confused too, and feeling himself under the necessity of saying something. 'And he'll want them soon. Sure you haven't seen them?'

'I'm a stranger here,' answered McCullough, swallowing a lump which, for some reason, came into his throat.

'How'd you get here? And where's your gear?'

'The truth is,' McCullough replied, scratching his head, 'that's just what I've been trying to find out.'

The man with the gun, though plainly a bit suspicious, could not question the doubt expressed in the face before him, for it was sincere enough. Men, he knew, could lose their memories; and in such cases anything was possible.

'You'd better hop down to the pub,' he said at last, 'and see what the boss'll do for you.'

'Then that building *is* a pub?'

'It is – the best on the peninsula.'

The best on the peninsula, thought McCullough. Then there must be others! He was again seized with a passionate desire to have a solution to this mystery.

'D'you know this place well?' McCullough questioned. The cloud of a few minutes back had already lifted magically from his spirit; and he felt a little of his old confidence again.

'Know it?' answered the man, with obvious pride. 'I know every turn and crack, every peak and precipice, of this patch – every foot of every trench, the ground of every engagement, of every victory – every boneyard I know too. If you want the history of this glorious battlefield,' he went on, with a flourish, 'I'm your man. That's my job. I'm a guide here.'

That puzzling construction on Koja Chemen, his companion explained, was a monument to commemorate the deeds of those who had fought, and those who had perished, on the peninsula. Housed in it, in a small temple, were the great books in which their names were recorded. This monument could be seen a long way off, and from all sides – it must have impressed, McCullough thought, the shipping of all nations in the Straits.

These records were the duplicates of similar records – housed also in a national temple – which were kept, for eternal remembrance, in the Australian capital. The peninsula, from Helles to the lines at Bulair, was British; and many thousands, Australians mostly, made pilgrimages to the place. Hence the large number of hotels and the guides for the battle-ground and all the paraphernalia for the use of sightseers.

Wattle had been planted and coaxed into growth, till the spot, in parts, looked a true piece of Australia. Military pundits had been busy there; and their many volumes, of many opinions, had been duly presented to the world. Every memory of that place, in short, was treasured as a national possession; and all existing records of the occupation were preserved as things sacred. These, and many other matters perhaps not so relevant, the man made plain to the astonished McCullough.

'And does Australia think so much of the job those fellows did here?' he asked, with a modesty lost on his companion.

The guide whipped out his book – for he always carried it – and, opening it with the skill that comes of much practice, he struck an attitude, and began an oration in this style:

'In these hills, on this holy ground, the sons of Australia, in deeds of the noblest heroism, achieved much in one of the greatest labours ever given to men. Here they fought and died in a way that shall grip the imagination, yes, and thrill the heart, so long as men walk upon this earth. Here they won that heritage which shall be prized, and not least by their own people, so long as nations are nations; for it was here that Australia first proved herself and became a nation. If all the great – '

'Hold hard!' McCullough interrupted. 'Got a smoke on you?'

The speechmaker, a little piqued at the interruption, felt in his pocket, produced a couple of cigarettes, and handed them over with some matches. He was about to return to his book when they heard the whistle of a steamer.

'Strike me!' said the late orator, thrusting the volume with haste into his coat, 'there's the *Australia Comes* putting in, full of tourists, I'd better look smart – guide business.'

At this the man's mind appeared to return suddenly to the present; and the incongruity before him – of this naked man. What could he do with him? The expected guests would have to be considered. At this juncture he could hardly take him to the hotel, clothed, as he was, only in whiskers.

'Hide yourself up here till I send some togs up,' he shouted, waving his hand; and he hurried off to be in place for the trade promised by the steamer's arrival.

McCullough pinched himself to make sure that he was thoroughly awake.

It seemed to him that he was thoroughly awake.

'So this's what it's come to!' he said to himself; and there was some bitterness in the reflection.

'Somehow I've lived long enough to see this. I've lived long enough to meet someone who knows this place better than the men did who made it ... Well, he's had a better chance than we had.

'Or has he?' he went on, after a moment. 'After all, he'll never know it. Only those who were here in my time will do that. We had the substance, others have but the shadow – though no doubt they'll be the richer ones.

'This fellow's a parasite,' he said aloud, considering it further, 'or perhaps I'm all wrong. Perhaps there's some right thinking behind all this after all. The shadow may be more than the substance.

'But, by God,' he concluded, 'I'd like to run into some who did their bit here, and pass the joke on.'

The steamer whistled again; and McCullough pushed back through the scrub to the spur which overlooked the beach. He saw a large vessel coming in under a good head of steam. Nearer and nearer she came – her decks alive with a freight very different from that carried in his time!

As he gazed, like one in a trance, the liner drew in cautiously to the pier; and the place, which before had seemed unpeopled, soon became crowded with men and women. Vehicles were making their way down to the landing place; and, guessing these to be the means of transit to the pub higher up, it struck McCullough that the dry throat must have been notably out of fashion in this later breed of Anzac.

It was a long time since McCullough had seen a crowd like that – in another existence, it seemed. There were men in holiday attire such as he had seen on the pier at Southport and women in clothes that were new and much changed in fashion since the casting-out of his soul into the wasteland ... but very becoming, he thought, for all that.

There were youths, too, and girls of all ages.

McCullough felt a great longing to get closer to that crowd.

So strong was this feeling that he pushed further out upon the spur which, being eroded and sandy like much of the land there, gave way suddenly beneath his weight. He made a frantic attempt to get back to safety – but too late. With a swiftness that completely blotted out his senses, he dropped, amidst a great welter of stones and dust, into the ravine below.

*   *   *

'I think he'll do well enough now,' said the doctor, as he turned, with something like a smile, from the bed in the hospital ship. 'He seems to be recovering and I think he'll beat the fish this time.'

McCullough opened his eyes. He could feel a heavy wrapping of bandages about his head and limbs. Above him, looking down into his own, he saw a woman's face, a nurse's face.

'So you've stopped dreaming at last?' she said.

ANZAC COVE

Leon Gellert

There's a lonely stretch of hillocks;
There's a beach asleep and drear;
There's a battered broken fort beside the sea.
There are sunken, trampled graves;
And a little rotting pier;
And winding paths that wind unceasingly.

There's a torn and silent valley;
There's a tiny rivulet
With some blood upon the stones beside its mouth.
There are lines of buried bones;
There's an unpaid waiting debt;
There's a sound of gentle sobbing in the South.

OUR SONS AS WELL

Jim Haynes

'Cheer, cheer, the red and the white . . .'

I'm belting out the Sydney Swans' victory song as we travel along the highway from Bursa, ancient capital of the Ottoman Empire, to the ferry station on the shore of the Sea of Marmara.

There are four of us driving back to Istanbul after a week on the road and the mood in the Mercedes minibus is one of comradeship and joviality. Two of us are Australian and two are Turkish.

The two Australians are my partner, Robyn, and myself. The two Turks are Ali, our guide, and Mehemet, our driver.

Mehemet is a small, wiry, bright-eyed man for whom nothing is ever a problem. He smiles and laughs a lot and smokes too much. We measure the time we spend exploring any one place by the number of cigarettes Mehemet smokes while he waits for us. At some places we joke and say that we stopped so long to look and explore that we are seriously damaging his health!

Although he has little English Mehemet is easy to communicate with and understand; he is a man of gestures and single words. A family man, proud of his clever daughter who is top in her year at the all-girls' school she attends in Istanbul, Mehemet is keen to tell us about her when he discovers Robyn is a teacher at an all-girls' school in Sydney.

Like myself, Mehemet is also a racing enthusiast, and Ali has been kept busy translating between us as we attempt to explain the subtleties of Australian and Turkish horseracing to each other.

Ali is a wonderful guide – companionable, well educated, efficient and hospitable. He is proud of his country and keen to help us experience all facets of its culture and history. At the same time he has a good grasp of the realities of Turkey's place in the world and the problems his nation still faces. With his encyclopaedic mind, he is the perfect guide for the curious, open-minded traveller.

Ours is a private tour and Ali is always accommodating and flexible. If we wish to spend extra time anywhere, or revisit certain places, as we did on the Gallipoli Peninsula several days earlier, Ali simply makes it happen with a smile. If we miss the regular ferry in order to spend more time on research, Ali always knows where the smaller ferry leaves from.

As an added bonus Ali also has a gourmet's knowledge of every town and village and seems to know the culinary specialities of every region and restaurant in Turkey. We have eaten very well in Turkey and it has been a satisfying and well-rounded trip, in more ways than one. We have been met everywhere with typical Turkish courtesy and hospitality, and extra friendliness every time we are introduced as Australians.

*   *   *

When we are not discussing history or the Gallipoli campaign or food, we discuss other things of universal interest, like football. Right now, as Mehemet steers us along the crowded highway, Ali is busy telling me how most right-thinking Turkish football supporters detest the silvertails of Turkish football, Fenebache. Any sensible Turkish football fan, he assures me, supports his own team and the one that's playing against Fenebache. I tell him that in Australian football we all support our own team and the one that is playing against Collingwood.

Ali and Mehemet both live in Besiktas, the old naval port area of Istanbul, and consequently they support Besiktas Football Club. Over the past week they have sung quite a few Turkish folksongs during long hauls between cities and now they sing a few Besiktas Football Club supporters' songs. Most Turkish men can sing, love to sing, and sing quite well.

I tell Ali that most Australian men don't sing in the normal course of daily events and singing is pretty much confined to the supporters of the winning side at the very end of an AFL game. Nevertheless, I sing the Sydney Swans song for them.

When I finish my raucous rendition I point out that the Turkish national colours of red and white are also the Swans' colours. Ali says that he will now become a Swans supporter whenever he meets other Australians.

*   *   *

Several days previously Ali and I stood at Anzac Cove and catalogued the similarities between the Turkish and Australian experiences on the peninsula in 1915:

- Both nations were involved in a war of someone else's making.
- The Turkish troops at Gallipoli were fighting as part of a larger army, the Ottoman Army, under German command. Our Australian troops were part of the Anzac force, under British command.
- The Ottoman Army was a part of the Central Powers' Forces. The Anzac Divisions were a small part of the Allied Forces.
- Turkish and Australasian troops displayed courage well beyond the call of duty.
- Both Turks and Anzacs respected each other as men of honour and decency.
- The campaign would become, for both nations, a defining moment in their national history. What happened in those eight months would become an essential element in each nation's heritage and a symbol of their national character, pride and independence.

For both Australia and New Zealand the Gallipoli campaign was the event that would stamp them as independent nations, both at war and in more general terms on the world stage. Even more significant, perhaps, was the effect the campaign had at home on the self-perception of both nations as independent entities with their own unique characteristics which were reflected in the character of their own fighting force.

The Anzacs represented a breed of men whose character, appearance, speech and attitude to life differed from that of their British ancestors and the other British troops at Gallipoli – and it is amazing to think that it was only a chance organisational move, a decision made while the troops were encamped in Egypt, that saw the Australian and New Zealand troops even fight as a separate, combined entity. They could have easily been spread throughout the other British forces as they had been in South Africa.

The way the forces were organised at Gallipoli actually made it possible for the Anzacs to be seen as separate from the other British forces. Thus their differences and characteristics were able to be perceived by all and sundry, including their allies, their enemies, and those at home.

For the modern Turkish nation the events surrounding the Gallipoli campaign represent significant milestones on the path to emerging Turkish nationalism. The Ottoman Empire was crumbling and the Turkish nation would rise like a phoenix from its ashes.

There are three elements that, in retrospect, make the Gallipoli campaign a very Turkish victory, rather than an Ottoman one: the defeat of the British and French fleet at The Narrows on 18 March 1915; the holding of the peninsula against the three-pronged Allied invasion at Helles, Anzac and Suvla; and the fact that Turkey's greatest national hero, Kemal Ataturk, rose to fame as a result of his involvement at Gallipoli.

Turks refer to the Gallipoli campaign as 'The Battle of Canakkale' and the significant date for them is 18 March, not 25 April. The eighteenth of March was the day the British and French fleet was defeated and turned back from its attempt to force the Straits by Turkish guns, mines and torpedoes. As a national day in

Turkey it is a celebration of Turkish nationhood – not a celebration of an old Ottoman Victory.

The holding of the peninsula against the Allied forces is also generally seen by Turks as one of the first acts of a Turkish Nation. Yet, Turks made up only a part of the Ottoman Army, just as Anzacs made up only a part of the Allied Army. In fact, two-thirds of the forces commanded by Mustafa Kemal on 25 April at Gallipoli were made up of Arab regiments, not Turkish ones.

For Turks, perhaps the most important element of the campaign is that it saw the emergence of their greatest national hero and the father of their nation, Mustafa Kemal, later known as Kemal Ataturk.

Ataturk was elected Turkey's first president and instituted sweeping social changes and reforms.

When you begin to consider these elements of the Gallipoli experience the seemingly strange bond between old enemies becomes a little easier to fathom.

© Embassy of Turkey

Kemal Ataturk, National Hero and Father of a Nation.

These days Turkey is still a poor nation by European standards. Many Turks have migrated over the past decades, one and a half million in fact. The bulk of these have relocated on a temporary basis as 'migrant workers' in European nations, especially Germany.

Turkish migration to Australia, however, has for the most part been by families wanting to settle permanently. Government-assisted migration to Australia began in 1968 and the early intake was of unskilled labourers and peasant families with little English. Since the 1980s this has changed and permanent visas are given only to highly skilled Turks and those qualifying under family reunion regulations. According to the 2002 census there are now some 53,000 Turkish-Australians.

*   *   *

In 1972 a Turkish migrant and former Turkish heavyweight wresting champion, Kemal Dover, decided to march with six other Turks in Sydney's Anzac Day March under a banner that read 'Turkish–Australian Friendship Will Never Die'. Their participation was apparently completely unofficial but well received by the crowd.

When official requests were made by Turkish groups to be involved in Anzac Day in the early 1980s they were denied. Victorian RSL president Bruce Ruxton famously stated, 'Anyone that was shooting us doesn't get in.'

The Turkish attitude to their old foe, the Anzacs, has always been generous, forgiving, and understanding. When our official Australian War Historian, Charles Bean, returned to the peninsula in 1919 to document and photograph the battlefields and the graves, he was received with courtesy and respect. Similar cooperation was afforded to the Commonwealth War Graves Commission which was assisted by the Turks in setting up the many beautifully laid-out and cared-for Allied graveyards on the peninsula.

Even though the Ottoman army lost over 86,000 men at Gallipoli, compared to 11,000 Anzacs and 31,000 British and French, there is

Cemetry, mosque and memorial to the 57th Regiment, Ottoman Army.

really only one Ottoman cemetery on the peninsula. It is a combined cemetery, mosque and memorial to the 57th Regiment.

The 57th was one of those under the command of Kemal Ataturk. An all-Turkish regiment, it happened to be on the parade ground ready for exercises when news of the landing came on the morning of 25 April. It was the regiment to which Kemal issued the famous order-of-the-day:

> I don't order you to attack, I order you to die. In the time it takes us to die, other troops and commanders can come and take our places.

In buying time to allow reinforcements to be brought up into place on 25 April 1915, the 57th Regiment was completely wiped out.

The Turks did build other monuments at various places on the battlefields at Anzac and at Helles. There is a gigantic statue of Kemal Ataturk on the spot where he turned the tide of the battle at Chunuk Bair. It stands beside the enormous monolithic memorial to the New Zealanders who died defending the hill.

Statue of Kemal Ataturk beside the memorial to the New Zealanders at Chunuk Bair.

There are a few isolated Turkish graves and other Turkish memorials and statues on the peninsula, including the statue of a brave Turkish soldier who carried a wounded British officer back to his trench during the fighting on 25 April. The bulk of the memorials and graveyards, however, are those of the invaders, not the defenders.

In 1934 Kemal Ataturk summed up many Turks' sentiments about the experience of 1915 when he wrote the words now enshrined on an enormous cement tablet above Anzac Cove:

> To those heroes that shed their blood and lost their lives ...
>
> You are now lying in the soil of a friendly country, therefore rest in peace.
>
> There is no difference between the Johnnies and the Mehemets to us where they lie side by side here in this country of ours.
>
> You, the mothers who sent your sons from far away countries ...

Wipe away your tears; your sons are now lying in our bosom and are in peace. After having lost their lives on this land they have become our sons as well.

* * *

In 1973 the Turkish Government designated 330 square kilometres of the Gallipoli Peninsula as the Gallipoli Peninsula National Historical Park. In 1997 this became a Peace Park with a rehabilitation plan organised by the International Union of Architects.

From the late 1980s there has been Turkish representation in Anzac Day marches in Australia and, in 1985, a small group of Anzac veterans returned to Gallipoli on Anzac Day as invited guests of the Turkish Government. At the same time Turkey officially renamed Ari Burnu Cove 'Anzac Cove', 'Anzak Koyu' in Turkish.

A larger group of Gallipoli veterans was there for the Dawn Service in 1990 to mark the seventy-fifth anniversary of Anzac Day, along with 10,000 others, including the Australian Prime Minister, Bob Hawke, and political leaders from Turkey, New Zealand and the United Kingdom.

Since that time the pilgrimage to Gallipoli for Anzac Day has grown to the point where new roads are having to be built to deal with the convoys of buses bringing in over 20,000 travellers each Anzac Day.

What is even more significant is that the crowd consists, to a large degree, of young Australian and New Zealand backpackers and school groups. The interest and involvement displayed by young people in the Anzac Day celebrations is fascinating and gives a true indication of the campaign's place in Australia's history, national pride and self-perception.

In my youth the conventional wisdom of the day was that Anzac would be forgotten as the veterans passed away. Despite the usual primary school lessons every April, as a young man I had little interest in the Gallipoli legend. My grandfathers fought at the Somme and in the Balkans as members of the British Army, not at

Gallipoli. Also, like many of my generation, I was busy in my youth protesting our involvement in the war in Vietnam.

It was only much later, after many years of researching, analysing and writing about the Australian character, that I became fascinated by the role of Anzac in our folklore. And for someone with no personal or family connection to the event itself, I was rather surprised to find that my September 2004 visit to the battlefields of Gallipoli was a deeply moving and emotional experience.

My idea had been to visit the area as research and background for this book. My main interest was to gain an understanding of the terrain and the landmarks that had become so familiar as I had collected and read and edited stories written about the campaign and its effects on the lives of Australians ninety years ago. My motivation for putting together this collection was more from a literary and sociological viewpoint than from any personal, military or historical perspective.

It wasn't until I stood at Ari Burnu point, where the first boats touched the shore, with the water lapping my shoes and uncontrolled tears running down my face, that I fully realised how much the Gallipoli experience is a part of the Australian psyche. I was rather glad the battlefields and beaches were virtually deserted when I was there.

I am sure many Turks feel the same about the 'Battle of Canakkale'. Former New South Wales RSL president Rusty Priest once said that 'Australia and Turkey are perhaps the only two countries in the world that have a strong friendship born out of a war'. He meant, of course, a war in which the two countries were enemies.

*   *   *

A few days before reaching Anzac Cove, we sat having lunch on the deck of a wonderful seafood restaurant in the town of Gelibulou. This town is the 'Gallipoli' after which the peninsula is named. It is situated well north of the battlefields and was untouched by the battles which bear its name.

'I stood at Ari Burnu Point, where the first boats touched the shore.'

The blue waters of the Dardanelles sparkled all around us in the September sunshine as Ali and I spoke of our differing perceptions of the events of 1915. We agreed to disagree on several points and Ali concluded by stating that, to his way of thinking, the Gallipoli campaign changed the history of many nations, but affected three in particular.

'It helped make the nation of Turkey and it gave your new nation an identity,' he said. Then he added, 'And if we had lost and you had won, supplies and arms would have reached Russia and there would probably have been no Russian Revolution. Imagine how *that* would have changed world history.'

Ali could well be right. It is certainly food for thought.

Ali also claimed the Turks probably knew about the withdrawal from Anzac Cove and Suvla, but let our troops go without further casualties because they were leaving. I think he is wrong on this point, of course. There is solid evidence that the Ottoman and German generals had no idea about the evacuation. It was one time when we actually got the better of the Turks at Gallipoli.

I can forgive Ali for this lapse. It would be impolite to argue every point with such a wonderful host. Ali is all that any visitor to Turkey could wish for as a guide and travelling companion.

* * *

Back here in Sydney, when I check the international football results in the paper every Monday, I find myself hoping that Besiktas has won on the weekend ... and Fenebache has lost.

Back in Istanbul, Ali Salih Dirik, long-distance supporter of the Sydney Swans, hopes that any other team has beaten Collingwood, and the Sydney Swans have been victorious in his nation's colours.

'Ali and I stood at Anzac Cove.'

TURKEY – AN ABBREVIATED HISTORY

Jim Haynes

The nation of Turkey as we know it today did not exist in 1915. The Anzacs, and the other Allied forces on the Gallipoli Peninsula, were fighting against an army assembled by the Central Powers and consisting mostly of units of the Ottoman Army, with some German officers and some German artillery. Although Turks made up a large part of the Ottoman Army, its troops were actually an ethnic mixture that reflected the extent of the Ottoman Empire.

The people known as 'Turks' or 'Seljuks' or 'Seljuk Turks' were Muslims from central Asia, east of the Caspian Sea. They invaded Anatolia in 1071 and defeated the Christian Byzantine army at the battle of Manzikert. From that time onwards, the Christian religion and Greek language were gradually replaced in Anatolia by Islam and the Turkish language.

Christians in western Europe sent a series of military expeditions called the Crusades to drive the Seljuk Turks from the Holy Land. However, the Seljuk Empire endured until 1243, when the Asian nomads known as Mongols invaded it.

The Mongol Empire was torn by internal struggles and soon fell apart. As a result, the Turks' influence in Anatolia grew. During the 1300s, a group of Turks who became known as the Ottomans began to build a mighty empire.

By the late 1300s, the Ottomans had conquered the western two-thirds of Anatolia, most of Thrace and much of the Balkan Peninsula, including Greece. In 1453, Ottoman forces led by Mehmet II captured Constantinople, ending the Byzantine Empire. The Ottomans called the city Istanbul and made it their capital. After Ottoman forces conquered Syria in 1516 and Egypt in 1517, the empire became the leading naval power in the Mediterranean region.

By 1566, under Sultan Suleyman I (known as Suleyman the Magnificent), the Ottoman Empire extended from Hungary in Europe to Yemen in the south, Morocco in the west and Persia in the east. Five years later, in 1571, a European fleet defeated the Ottoman navy in the Battle of Lepanto, near Greece. The Ottoman Empire was in steady decline from that point until 1918.

In 1774, the Ottomans lost a six-year war against Russia and were forced to allow Russian ships to pass through the Dardanelles, the waters linking the Black Sea with the Mediterranean. The Ottoman Empire lost the Crimea, a peninsula in the Black Sea, to Russia in 1783.

The empire also lost more territory during the 1800s. The Treaty of Adrianople acknowledged the independence of Greece and gave Russia control of the mouth of the Danube River. The Ottomans then lost other Balkan territory in a series of wars with Russia and lost Algeria and Tunisia to France and Cyprus to Britain.

During the late 1890s, small groups of students and military officers who opposed the empire's old, harsh policies banded together secretly. They were known as the Young Turks and the most influential group was the Committee of Union and Progress. In 1908, members of this group led a revolt against Sultan Abdulhamit and then ruled the empire using his brother, Mehmet V, as a puppet Sultan.

Some Young Turks, such as Enver Pasha, wanted to restore the greatness of the Ottoman Empire. Others, like Mustafa Kemal, no longer cared about the idea of maintaining an empire and wished to establish a new Turkish nation.

And so the Ottoman Empire continued to crumble. Soon after the revolution in 1908, Bulgaria declared its independence, and

Austria-Hungary annexed Bosnia-Herzegovina. Italy took Libya in 1912. In 1913, the Ottoman Empire surrendered Crete, part of Macedonia, southern Epirus, and many Aegean islands to Greece. By 1914, the empire had lost all its European territory except eastern Thrace.

Enver Pasha, leader of the governing committee, had strong links with Germany and, in 1914, the Ottoman Empire entered World War I on the side of Germany and Austria-Hungary in an attempt to regain lost territory.

Many nationalists saw this as a bad move. Mustafa Kemal was of the opinion that it was a 'no-win' situation for Turkey. If the Central Powers won, Turkey would be a satellite of Germany. If the Central Powers lost, Turkey lost everything.

In 1915, the British, French and Russians, with support from Greece, tried to gain control of the Straits so that aid could be shipped to Russia.

The Ottomans, with German help, defeated the British navy's attempt to force a passage through the Dardanelles in March 1915 and then successfully held the Gallipoli Peninsula, dealing the Allies a crushing defeat in their attempt to invade which lasted from April to December 1915.

The Allies, however, won the war in 1918.

After World War I, the Allies set out to break up the Ottoman Empire. Allied troops occupied Istanbul and the Straits. In May 1919, Greek troops, protected by Allied fleets, landed at the Ottoman port of Izmir and advanced into the country. Turks deeply resented the Ottoman Government's inability to defend their homeland.

In August 1920, the Sultan's government signed the harsh Treaty of Sevres with the Allies. The treaty granted independence to some parts of the empire and gave other parts to various Allied powers. The empire was reduced to Istanbul and a portion of Anatolia. As a result of the treaty, the Sultan's popularity among the Turks declined further, while the power of the nationalists grew.

Mustafa Kemal was a Turkish military hero as a result of his bravery and leadership during the Gallipoli campaign. He quickly organised a nationalist movement. Under his leadership, a series of nationalist congresses met in Anatolian cities and formed a provisional government. In April 1920, a new Turkish Grand National Assembly met in Ankara and elected Kemal as its president.

In September 1922, the nationalist forces finally drove the Greeks from Turkey. The Allies agreed to draw up a new peace treaty with the nationalists. The Treaty of Lausanne, signed in 1923, set Turkey's borders about where they are today.

The Grand National Assembly proclaimed Turkey to be a republic on 29 October 1923 and elected Kemal as president. Kemal and other nationalist leaders believed that the new nation could not survive without sweeping social changes.

During the 1920s and 1930s, the government did away with such traditions as Muslim schools, the Islamic legal system, and the wearing of the veil by women and the fez by men. It abolished the religious and civil office of the caliph. Polygamy was outlawed and women received the right to vote and to hold public office.

One of the reforms to Europeanise Turkey was that all Turks were required to choose a family name. At the same time, the Grand National Assembly gave Kemal his surname, Ataturk, 'Father of the Turks'.

Ataturk served as Turkey's president until he died in 1938. His memory is still revered today and his photograph hangs in all public buildings.

Mustafa Kemal was born on 12 March 1881, in Thessaloniki, Greece (then part of the Ottoman Empire). He attended military schools and rose to the rank of general during World War I. He became famous for his role in defeating the Allies at Gallipoli Peninsula.

Kemal had originally been active as a Young Turk but he disagreed with Enver and others on such issues as maintaining the empire and, later, joining the Germans in the war against Britain, France and Russia. As a result he was never part of the ruling group and was sent as military attaché to Bulgaria in a form of exile.

It is ironic that the man who defeated us at Gallipoli was opposed to being involved in the war on the side of the Central Powers.

It can be argued that Kemal was the one man who stood between Allied victory and defeat at Gallipoli. It was he who anticipated the Allied moves and read the situation and reacted fastest on 25 April. It was he who ordered the 57th Regiment (significantly an all-Turkish Regiment of the Ottoman Army) to die in order to halt the Anzac advance. It was he who drove the New Zealanders and British from Chunuk Bair on August the 10th and thus finally rendered the Allied August offensive futile.

Victory at Gallipoli was what gave Ataturk the kudos, credibility, popularity and power base to later lead the Turks to independence and create the nation we know today as Turkey. There is a certain irony in the fact that Kemal's own birthplace, Salonika, in Macedonia, part of the old Ottoman Empire, was not included in the Turkey he helped create and is now part of Greece.

Upon the death of Ataturk, Ismet Inonu became president and kept Turkey virtually neutral during World War II by avoiding entering the conflict until February 1945.

Turkey struggled to come to terms with its new identity as a democratic republic through the twentieth century. By the late 1950s, a rise in the national debt and restrictions on freedom of speech made the ruling Democrat Party government unpopular and, in 1960, army units seized control of the government. Prime Minister Menderes was hanged for crimes against the nation and President Bayar was sentenced to life imprisonment but later released.

In 1961, Turkey adopted a new constitution and the provisional government then held free national elections. No party won a majority in the legislature. In the late 1960s, radical groups of Turks began staging bombings, kidnappings, and murders in an attempt to overthrow the government.

In the 1970s, deep divisions developed between secular and religious groups. No political party could form a stable government. In 1980, the military again seized control of the government and ruled until Turkey returned to civilian rule in 1983.

The Motherland Party controlled the government from 1983 until the True Path Party won the most legislative seats in the 1991 elections and Tansu Ciller became Turkey's first woman prime minister.

In the elections held in 1995, the Welfare Party, a strongly pro-Islamic party, won the most seats in the legislature but, in 1998, the Constitutional Court banned the Welfare Party, ruling that its goal of creating an Islamic state was unconstitutional.

This type of instability has been the norm in Turkey over the past seventy years, with political parties forming, merging and re-forming constantly.

Turkey has also been beset by other problems. Since the 1960s there have been problems in Cyprus which remains politically divided. The government has battled Kurdish guerrillas in south-eastern Turkey and, since the 1980s, 30,000 people have died in the fighting. In August 1999, a powerful earthquake struck north-western Turkey, killing more than 17,000 people. In 2001, the national currency lost about half its value, thousands of businesses closed, and hundreds of thousands of workers lost their jobs.

In 1999, the European Union accepted Turkey as a candidate for membership but political and economic reforms are required before the EU will set a timetable for membership. In 2002 Turkey abolished the use of capital punishment during peacetime and expanded civil rights.

Turkey is a nation torn between old traditional values and the modern world. It is both European and Middle Eastern, sectarian and Muslim. The long process of evolution into a successful and independent nation, begun by Kemal Ataturk, is not yet complete but Turkey is a proud country with a unique heritage and at least her future is now in her own hands.

BIBLIOGRAPHY

Askin, M. *Gallipoli A Turning Point*, Mustafa Askin, Canakkale, Turkey, 2002.

Baylebridge, W. *An Anzac Muster*, Angus & Robertson, 1962 (first published in 1921).

Bean, C.E.W. (ed.) *The ANZAC Book*, Cassell, London, 1916.

Bean, C.E.W. *The Story of Anzac*, Vol II, Angus & Robertson, Sydney, 1935.

Beeston, J. L. *Five Months at Anzac*, Angus & Robertson, Sydney, 1916.

Birdwood, W. *Khaki and Gown – An Autobiography*, Ward Lock, London, 1941.

Bridges, R. *The Immortal Dawn*, Hodder & Stoughton, London, 1917.

Buley, E.C. *Glorious Deeds of Australasians in the Great War*, Andrew Melrose, London, 1915.

Carlyon, L. *Gallipoli*, Pan MacMillan, Sydney, 2001.

Cavill, H.W. *Imperishable Anzacs; A Story of Australia's Famous First Brigade from the Diary of Pte Harold Walter Cavill No. 27 1 Bn.*, William Brooks & Co, Sydney, 1916.

Coulthard-Clark, C. *The Encyclopedia of Australian Battles*, Allen & Unwin, Sydney, 1998.

Dinning, H. *By-ways On Service: Notes from an Australian Journal*, Constable, London, 1918.

Fahey, W. *Diggers' Songs*, AMHP, Sydney, 1966,

Fewster, K., Basarm, V. and Vasarm, H. *Gallipoli, The Turkish Story*, Allen & Unwin, Sydney, 1985/2003.

Hanman, E. F. *Twelve Months With The 'Anzacs'*, Watson, Ferguson & Co, Brisbane, 1916.

Hogue, O. *Love Letters of An Anzac*, Melrose, London, 1916.

Hogue, O. *Trooper Bluegum at The Dardanelles*, Melrose, London, 1916.

Kent, D. *From Trench and Troopship*, Hale & Iremonger, Sydney, 1999.

Kent et al *Kia Ora Coo-ee*, Cornstalk/Angus & Robertson, Sydney, 1981.

Kinross, P. *Ataturk – The Rebirth of A Nation*, Weidenfeld/Phoenix, London 1991/1993.

Livesey, A. *Great Battles of World War I*, Guild, London, 1989.

Loch, F. S. *The Straits Impregnable*, John Murray, London, 1917.

Perry, R. *Monash – The Outsider Who Won A War*, Random House, Sydney, 2004.

Phillips, W. *Australians in World War One: Gallipoli*, Phillips, Coffs Harbour, 2001.

Pope, E. and Wheal, E. *Dictionary of the First World War*, MacMillan, London, 1995.

Pugsley, C. *The Anzacs at Gallipoli*, Lothian, Melbourne, 2000.

Rudd, S. *Memoirs of Corporal Keeley*, University of Queensland Press, Brisbane, 1971 (first published in 1918).

Skeyhill, T. *A Singing Soldier*, Knickerbocker Press, New York, 1919.

Skeyhill, T. *Soldier Songs From Anzac,* George Robertson & Co, Melbourne, 1915.

Steel, N and Hart, P. *Defeat At Gallipoli*, MacMillan, London, 1994.

Travers, T. *Gallipoli 1915*, Tempus Publishing, Stroud, UK, 2001/2004.

Uluarslan, H. *Gallipoli Campaign*, Zeki & Uluarslan, Canakkale, Turkey, 2001.

Various, *An Anzac Memorial*, Returned Sailors and Soldiers League, Sydney, 1919.